W9-CVZ-204

(continued from front flap)

Brough and his nephew are plunged into a horrifying odyssey—a hair-raising investigation into the supernatural and the strange possibilities of the soul. Drawn to Rogano itself, they ultimately uncover the crucial link in a chain of violence and death reaching back to the ancient world—to a chilling controversy buried but not forgotten through the ages.

Stephen Knight is twenty seven years old, and left school at the age of sixteen, to try a career as a journalist. He was a reporter on several weekly London papers, and by the age of twenty had become chief reporter of one of them. In 1973 he met a man who claimed to know the truth about the Jack the Ripper murders, so Knight investigated the case, obtaining access to previously closed files of the Home Office and Scotland Yard. This led to his first book, a nonfiction work entitled *Jack the Ripper: The Final Solution.* He began to write ROGANO in 1976. He is now at work on a second novel, and on a nonfiction book about unsolved murder crimes in history. He is married and has three daughters.

JACKET BY PAUL BACON

Books by Stephen Knight

ROGANO

JACK THE RIPPER: THE FINAL SOLUTION

ROGANO

Rogano

A NOVEL BY

Stephen Knight

DOUBLEDAY & COMPANY, INC.
GARDEN CITY, NEW YORK
1979

This book was published in Great Britain
under the title *Requiem at Rogano*.

Library of Congress Catalog Card Number 78-22335
ISBN: 0-385-14763-5

For my dear friend
David Newnham

THANK YOU: David Richardson, Andrew Hewson, Anna Cooper, Leonard Knight, Adrian Knight, John Wilding, Bernard Taylor, Bob Woodings, Chris Hollifield, Kate Medina, Peter Jeffery, Nigel Coombs, David and Mary Pownall. Thank you, especially, Margot Kenrick, my most loving wife.

ROGANO

Retirement, thought ex-Inspector Brough, is all very well if your heart is in it. He settled himself into his favorite fireside chair and looked out at the mist creeping slowly up from the Thames. The cabs rattling along Jermyn Street already looked indistinct and spectral in the December dusk.

An early edition of the *Star* lay open on his lap. "Fourth Man Strangled by Mystery Assassin" declared a headline at the top of the page.

Brough reached for his pipe and began to fill it.

"A university professor done to death in Camden Passage, the Yard running around in circles not knowing who to arrest next, and me sitting here sinking into my dotage," he muttered. "It just doesn't make sense."

Brough had been melancholy and shiftless for more than a month, ever since the strangler's first appearance at Deptford had sent the press into hysterics and the Yard into confusion.

My brain is as sharp as it ever was, he thought. But the great god Regulations is not concerned with brains.

Daily physical jerks and a few Sufi exercises learned during his army days in India kept his body as sound as his mind. He was as fit now as when he had taken over the metropolitan murder division of the CID back in '91.

But Regulations said an officer must retire at sixty, and no one —not even the commissioner—could defy Regulations. When, on the threshold of retirement, its depressing reality had at last become plain to him, he had tried hard to bend a few rules. But it was hopeless. He might just as well have sought the Holy Grail in the men's locker room. On his sixtieth birthday, not a day sooner or later, the ax had fallen.

Oh, he had tried to make the best of it. He had tried to tell himself that detective work was just another way of saying donkey work. And, to a point, that was true. Every startling solution that hit the headlines, every dramatic arrest, was the product of weeks or months of often tedious legwork.

Donkey work, legwork, bloody hard work.

But it was hopeless. All those arguments appealed to the mind. They didn't really *touch* him.

How could they? Reginald Arthur Brough had never troubled about hard work. He had savored every moment of it. In twenty-six years with the uniformed branch and eleven with the Detective Department he had earned the reputation of being one of the most single-minded men at the Yard. And donkey work or not, no man on the force had relished his duty more than Brough.

Never one to be defeated easily by misfortune, he had striven valiantly to fill the empty weeks and months of his retirement.

But that hadn't worked either. In eighteen months he had accomplished much of what he had imagined would take years. Since leaving the Yard in June of the previous year he had read the complete works of Mr. Dickens—apart from *Bleak House*, which he couldn't begin to get his teeth into; he had endlessly haunted the Natural History Museum; and he had photographed the scene of almost every notorious murder that had ever taken place in his beloved London. He had trudged from the splendid Kensington mews where Mrs. Cheyney-Loring had met her come-uppance in the shape of Spider Bill (to whom she had been married for twelve years without suspecting his identity) to the very house where the horrible Ratcliffe Highway murders had been committed, and he had taken hundreds of pictures en route. The sepia prints now occupied every inch of space on the walls, and, together with a formidable array of gruesome knick-knacks from a lifetime spent chasing criminals, they turned his gaslit rooms into a veritable museum of murder. He looked around him. Between the books and the murderers' bric-a-brac, strange Buddhist gods peered at him out of the shadows. He dropped his gaze to his hands and ran his eye along the crease that the palmists called the life line. How far have I traveled along it? he pondered. I see its beginning. And its end. And all its tributaries. But whereabouts is *now?*

God, how he ached to be back on the job. Other men, not yet sixty, nudged him in the ribs and chortled about the freedom of retirement. Well, they could have it. The only freedom he wanted was about the only freedom he couldn't have. Freedom, real freedom—carte blanche—to set up the machinery to snare this bastard strangler.

But what use were dreams? Sitting there alone in the flickering firelight of his rooms, he felt adrift like a dinghy that had broken its moorings. Botany, reading and amateur photography never had and never would replace the thrill of the chase. And learned men getting strangled in dark alleys miles from where they lived aggravated his dissatisfaction with life.

Such incidents made him yearn to wind back the clock and show these youngsters with three stripes on their arms before they were thirty how a criminal investigation should be handled. Dreams again. Empty, useless dreams.

Now with a little woman beside me, he reflected, I wouldn't feel so cut off from life. I wouldn't feel the need to fill my days with so much doing. Just *being* would be a fine thing.

He yawned. Troubled nights for the past few weeks had added to his misery.

He looked again at the unopened letter lying on the table by a plaster bust of his old sparring partner Charles Peace. It had arrived with the second post, but he had been so involved in developing some photographs that he had had no time to open it. Later, when the prints were hanging up to dry in his makeshift darkroom, he had been too immersed in mourning his lost past to give it a thought. Rising, Brough picked up the letter, walked to the window and opened it.

> Grand Hotel de New-York
> Palazzo Ricasoli
> Florence
>
> 29
> NOV
> 1902

R. A. Brough, Esq.
35a Jermyn Street
London W.

My Dear Uncle,

Forgive my using the typewriter, which at best seems cold and impersonal, but in three years of newspaper work my handwriting ability seems to have atrophied.

Journalism is a pretty precarious existence, as you warned me it would be—more so when you sell what you can on the open market rather than buckle down to an eight-to-seven drudgery with a regular employer. There's not a great deal more to be made writing books, as I found with *King Teddy*, but the odd literary venture does swell the coffers a bit. And perhaps more importantly it helps me keep my hand in with the king's English, which my twopence-a-lining for the dailies rather abuses. As an indignant professor of English told me before I came down from Oxford, any similarity between journalese and the English language is purely coincidental!

I know *Teddy* wasn't the hottest seller of the year, but it did moderately well and I have enough confidence to think my style will improve with experience, so I've decided to start work on another book.

How does the idea of collaborating with me on *A History of Murder* appeal to you? I realize I have been rather aloof of late and I must have seemed ungracious in my neglect of our old friendship, but life takes some queer twists and the course of our existence is so often outside our control, as you have told me often. No matter. I shall be lodging with my parents for the foreseeable future when I return home and for my part I should dearly love to revive our old association. And after a year and a half of forced inactivity you must long to get your teeth into something challenging and fulfilling. You might be out for the count as far as new cases are concerned, but who better than a man of your experience to tackle a proper account of the great murders of the past—and to have a crack at clearing up a few of the unsolved ones? Writers with no training in detection are producing books every year with ingenious and widely discussed theories on old mysteries from the identity of the man who wrote Shakespeare's plays to the riddle of the little princes in the Tower. Andrew Lang has made a career out of mystery.

As far as I can discover there has been no well-researched history of murder from the earliest times to the present day, and old Harris at Methuen & Co. thinks there could be a good market for it. Not knowing my plan to ask you to collaborate with me, Harris suggested that a foreword from you would give the book a sort of imprimatur. Imagine how the reading public will sit up and take note if the title page is inscribed "By Former Scotland Yard Inspector Reginald Brough. . . ."

I thought we could start with Tiberius Sempronius Gracchus, who was clubbed to death in the Roman senate in 133 B.C., and document every notable murder that's been committed since—

reporting facts, commenting, and where possible offering new explanations for stubborn mysteries. I have already done six months' work on a synopsis and I've been digging into some pretty bizarre cases.

I have stumbled on one case the like of which you've never seen. It must beat anything they ever handed you at the Yard. That's really why I am in Italy. If we can get to the bottom of this one it will be the highlight of the book.

I still have a lot to do here but I expect to be back in London by Wednesday, December 10th, at the latest. If I don't contact you before, I shall be at the Beggar's on Thursday the 11th at six if you should care to join me.

> With great affection
> Your nephew
> Nicholas

P.S. I'm not staying at the Hotel de New-York. I just nipped in for a cup of tea and to pinch some stationery.

Nicholas Calvin. My God, it must be nearly two years.

Before Oxford, Nicholas had been Brough's companion through many long evenings. They shared a number of interests, notably the detection of crime, and each enjoyed listening to the other expound on his own subjects. Despite the thirty-odd years that separated them in age, a warm friendship had grown up between them. Nicholas was the only son of Brough's sister Alice, so the old man had known his friend almost since he had drawn his first breath.

There had been a grand reunion when Nicholas came down from university and another a short time later when his biography of the new king was published, but since then nothing. Brough was not so unsympathetic as Nicholas seemed to fear. He had treasured their friendship, but for at least four years before it ran down he had expected his place in his nephew's affections to be replaced, quite properly, by the tenderer charms of a young woman. As far as the old man knew, no serious love had as yet materialized. Doubtless there had been mistresses, but *the* lady in Nicholas' life had turned out to be his work, and Brough no more resented that than he would have resented a woman.

The letter had taken nearly a fortnight to arrive, and by Nicholas' calculations he would have arrived home last night.

A History of Murder. It was quite a thought.

Of course, Nicholas would have to do the writing. And Brough would insist that his own name came second on the title page—"By Nicholas Calvin and Reginald Brough."

But the unsolved murders of the past exerted a peculiar fascination. . . . As Nicholas said, it would be unique for a respected detective to turn his training to that sort of use. . . . Mr. Dickens and botany could go to the devil, or at least to the old folks' infirmary where they belonged. . . . The work involved would be immense. . . . But it would certainly put the mockers on this mental stagnation, this so-called retirement. Retirement? More like a slow march to death.

"Yes, Nicholas, I'll do it," he said aloud. "God bless you, I'll do it."

2

He took out his watch. Twenty minutes to six. If he was to be on time he would have to forego the pleasure of walking, generally his only way of travel in the capital, and take a cab. Putting on a sturdy greatcoat that had served him for a dozen snowy winters, he went down to the street, set off for Piccadilly at a brisk pace and there hailed a cab heading down Coventry Street.

The cries of a newsboy in Leicester Square made him call to the cabby to halt.

"Special! Evenin' paper!—'Nuvver Stranglin' in London!—Maniac Kills Again!—Special!"

Brough stepped smartly across the pavement and bought a copy of the *Evening News*.

"Full story on the Camden Passage bloke, mister," said the newsboy.

"Thank you," said Brough, and bidding him a cheery "good night," he returned to the cab.

The glimmer of the lamp on the side of the hansom was too dim to read by, so he nestled down beneath the covers and reviewed the problems posed by the newcomer to the criminal scene.

"The Deptford Strangler." A promising subject for the last chapter of the *History*. Nothing like being bang up to date.

His tongue worked away at a back tooth where a particle of meat had lodged at lunchtime.

The underworld must be running alive with rumor and speculation, he thought. The copper in charge of the inquiry would do well to collar a few criminal contacts. After all, even villains disowned a mad killer. When it was one against society like this, the criminal element nearly always crossed the line and allied itself to the forces of law. This was part of the reason why Brough had managed to forge a tolerable working relationship with a number of men who should strictly have been regarded as the enemy. In his last decade on the force he had been concerned solely with the detection of murder, so in practice he posed no threat to the pickpocket or the fence, or even the robber or cat burglar providing he avoided violence. As such he could pick their brains when their world spawned a specimen too nasty even for their taste.

He sighed miserably and longed once more for the past to return. Even the drudgery, the long hours, the cold, the drizzle and the darkness of his old job took on a romantic aspect as his mind dwelt on the excitement of cases now long solved or long closed.

As the cabby's horse picked its way through the confusion of traffic at the corner of Charing Cross Road, he turned over in his mind the known facts of the murders which had London peering over its shoulder in fear. He was still ticking off points on his fingers when the vehicle came to a creaking halt outside the Beggar's Alms.

3

Nicholas Calvin sat in the farthest corner of the saloon bar and sipped at a glass of brown ale. A pile of dusty papers was spread out before him on the table.

He liked the Beggar's. He had been introduced to it years ago after a nocturnal expedition with Brough to the cellar that had become notorious for its grim connection with the "Clerkenwell Poisoning Mystery." Four bodies sitting side by side in a damp cellar and all perfectly preserved by the massive doses of antimony each had absorbed. Suicide pact or murder? Publicly, no one had even been able to establish who the three men and one woman were, although some spoke guardedly of a latter-day Hell Fire Club and there had been much talk of a certain demented nobleman.

"The truth of that one will never come out," Brough had said, "but that doesn't mean the truth is not known." And with those enigmatic words echoing in his mind, Nicholas had followed his uncle through gaslit courtyards and dingy alleys to the lowest pub in Seven Dials. The Beggar's Alms was the haunt of criminals, pimps, prostitutes and all manner of outcasts, from the unfrocked clergyman who sat day and night by the open fire saying nothing and drinking almost without rest, to the circus dwarf who had grown too old to do somersaults and so outlived his usefulness. Bruno, found distracted and starving by Brough four years earlier, had been brought by the detective to the sanctuary of the Beggar's, where he now played to a less discerning audience. His pathetic little one-man show had become a nightly event at the farther end of the bar, which all but a few ignored. At the end of it he would curl up in a ball on the straw-covered floor and sleep until opening time in the morning.

At least it keeps his belly full, Brough thought whenever he saw the dwarf in action.

Despite the ceaseless noise of the place, Nicholas found he could relax and be himself. The beer was good and the clientele appealing in a perverse sort of way. It was certainly a refreshing contrast to his parents' whitewashed vicarage.

The wail of a broken barrel organ drifted across from somewhere in St. Giles as Brough paid the cabby and walked toward the raucous chatter and garish lights of the pub. He stepped inside and looked around the crowded bar for his nephew.

A wiry little man with red side whiskers was emerging from a lavatory to his left. "Sam Croker!" said Brough, and shook the man's hand. "I thought I might see you here."

"You thought right, Mr. Brough, sir," Sam grinned from behind a great glass of frothy beer that had accompanied him to the urinal. "Never stirs outside these doors till closing."

"Then it's off to work, eh?" said the old detective with a smile. Sam had been one of his better underworld contacts in days gone by. A burglar by profession, he knew virtually every London villain north of the Thames. Since plowing through *Notre Dame de Paris* three summers ago, Brough had always thought of Sam as the King of the Beggars.

"What's the score, Mr. Brough?"

"Oh, just a social visit, Sam. There's no chance of the Yard taking back an old codger like me."

"That's too bad. We need a few more good coppers, not less of 'em. Bet you'd soon lay this strangler character by the 'eels."

"Maybe, Sam, I don't know. Perhaps we could have a talk about him sometime. Keep your ears open on that one though, won't you? You know my address if you get anything."

Brough knew no one else at the Yard had cultivated Sam as an informant and he assumed that Daubeney, his successor, would have no objection to a bit of free information from his old boss if the situation arose.

He gave Sam a wink and pushed farther into the crush of bodies. Bruno was sitting on a brandy barrel at the end of the bar, pulling faces to amuse the crowd. At the sight of Brough his face opened in a gaping childish grin. Brough smiled and waved. He saw Nicholas in his corner and gently elbowed his way toward him.

"Uncle!" said Nicholas, jumping up and extending his hand. Brough shook it heartily.

Nicholas' frock coat was crumpled and dusty, and looked as if he had been wearing it day and night for a week. His face was dappled with the stubble of a good three days and there were dark pouches under his eyes, but he beamed with excitement and pleasure.

Brough did not remark on his nephew's shaggy appearance, although it intrigued him. Before he could say anything at all, Nicholas said, "I've been longing to see you. I haven't slept a wink since Saturday but I had to talk to you before I turned in."

"Have you just got back?"

"No. No, I arrived in London last night."

"I'm delighted to see you, Nicholas, but what could be so urgent that it can't wait until you've had some sleep?"

Smiling, the young man looked at the pile of papers on the table in front of him.

"This," he said. Then, once again before Brough was able to speak, he asked quickly, "What do you know of the Inquisition?"

Brough pulled up a chair and sat down opposite his nephew.

"The Inquisition?" he replied thoughtfully. "Not much at all. You're the historian of the family, I'm just a pensioned-off bloodhound."

He thought for a moment.

"The Spanish Inquisition. Now let me see. I think I'm right in saying it did some pretty bloody deeds in its day, mainly persecuting Protestants and heretics."

"Which of course were one and the same to the Inquisition," replied Nicholas. He hunched forward in his seat and rested his forearms on the table. "It's interesting you should add the word 'Spanish.' Whenever we speak of the Inquisition we always seem to think of the *Spanish* Inquisition, chiefly I suppose because it was the most wicked and ruthless branch of the so-called Holy Court. But the Inquisition spread its tentacles all over Christendom. There was an Italian Inquisition, a French Inquisition. Even, for a time, an English Inquisition."

"Really?" said Brough. "I didn't know the blighters set foot here."

"Very much so, though only for a short time at the trials of the Templars at the beginning of the fourteenth century. Another thing most people don't know is that the Inquisition was not finally suppressed until 1808. And its successor, the Tribunal of Faith, was not abolished until 1834, less than seventy years ago. In its six hundred years the Inquisition tortured and murdered thousands in the name of Christ."

Nicholas' fatigue seemed to dissolve as he became more involved in his subject, and his enthusiasm gave new life to his whole body.

"Is this part of the *History of Murder?*" asked Brough.

"We must abandon the *History of Murder.*"

"Why?"

"Because we are going to write a book on one single crime and its aftermath."

"Ah," said Brough, still uncertain where the conversation was leading.

"We shall also tell for the first time the true story of the Inquisition and its inner workings."

He picked up a sheaf of documents in his left hand.

"I have here," he said, "actual documents from one of the Inquisition's courts. They include verbatim reports of proceedings, statements of witnesses and copious confidential memoranda. They build up a remarkably detailed picture of one of the most astonishing criminal investigations ever."

He rose and walked silently to the bar, leaving Brough to ponder what unexpected turns his disclosures might yet take. He returned with a tall glass of orange and lemon juice, the closest thing to alcohol Brough ever drank. The former policeman had always maintained that nicotine relaxed and sharpened the senses where alcohol dulled them. He had begun to revise his thinking over tobacco in recent years since a hacking cough had rendered his alarm clock redundant, and he had abandoned cigarettes for the more gentle poison of the pipe. But about alcohol his views remained unchanged. He thanked Nicholas for the drink and looked at him pensively.

"I am disappointed," he said.

"Don't be. In dealing with the whole panorama of murder we should have been able to investigate none of them deeply. Theories are the best we could have produced. Whereas by concentrating on just one case we shall produce no theories but the truth."

"That does sound a shade overconfident."

"Why? Answer this. Why should the approach to a four-hundred-year-old mystery differ from that of a modern investigation? Surely, with our scientific methods of detection we are now more likely than ever to succeed in solving the riddle."

"Assuming we had all the facts, yes. But we are not present at the scene. We cannot go over the ground. We cannot get the feel of the place and the people. We cannot analyze the reactions and behavior of witnesses as we can in a case that occurs today. Instinct and intuition are often as important in solving crimes as are solid facts, you know that as well as I."

"Yes, but the answer must lie in the facts. All the clues must be there. It simply needs a trained and methodical mind to sort the wheat from the chaff."

"I challenge the word 'simply.' In detection there is very little that is simple."

"Point taken. But my instinct tells me there *is* an answer to this mystery, and that it is contained in the facts still available. I am surprised how minutely the whole affair was documented. There are gaps, some of them quite large, but I have every hope that these can be filled in with records still to be obtained. I cannot explain why, but from the beginning I have felt an odd compulsion to get to the bottom of this case, and an intuitive certainty that I shall actually do so."

Brough nodded silently. "Well," he said at length, casting a glum look at the papers before him, "as you've raised my spirits and knocked them down again all within the space of half an hour, perhaps you'd better tell me about this wondrous crime."

Nicholas did not react to the sarcasm. Swallowing the last of his beer, he launched into the story that had filled his mind and robbed him of sleep for months past.

4

"On the night of October the thirtieth, 1454," said Nicholas, looking steadily into Brough's tawny eyes, "Lorenzo di Corsa, Duke of Rogano, was murdered by an unknown assassin as he lay sleeping in his bed. It was the first of a series of killings that was to convulse half of Italy with fear.

"The town of Rogano lies in a narrow cleft of lowland between two great spurs of the Dolomites, in a fertile region known as Cavenna. Rogano evolved as a settlement after the Romans built a fortress high up in the valley to guard the perimeter of their embryonic empire from incursion by the barbarians massing beyond the Brenner Pass.

"Lorenzo was the second duke. His father, who rose to prominence as a banker and merchant, amassed a fabulous fortune and wielded enormous political power within Rogano. He was eventually invited to run the affairs of the town as Chief Citizen. After fourteen years of benevolent dictatorship, and with virtually no opposition from the city elders, he declared himself duke. He built himself a grand palace in the center of Rogano and ruled with apparent wisdom and mercy for another five years. He died in 1446 after being thrown from his horse while hunting in the hills above the city.

"He was succeeded by his son Lorenzo, then aged twenty-two, a handsome fellow judging by portraits of him. A pious man, he was both more intelligent and more studious than his father but at this time at least he was wildly undisciplined. At university he had nearly killed a fellow student in a brawl over a woman, and rarely a week went by without his challenging some rival to a duel. After succeeding to his father's title he began to channel his excess energies into more socially acceptable outlets for aggression like field sports. He was a fine wrestler and an acknowledged master of falconry.

"In a falconry accident outside Rogano shortly after his marriage in 1451 he lost his left eye and ever after wore a white patch over the empty socket."

"What happened? Did the bird peck it out?"

"Yes, I think so." Nicholas paused. "In his short reign Lorenzo was as merciful an administrator as his father. But he lacked his father's financial wizardry simply because he could summon up little enthusiasm for the aimless accumulation of wealth. Nevertheless, he became the most popular leader Rogano had known, his chief bequest to the town being one of the most magnificent libraries of medieval illuminated manuscripts anywhere in Italy. Unaware of the revolution the newly invented printing press was about to bring to the worlds of learning and communication, he commissioned the most beautiful manuscript versions of Aristotle, Socrates, Plato and the rest from calligraphers in the Cavenna monasteries.

"As Lorenzo reached the peak of his popularity something

strange happened. As I said, he was a most pious man, and toward the end of 1453 he had led a great pilgrimage to the Holy Land. Shortly after his return a great change took place in his character. At the beginning of 1454 he shocked the Roganese by refusing for no apparent reason to allow his newborn son, Lothario, to be baptized. He would give no explanation for his unforeseen *volte-face*, which in the eyes of his people amounted to the most arrant blasphemy. The storm clouds gathered over the di Corsa Palace, and after a savage quarrel with Lorenzo, his wife fled to her family in Florence.

"Thereafter Lorenzo was rarely seen outside the grounds of the palace, and his sole companions were two Sicilian dwarfs who had joined his household shortly after the birth of his son. There was some idle talk that they were minions of the Vatican sent to spy on him and discover the reason for his strange conduct, but nothing was ever proven.

"By the autumn it became clear to the leading citizens that something had to be done either to stir Lorenzo from his hibernation or else to resort to law and set out on the miserable road to impeachment. One thing seemed certain—Rogano needed a strong and active leader to withstand the threat posed by the rapidly expanding dukedoms to the south and west. From that viewpoint Lorenzo was a dangerous liability. Before any formal moves were made fate took a hand. One of the dwarfs, a deaf mute, discovered his master murdered on the morning of October 30th when he entered the duke's chamber with his toilet articles."

"How was he killed?" interposed Brough. At that moment Bruno began wheeling about the farther end of the bar and singing broken verses of half-forgotten circus songs in his piping childish treble.

"Let's find somewhere quieter to talk," said Brough, snatching up an armful of Nicholas' papers and marching through a doorway hung with a threadbare blanket behind the bar. Nicholas followed obediently as his uncle walked unannounced into the landlord's dwelling place at the back of the pub.

"Leon, we want to be alone out of the noise. Upstairs O.K.?" said Brough. A growl rather than a word of assent brought the old policeman scurrying back along the passage and up a flight of steep wooden stairs. He led Nicholas to a dingy back room with green paint peeling from the door. The room contained a deal table, two chairs and a tumbled bed.

"This'll do," said Brough, motioning Nicholas to be seated. As Brough himself stooped to sit he squinted his eyes and twitched his nose once like a rabbit.

"Peterson's out," he said under his breath.

"Out where?" said Nicholas. "And who's Peterson?"

"Peterson the mine-shaft killer. He's out of nick and he's been here."

"I thought you said when he went down for manslaughter that they'd never let him out."

"They must have sprung him."

"When?"

"I don't know. But I can smell Peterson. He's been here in the last four or five hours."

Nicholas gave a nervous little laugh. The thought that the revoltingly brutal Peterson was possibly still within killing distance made him feel decidedly uncomfortable.

"Are you sure?" he asked, quite certain Brough was.

"The human scent is as infallible a way of identifying criminals as fingerprints if you can only isolate it. Now my eyes get a bit cloudy as old age rolls on, my ears sometimes feel as if they're bunged up with pipe tobacco, but one thing I know—my sense of smell is remarkable. Pity there's no way of recording different aromas. I might have set up a huge index at the Yard—or even gone into the phonograph business and made my fortune writing symphonies of smells."

"His Master's Odor?" said Nicholas.

Brough smiled at his own folly. "No," he pronounced with a sudden seriousness, "I'd know that man's scent anywhere. There are some you just don't forget. I could identify him in a crowded room at a range of fifty feet."

"Is he likely to come back?"

"Not now we're here. But I'd like to know what devilry went on up here today."

He sat down. "Now," he said, switching with hard-won discipline back to the matter in hand. "Back to Rogano."

"What about Peterson?" said Nicholas.

"His goose is cooking. We needn't disrupt our plans for his

sake. The man's an amateur. By now he'll be with the professionals who snatched him from the clink. Why they should want him is the puzzle. But we'll find neither Peterson nor the answer to the puzzle tonight, so we'd profit nothing by abandoning our talk."

"Suits me," said Nicholas, startled as always by his uncle's ability to relegate the most staggering information to the right pigeonhole and not get overexcited about it.

"So." He composed himself. "Lorenzo was dead. Despite desperate attempts to find his murderer, no scrap of evidence that pointed anywhere sensible could be adduced. The manner of the man's death wiped out all the discontent the townsfolk had been nurturing about his conduct, and no pains were spared to find a solution.

"Just a week later, on November 6th, the city's chief architect and engineer, a man called Pietro Gatta, was abducted from his house at night and done to death. Gatta was a well-traveled man who had spent several years in a high civic position at Mainz in Germany before returning to Rogano about 1452. His body was found floating in a canal that led from the city center to the Pergino River at the perimeter of Rogano.

"On November 11th a leading banker, himself the owner of a great palace in Rogano's financial heart, was found stretched out, dead, on the floor of his wine cellar. Again, no motive could be discovered.

"After this orgy of killing there was a brief lull, during which there was intense activity by day to prosecute inquiries and scour the town for clues. By night no one stirred out of doors. Just as a few optimists were beginning to whisper that the killings were at an end, an old monk was discovered murdered in the cloister of the monastery where he had dwelt in poverty, chastity and obedience for fifty years. That was November 30th. The body of Brother Domenico was conveyed to the crypt of Rogano Cathedral for examination by surgeons. The excitement caused by this fourth murder had scarcely begun to abate when, two days later, a fifth was committed. On the night of December 1st a nineteen-year-old girl, daughter of a well-to-do merchant and a pillar of the church, vanished from her bed in the wealthy town center of Rogano. The disappearance was inexplicable. The house was locked and none of the windows or doors had been forced. When her absence was discovered on the morning of the second her father had the servants search the house, which faced the Piazza del Santa Maria. When that proved fruitless he organized a search of the whole town. That morning her body, dressed in a strange black garment, was discovered in the foundations of a partly built house."

"What sort of black garment?" said Brough.

"I'll come to that in a minute."

"A society without police," said the old man. "Clues everywhere and nobody to follow them up."

"Exactly," said Nicholas. "In the absence of any real leader the people turned naturally to the Church, and a rider was sent posthaste to Sandrio, a town twenty miles along the valley where the Bishop of Rogano was lodging with his family and recuperating from an attack of dysentery. The following night the ashen-faced bishop rode into Rogano under heavy guard to set up a court of inquiry.

"Two days after the murder of the girl an old man who dabbled in astrology met the murderer as he shambled up a steep alleyway from the main street to his garret in the shadow of the campanile. It was noon. All the houses were shuttered and everyone was indoors. No one saw what happened. When the old man's corpse was found by some children later it was still warm.

"The leading citizens of the town gathered to debate the crisis. But if the bishop could do nothing, what positive steps could they take alone? A deputation of elders set out the next morning for the vast Abbey of Alba d'Amprizio to seek the guidance of the revered abbess, Mother Maria d'Aprillia. The abbey still stands today. Let me read you what the guidebook says."

He rescued a dog-eared pamphlet from the pile of papers and flicked carelessly through the pages.

"Here we are," he said, "listen to this. *The Abbey of Alba d'Amprizio was built as a castle in the tenth century on the ruins of the ancient Roman fortress. It stands on an outcrop of rock half a mile above Rogano. A single steep, winding road leads up from the town. Travelers approaching the abbey are unable to detect where the man-made wall becomes the foundation of rock on which it is built, for both are of the same black granite. The rock*

*falls sheerly for fifty feet before disappearing into the trees of the
great Forest of Amprizio."*

Brough nodded sagely.

"According to the diary of one of the leaders of the deputation"
—Nicholas thumbed through his papers and produced a grubby
notebook—"the holy mother looked desperately miserable. Her
unhappiness was painful to see, wrote the diarist, because it con-
trasted so sharply with her usual effervescent warmth and humor.
Encouraging words and a plea for constant prayer were the sole
comforts she seemed able to offer.

"Then she said something they could not really understand.
Quietly, almost in a whisper, she said, 'Ask no intercession. Pray
with all your souls directly to the Father and to the Father alone.'
As they left her she was sitting at her window looking down at the
orange rooftops of Rogano. The diarist recorded that her eyes
were full of tears."

Nicholas handed Brough a sheet of typing. "I've put together a
summary of the next bit," he said. "Shall I read it aloud or do you
want to look at it yourself?"

"I'll read it," said Brough, taking out his silver half-moon read-
ing glasses and setting them on the tip of his nose.

*The populace generally concluded that some supernatural force
had been at work. Perhaps even the devil himself was abroad in
Cavenna. Some, however, speculated on a more worldly level and
placed the blame fairly and squarely on the shoulders of a band of
Romanies who had wandered into the region several weeks before.
Almost everyone, of whatever opinion as to the identity of the
killer, seemed agreed that God must in some way be displeased
with the people of Cavenna to allow such ill fortune to beset
them.*

*Once again, as the days passed with no development in the
case, and as the days lengthened into a week, life at Rogano re-
turned more or less to normal. The terror had spread far beyond
the walls of Rogano, but after twelve days prosperous merchants
began to ride once again between the towns and villages of Ca-
venna. Citizens began to talk again of venturing out at night,
though few as yet actually did so. Many felt the nightmare had
passed. It was a short-lived deception.*

Brough looked up. Nicholas consulted his papers again.

"On December 17th another disappearance occurred," he said, "this time from the abbey. A twenty-eight-year-old sister disappeared from her dormitory in the West Tower in the dead of night, apparently in just the same circumstances as those in which the young girl had vanished. No one heard or saw anything and all the doors of the place were bolted on the inside. No one could explain how the kidnaper or kidnapers had scaled the wall of the abbey, for the drawbridge, which was its sole link with the world beneath, had been raised hours before, and would have been heard had it been lowered. The mother abbess was emphatic that nothing had been seen and no sounds had been heard.

"Men from surrounding towns and villages, principally Rogano, set up vigilante groups to patrol each township and guard the road to the abbey to prevent a repetition of the episode. They searched for the lost sister all over the great abbey and the rugged countryside around it, all to no avail."

Nicholas broke off to give his voice a rest.

"Another drink?" said Brough.

"No, water will be fine for me," Nicholas replied, and he crossed to a cracked sink and filled a none-too-clean mug he'd found by the bed. "What about you?"

The old man didn't seem to hear him. "What happened next?" he said.

"The next day an apothecary called Mercurio Ferruccio, a bachelor, was found murdered near the East Gate of Rogano."

"And then?"

"Two days after that, on December 20th," said Nicholas, coming back to the table, "a woodman was on his way home to a village outside Rogano from his place of work when a sudden mist enveloped him on the hillside and he lost his path. Climbing the hill in the hope of rising above the mist, he went into a clump of trees which he had never before explored. He had not taken many steps into the gloomy wood when he stumbled across a dark object on what turned out to be an overgrown track, long disused, that ran around the hill parallel to the path he normally used."

"What was it?"

"The body of the sister of mercy from the Abbey of Alba d'Amprizio. She would have been twenty-nine that day. She was dressed in a dark-colored garment that at first glance looked like the deep-blue habit of her order. Only later did the woodman realize that she now wore no wimple and the white cotton garment normally worn beneath the outer habit and visible at hem, collar and cuffs was also absent. Finally, when the body was dragged from the undergrowth, he saw that her dark clothing was not blue but black. It was no nun's habit but a sort of uniform in coarse cloth, with breeches instead of skirts. It was identical to the singular garb in which the body of the young girl, Maria Bellini, had been clothed.

"The discoveries confused the poor woodman beyond endurance and sent him running blindly down the hill into the swirling mist, desperately chanting the Angelus as he went. What it all meant he could not begin to understand. But he knew that it was blasphemy for a woman to be dressed in man's garb, and in his simple mind stirred the beginnings of a suspicion that was eventually seized upon as a certainty by the population, and which grew into a widespread panic. He feared that the sister had been snatched from the house of God in which she dwelt by worshipers of the devil, and that she had been used in their evil rites.

"He ran without rest down the hillside, colliding with trees and tripping over creepers. But he believed the legions of hell were behind him and he did not stop until, bruised and gasping for air, he collapsed upon the steps of the cathedral at Rogano.

"A search party was sent into the hills, and the woodman, as the only available suspect, was thrown into prison. No record of his fate has survived. Later events turned suspicion from him, and it is likely that after weeks in the dungeons beneath the cathedral crypt he was released.

"Rumor now flew hither and thither. The Rogano murders were almost the sole topic of discussion in towns and villages for fifty miles around. It was then remembered that about six weeks earlier a herdsman from the hills outside Rogano had seen lights flickering high up on the hillside at night. His talk of men with torches had been carried to the town by some children who had met him while playing by the river where he daily washed and drank, but it had been dismissed by those who had heard of it as the ramblings of an old rascal. Now the people of Rogano were not so skeptical.

"The Bishop of Rogano, ensconced again at the cathedral with his reconstituted court of inquiry, now stood aside and surrendered his responsibility for the case to a formidable man called Vincenzo Palestrina, Bishop of Coranta and the most ruthless holder of the title Grand Inquisitor in all Italy. According to the same diarist who had written of the interview with the mother abbess, Palestrina had been a guest in the house of the Bishop of Rogano since October. The reason for his making the arduous journey from Rome became clear later.

"The Grand Inquisitor's first action was to send mounted officers to bring the herdsman before him. The old peasant was interrogated by Palestrina and the Bishop of Rogano. He repeated his story confidently. He had not only seen lights, he claimed, but on two occasions he had seen men too. They had been dressed in black and they had moved quickly along the top of the Santine Hill, upon which the body of the nun had been found. He had been surprised at their presence there because it was widely believed that the crest of the hill was haunted by the ghost of a medieval hermit who had lived there and died at the age of a hundred and twenty while conjuring up the devil to help him turn stones into gold. The place was avoided like the mouth of hell after the fall of darkness, even in secure times. He said that on every occasion when he had seen the lights they had moved along the crest of the hill and then disappeared down the opposite side. He had seen this strange activity on about five occasions only. Later he identified the clothing found on the bodies of Sister Ruffo and Maria Bellini as similar to that worn by the nine figures on the hill."

"Nine?" said Brough. Nicholas nodded. The detective penciled a note on a scrap of paper.

"Events now moved rapidly," said Nicholas. "Living in a narrow house by the East Gate of Rogano were two brothers, scions of the noble Aquilina family of Naples. It seems that a feeling of antipathy existed toward them, Antonio the elder and Giuseppe the younger, because they remained aloof from the mass of townspeople and had no interest in civic functions and the gatherings of the money-oriented merchant class which dominated Rogano.

"An individual of the town, recently offended by the brothers' refusal to take part in a masked ball he had organized for the town's elite, came forward with a story. He reported to the Holy

Court of Inquiry that he suspected one of the brothers was responsible for the recent murders. But he was unable to say which. He claimed that he had long entertained the suspicion that one of them was a heretic who communed with evil spirits. He had seen him leave the house by the East Gate on many occasions late at night. He said the brother had 'stolen from the town like one who fears the eye of God' and that his return was often hours later when the town slept. He was unable to identify the brother who had made these nocturnal expeditions, he said, because both were of similar height and build, only eighteen months separated them in age and there were marked similarities in both their appearance and in their styles of walking.

"One night, hoping to discover evidence that would both settle the question of identity and confirm his suspicions, the townsman decided to follow the brother. This he did at a safe distance.

"The brother tramped out into the countryside and into the hills. The informant followed him as far as the base of the Santine Hill, and there he stopped for fear of the curse that hung about the place. But from a hiding place behind a large boulder he watched the brother ascend the hill without any apparent apprehension, and he made his way toward the very spot where the strange lights had flickered and where later the corpse of the sister of mercy would be found. He was unable to tell even now which brother he was shadowing, but he was able to produce one crucial piece of evidence. For a brief moment as the suspect climbed the hill, the moon shone out from behind a cloud that had obscured it all night. In that second the townsman saw that the brother was clothed in an odd black uniform, with breeches that extended to his ankles. The value of this testimony was that it was given *before* the details of the murdered women's clothing were made public. The man disclosed that he had kept a calendar of the days the brother took his night walks, planning to denounce him as a heretic and to present the case against him to the Inquisition. The record proved that the last night he had made the journey was on December 17th, the very night when the sister of mercy had disappeared.

"On the Sunday following, a startled congregation heard the Bishop of Rogano explain what he described as 'the solution to the dark mystery that has cursed us.' He said that in early October

Vatican agents had uncovered a frightful conspiracy to assassinate the Pope and destroy the Church. The threat came from a band of heretics who within months of the martyrdom of their leader, a fanatical ex-priest from Etruria, had gained enormous influence, especially in northern Italy and southeast France. This evil sect, said the bishop, called itself the Gormini. And the center of its horrible activities was Rogano. Its initiates professed to have solved the riddle of existence. They conceded that the world had been created by the God of the Christians and Jews, but that he was dead, murdered by Satan. Jesus Christ, said the Gormini, was not the Son of God but the devil incarnate. He now ruled the world and had to be worshiped on his terms, not those mistaken lines adopted by the Catholic Church. All this had been discovered by the ingenious and holy work of the Grand Inquisitor and his promoter fiscal. The Pope had ordered the rooting out and extermination of the sect, which sought spiritual power by violence, murder, sacrilege and sensual perversion.

"In a dramatic oration the bishop revealed that the Gormini had insinuated its evil influence into the very congregation to whom he now spoke. That now, listening to his words and all the time secretly cursing God, were members of that reviled sect posing as Christian men and women.

" 'The leader of this hellish gang sits even now among us,' said the bishop, turning fiery eyes toward the Aquilina brothers—who sat, as befitted their status, on a marble balcony in a part of the cathedral occupied by tombs of their family.

"The bishop gave a sign and the brothers were arrested and conveyed under heavy guard to the dungeons beneath that very building.

"Strenuous efforts were made to identify the brother who had made the sinister trips into the hills. Under the supervision of the Grand Inquisitor, officers of the Inquisition mercilessly tortured both in the hope of wringing a confession from one. When this failed, and amid great rejoicing in the streets of Rogano, the Inquisition burned them both at the stake. In sentencing the brothers for the crimes only one of them had committed, the Grand Inquisitor disclosed that his officers had discovered a cave near the top of the Santine Hill in which was found all the devilish paraphernalia of the Gormini.

"A pendant bearing the crest of the Aquilina family lay among the relics. Their house by the East Gate had also been ransacked and in a cubbyhole beneath the floor of an upper room a black garment was found as final proof of guilt. The garment was held up in court and described as the universal uniform of the Gormini. The Bishop of Rogano justified the court's actions with the public statement from the steps of the cathedral that the guilty man would receive eternal damnation in hell while the innocent brother would be compensated for the loss of his mortal life with life everlasting bestowed by a merciful and loving Father.

"The knowledge that one of the condemned was innocent of the abominations committed by the other in no way diminished the outcry of the populace against both. As they were led from the cathedral to the place of execution they were pelted with stones and beaten with sticks by a frenzied crowd. They died horribly. At the end of it, the bishop made the sign of the cross over them and pronounced the prayer for the dead. *Requiem aeternam dona eis, Domine.*"

"Which meant what?"

For a moment Nicholas did not seem to hear. His thoughts were far away in another time.

"What?" he said absently. "Oh, yes. It means, 'Grant them, O Lord, eternal rest.' "

"A lot of comfort that must have given them. Still, the thought was there, I suppose. Was that the end of the matter?"

"No. Three weeks after the execution, Mother d'Aprillia, devastated by the death of Sister Ruffo, committed suicide by throwing herself from the window of her cell."

5

Bruno the dwarf had long since finished his nightly act by the time Nicholas came to the end of his story, and only the murmur of pub talk filtered through the floorboards to the shabby room where the two friends sat immersed in the fifteenth century.

Brough said nothing for several minutes, but sat staring at the fading embers in the bowl of his pipe. He opened his mouth as if to speak, then decided against it and sank back into his reverie. Nicholas knew better than to interrupt his uncle during a pensive mood.

"I like it," the former detective said at length. "It has certain classic qualities rarely found in present-day murder mysteries."

Again he paused thoughtfully and drew deeply on his pipe. Then, without removing it from his clenched teeth, he said, "How did the victims die?"

"That," said Nicholas, "is one of the major gaps I spoke of. In none of the papers I have so far obtained is there any mention of the killer's method. But there is one further source of information in which I have great hopes. The cathedral at Rogano was destroyed by fire in 1781. As it was beyond repair the Vatican ordered its immediate demolition, and a hospital was built on the site shortly afterward. The hospital was badly damaged in an earth tremor that shook northern Italy in 1819. The guidebook to Rogano, produced by the town council, says that about seven years after the tremor a German scholar was given permission to excavate the foundations of the hospital to see if anything remained of the crypt of the old cathedral. The foundations proved to be far more solid and deep than he had anticipated but eventually his team uncovered the remains of the crypt. It contained several well-preserved tombs, the main structure remained and apparently there was a lot in the way of old registers and cathedral records. The scholar was attached to the Museum of the Renaissance in Bonn, and I have written to the present director of the museum asking if anything touching the Aquilina case exists there. Most of my other avenues of research have turned into blind alleys, but I am almost sure—"

Brough cut him off with a sudden movement of his hand. He placed his finger on his lips and tiptoed to the door. Grasping the handle firmly, he pulled the door open with a jerk. There was a brief vision of a startled white face and then only the sound of echoing footsteps as the eavesdropper beat a hasty retreat along the corridor and down the stairs. Brough went to the window and watched the bent figure emerge into the street and vanish into the fog.

"Peterson?" Nicholas asked tensely.

"No," said Brough, loud with impatience, "it's that ruddy un-frocked priest from downstairs. God knows what mischief he had in hand."

"I didn't hear him outside."

"Nor did I. I smelled the beggar. His combination of whiskey and incense is unmistakable."

"How long was he there?"

"Not more than about a minute."

"What's so interesting about us?" asked Nicholas, but Brough was back in Rogano.

"Where did you come by the documents you already have?" he asked.

"Florence mainly. There was a big Inquisition headquarters there. But I found a batch of witnesses' statements at the Public Record Office in London. Don't ask me how they got there all the way from Rogano. It was finding those that started me on the trail. Since then I've made one trip to Rome and this latest one to Florence, collecting papers and translating them from the un-wieldy legal Latin they used in those days."

"Can you prepare me a chronological report of the case from the first crime to the execution of the brothers?" asked Brough.

"Of course."

"I'd like all possible detail in as few words as you can manage. Include full descriptions of the victims—names, ages, addresses if possible, dates on which they disappeared, dates on which they were found—you know the sort of thing."

"I can let you have it by tomorrow night," said Nicholas.

"Excellent. We shall also need to look closely at the background of the two brothers."

"That shouldn't prove difficult. They were of fairly high birth. Their family history shouldn't be hard to trace."

"Now a few more questions. This cave on the hill, where it was thought the devil worshipers gathered. You mentioned that the officers of the Inquisition discovered 'paraphernalia' there. What exactly did they find?"

"According to the Bishop of Rogano in his speech to the people, it consisted of inverted crucifixes, books of magic spells and incantations, disfigured idols and something he described as an 'infernal machine,' whatever that was."

"And what happened to these items?"

"They were left in the cave and the entrance was sealed up."

"And the cave itself?"

"I suppose it became overgrown with trees and weeds and was simply forgotten. There's no mention of it in any of the guidebooks of the area. But to this day the people of Rogano are a superstitious bunch and they still believe the Santine Hill is accursed. No one ever goes near it. I dare say, from the descriptions we have of the cave's position, that it would be possible to find it."

"Did Mother d'Aprillia leave any sort of letter explaining her suicide?"

"No."

"We have a riddle on our hands and no mistake," said Brough. "From a purely professional point of view I find it intriguing. But I still don't see why it can't form the centerpiece of our *History of Murder*."

"No, Uncle," said Nicholas. "We simply won't do it justice if it becomes just one of hundreds, even if it were the main one."

"Why does it mean so much to you?"

"I'm not sure. I don't mind admitting that I've become obsessed with it. Of course, I stumbled on the whole thing and brought it to light, and that in itself gives me a strong personal involvement. On top of that it will make a gripping book. But there is another dimension that I can't begin to explain. It's all bound up I think with my instinctive knowledge that we shall solve the case. I can't say how I know that or why it should mean so much to me."

"All right," said Brough. "I accept the challenge on one condition. That when we have finished we embark upon the *History*."

"Done!" said Nicholas, but it was a transient jubilation. The energy that had sustained him while he related his story was spent. It was a sober, thoughtful Nicholas who said, after a pause, "I shall not rest until I find out which of those brothers was an innocent victim of events and which a vile murderer."

6

Nicholas delivered the promised report to his uncle the following evening at about nine o'clock. In addition to tabulating the main facts about the Rogano murders as requested, he had managed to get twelve hours' sleep and a hearty meal, both of which had been long overdue. After rapping on the front door, he let himself in with his own key. He found Brough poring over a mass of documentation and making hurried notes on scraps of paper. A pile of books teetered precariously near the edge of the table, threatening at any moment to fall and decapitate Charlie Peace.

Brough looked up quickly. "Ah, Nicholas," he said without getting up, "I'm glad you're here. Have you got it?"

Smiling, Nicholas handed over the report.

"Good," said the older man. "This is the solid foundation of fact upon which we build our case. As you can see, I've not been idle. I have selected a dozen books from the London Library on a variety of topics that touch upon our subject, all of them providing details of the people of northern Italy at the time in question. I've been at it all day, getting the feel of the world as it was then —politics, religion, geography. So far I've managed to build up only a very sketchy picture, but at least I begin to see the colors, and every new detail helps. Any news your end?"

"No. I was hoping to hear from the museum in Bonn by now. If they do have anything it could be vital and it would be good to get an early look at it."

"You know, I think you're more interested in injustice than in crime."

"You're probably right, but what brought you to that conclusion?"

"I think it explains your passionate concern with these Aquilina boys. Look how excited you got about poor Mrs. Maybrick and what a crusader you became when old Fulton had Adolf Beck carted off to quod."

"*Poor* Mrs. Maybrick? Uncle, that woman is a victim of barbarism. How can you be so mild about it? She was condemned to death for poisoning her husband. The crown had not begun to prove she was a killer—they didn't even establish that Maybrick had died from poison. The jury was bigoted and the judge was mad. She rotted in prison for fifteen years. Not because she was a murderess but because she had taken a lover. That is the sort of iniquity with which our legal system is riddled."

"What about Beck? Do you still feel as strongly about that Norwegian shyster?"

"I feel as strongly as I ever did. An unsavory character he might be but no one has shown him to be a criminal. One day I am going to prove his innocence with a proper account of the case."

Beck had been imprisoned for five years in 1896 for a series of crimes Nicholas was convinced had been committed by someone else. After the verdict he had lain awake night after night turning the facts over in his mind. The evidence proved it was a case of mistaken identity. Why couldn't anyone see that?

Such cases captured his imagination far more than cut and dried issues full of grisly details like the psychopathic escapades of Dr. Thomas Neill Cream. He wondered how society could be so blind, and was appalled at the frequency with which injustice was dispensed by the courts. But search his mind how he might, he could think of no practical way of improving the legal system that had evolved over a thousand years in Britain.

Quite how his concern with the psychology of injustice had arisen he never really knew. Certainly his childhood had been basically happy. There had been no wicked stepmother venting her cruelty on young Nicholas. But while he had been spared the sort of Dickensian upbringing that might even have been an advantage to his creative writing of later years, he was nevertheless sure that his interest in injustice, its power and its effect, stemmed from his youngest days. He could remember the poignancy with which he felt wronged on several occasions during his childhood. None of the incidents was particularly dreadful: each had been experienced in one way and another by his many school friends. But somehow Nicholas suffered more than his contemporaries at being called a liar by his parents, and at being shunned, albeit for only a couple of hours, for something he had not done. The memory of those incidents had remained with him ever since.

"I think my interest in crime developed from my preoccupation with injustice," he said after a long pause. "Rather than being the stronger of the two interests it is the *foundation* of my fascination with crime."

"What time is it by the way?"

"Just after nine."

"My God!" said Brough with uncharacteristic agitation, "I've been wandering around in the fifteenth century for hours without realizing the time. I had an appointment at the Yard at eight-thirty."

"At the Yard?" said Nicholas in surprise.

"Something very interesting has happ—well never mind. It's nothing to do with the case in hand. I'll tell you tomorrow. Shall we say breakfast here about eight?"

"Fine."

"By the way, I found out today that Peterson has been out of Princetown for five weeks. How I missed it I don't know, but the Yard are grateful for the news that he was at the Beggar's yesterday."

"It never ceases to astonish me how convicts can escape from a place like Dartmoor. Was it a big professional job?"

"I don't know. Daubeney was cagey on the phone. I'll see what I can find out. Ring me here if you come across anything startling about Rogano between now and breakfast," he said, heaving on his greatcoat, and with a cursory wave as he passed through the door, he was downstairs and in the street hailing a cab before Nicholas could say another word.

7

The Scotland Yard building in Whitehall was cold and drafty, and tiny offices were bordered by echoing, prisonlike corridors. Yet as he climbed the steps from the street to his old office, Brough thought it compared favorably with the overcrowded rabbit warren which the Metropolitan Police had occupied until the eighties.

Daubeney had more humility than Brough had ever given him credit for, and Brough felt vague pangs of remorse that the man now asking his advice he had judged proud and stand-offish through all the years they had worked together.

He had taken Daubeney under his wing eight years before and trained him as well as he could train any man. Many a long evening at the end of a hard day had been spent coaching Daubeney in the sort of subtleties of detection that were not easily passed on during working hours. Daubeney, then a sergeant, had responded well to his superior's efforts. But the two men had never really hit it off. Not that there had been friction. Relations between them had been very proper. Too proper, Brough had always thought. Stiff even. He had interpreted this inability to unbend on Daubeney's part as a sign of antipathy. In reality it was an uncontrollable nervousness that overtook the younger man whenever he was in Inspector Brough's presence. He was awed by the reputation and the genius of his governor, and despite Brough's informality he felt decidedly inferior. It was a fault in Brough that he had never been able to see the effect he had on the other man. Only when Brough retired and recommended Daubeney as his successor did the protégé begin to develop real confidence in his own abilities. Within two months of taking over as head of the department he had cracked three difficult cases in succession. It was then that he had begun to miss old Brough, and to regret his own inability to relax with the Old Man. Now, he thought, he could make some amends and do himself a good turn at the same time. He knew he was a good copper. He had a string of successes to prove it. But his basic modesty never allowed him to forget that for every good copper there was a better one not far away. In his own case the better man had always been, and probably always would be, Reginald Brough. Retired or not, Brough was the finest policeman Daubeney knew. And right now that was just what Daubeney needed.

When he had telephoned Brough earlier that day he had felt no shame in confessing that the Deptford Strangler had him beaten. It was with relief that he found himself inviting Brough to help him out on the case. It had to be in a purely unofficial capacity so that no Regulations were flouted, but that should present no great difficulties.

Brough, of course, was thrilled. As his footsteps echoed along the stone corridor that led to the Murder Division, his blood coursed through his veins with elation at the impending chase.

Daubeney, now an inspector, was alone in the office when Brough entered. Brough looked around the room and noted several minor changes carried out by his successor. The filing cabinet was now near the door instead of under the window; the picture of the Queen—which even after her death Brough had not the heart to remove—had been replaced by a picture of the King; the potted plants that once ranged along the window sill had been replaced by an untidy pile of directories. And there, in his old chair, was Daubeney.

"Ambrose," he said, extending his hand, "I do apologize for my lateness."

Daubeney was a huge man, like a gigantic Teddy bear. He was at least six feet five and beefy. He had a smooth boyish complexion that gathered into round patches of deep pink on each cheek. His relief that Brough had arrived at all outweighed any impatience at being kept waiting.

"Think nothing of it, sir. I am more than pleased you could come," he said, standing up.

He offered Brough his old seat, but the older man demurred and sat in the visitor's chair.

"This 'sir' business will have to stop," he said. "Dobbin's a better name for those who've been put out to grass. Call me Brough like everyone else. Or Reginald if you prefer."

"I think I shall have to work up to that—er—Mr. Brough," said Daubeney, who seemed to find the prospect of equality with his old boss almost as intimidating as coping with the strangler.

To cover his embarrassment he put through a call to the staff canteen and ordered two mugs of tea and some biscuits. Then, maintaining the momentum, he plunged into business.

"As you already know, there have been several murders so far attributable to this so-called Deptford Strangler. He got the name because it was Deptford where he first struck, though all his crimes since have taken place north of the river. The first victim was Henry Antrobus, a schoolmaster aged thirty, who lived in lodgings near Drury Lane. There seems some evidence that he was a homosexual. He was found dead in Rope Walk, Deptford, on November 9th. We've looked into his background, interviewed his colleagues, neighbors, family and friends. Nothing. No glimmer of a motive among any of them. What he was doing south of the Thames we don't know. We've not been able to discover whether he knew anyone there. All things considered, it looks like madman's work.

"All the asylums and hospitals have been checked. One or two came up with names of apparently cured lunatics recently let out. But none of them looked even remotely like a potential strangler, and when we checked they all had alibis."

He paused as a uniformed constable brought in the ordered refreshments, which gave Brough a moment to ponder with a tinge of sadness on the rapid and irreversibly changing nature of time. A year ago there would have been no P.C. in the building who did not know him. Now this young recruit could sail blithely in and out with his mugs of tea and not know him from Adam.

"He struck again on the sixteenth. Victim—the historian and freethinker Dr. Colin Manders, aged fifty-nine. 'Godless Manders' they call him. Created a hell of a stink last year when he published a paper suggesting there was no historical basis for belief in Christ. He was working on a massive biography of the Roman emperor Constantine the Great when he died. Found in some shrubbery at Hyde Park. Five days later it was Patrick Lovell the explorer, forty-seven, of New Cavendish Street, Mayfair. He was found on a towpath behind Farringdon Road. He'd been dead about half an hour when found. That brings us to Wednesday. Just as we thought the strangler had called an end to his fun and games he struck again in Camden Passage. This time it was Maurice Dakins, a Cambridge University professor, sixty-three years of age."

"Four in less than a month," said Brough.

"Five," said Daubeney.

"Five? You mean . . . ?"

"A young woman who went missing last night was found strangled on some dustbins behind Piccadilly this morning. Name—Jessica Twomey, a lass who lived with an uncle and aunt out at Leytonstone, aged nineteen. It was the same method on every occasion. The throats of all five victims bore identical bruising. The marks around the right side of each neck were deeper and more pronounced than those on the left—which, assuming the murderer approached the victims from the front, leads us to think we are looking for a left-handed man."

"It seems a reasonable assumption," agreed Brough. "The hand we are most accustomed to using in everyday life is almost invariably the stronger of the two."

"Beyond the fact that we are looking for a maniac who is almost certainly left-handed we are stumped. How can you begin to build a scientific hypothesis on the motiveless work of a random killer?"

"You are quite certain this is the work of a maniac?" asked Brough offhandedly.

"Of course," said Daubeney with greater confidence than he felt. "How else could such motiveless killings be explained?"

"You are sure the killings are without motive?" asked Brough, consciously varying his tone and striving not to appear patronizing.

"Well," began Daubeney. He faltered and looked dejectedly at a mass of doodles, the product of frustration, that adorned his blotter. "To tell you the truth, sir, I am not sure of anything. I was hoping you could tell me."

8

He read through the poem again:

> Deep inside the mind of Man
> Beyond the reach of thought
> Past untold byways in his brain
> In regions still unsought
> Beneath the depths of joy and care
> And memory and sin
> There is a world but half awake
> Where no light enters in.

Within this sea of future traits
Where true ego doth abide
Where embryonic loves and hates
Are washed on a foetal tide
Within this ocean of our soul
Our future selves are framed
And rise in parts or in a shoal
To the dry land of our brain

All along the whispering shore
Between the Conscious and the deep
The waves of newborn reason roar
On this borderland of sleep
And there it was that in a dream
I plumbed that swirling sea
And my poor human eyes have seen
Invisibility.

I saw with mounting awe a cord
Of purest holy white
Joining my present love for you
In the dark subconscious night
To a greater love that's yet to be
Which will entwine our souls
And keep us one eternally
Yet free as breeze-blown gulls.

Promising, he reflected, but he'll not win any prizes for his scansion.

He had realized after reading the first few lines jotted on the scrap of paper that had fallen from the leaves of Nicholas' report that he had found something intensely personal, something that had plainly been scooped up with the rest of the papers by accident. But some impulse had compelled him to read on, a sort of adolescent curiosity quite foreign to his ingrained sense of propriety.

"The dark horse," he muttered with a smile. "There is then a lady in his life more precious than his work. Not before time, I'm thinking." His smile broadened into a grin.

He was undecided how to approach the problem of returning the poem to his nephew. He had no wish to embarrass him but he was equally averse to cheap deception.

I'll come straight out with it, he decided as he slid six rashers of bacon into the frying pan. Sorry, Nicholas, I found your poem and

I couldn't stop myself reading it to the end . . . that sort of thing.

He paused and weighed the idea in his mind.

"It's the truth," he argued aloud with the devil's advocate resident in his conscience. "It's also a compliment," he said in final dismissal of what he had decided was much ado about a trifle.

Just then the telephone rang. It was Nicholas. He sounded subdued.

"I feel badly under the weather," he said. "I really can't get around for breakfast. All these long hours and lack of sleep are beginning to tell. I think I'll stay in bed this morning and see you later today."

"Come around about seven if you're feeling better. And make sure you do rest. My visit to the Yard was profitable to say the least of it. I'll give you the rundown when I see you."

Rather than let the double ration of bacon go to waste, Brough slapped it between four hunks of bread and butter and ate it himself.

At nine minutes past two Nicholas rang again. He seemed much better.

"I've received a letter from the museum in Bonn," he said. "It seems they do have quite a lot of stuff from the old cathedral at Rogano. They suggest I go over and take a look."

"I think you should do that if you are well enough. How soon can you collect what you need and get back?"

"Within ten days I should hope, depending upon the amount of stuff to be copied. I can start translating it on the journey home and finish the job when I get back to London."

"That's admirable. Will you leave tomorrow?"

"There's a steamer leaving Harwich at nine o'clock tonight, so if I get myself organized I can catch that. I'll be in Bonn by early Monday morning."

"Wonderful," said Brough. "Happy hunting."

9

In the next week Brough was in daily contact with Daubeney. Apart from spending an hour or two each night studying his library books, he devoted his entire energy to assisting his erstwhile apprentice track down the elusive strangler. He realized that until Nicholas returned he could contribute nothing concrete toward the more picturesque of his two inquiries. After all, he mused as he paced across St. James's Park toward Scotland Yard on the morning after his nephew's departure, a mystery that has remained unsolved for four hundred and fifty years isn't likely to go stale in a week.

He liked his new role as unpaid consultant. As he was receiving no remuneration except his expenses, and those by way of the staff tea-money box, it put no undue pressures upon him. And as he was not answerable to anyone but himself concerning the way he conducted his inquiries, he felt freer than he ever had as head of the Murder Division. As a bonus, all the donkey work was being carried out by Daubeney and his merry men, and Brough could concentrate on the most positive and enjoyable aspects of the case. Visions of a visiting card inscribed "Reginald Brough, Consulting Detective" arose in his mind, and he smiled in mild amusement at his own egotism. When the visiting card evaporated to be replaced by a brass plate he laughed aloud and thrust the daydream from his mind.

As old buffers go I must be one of the most fortunate, he thought, and broke into a spirited whistle.

That evening he took a train from Charing Cross to Deptford, and haunted some of the meanest ale houses in the hope of picking up a scrap of drunken gossip that might prove useful. He knew it was a slender chance. The man he was after was almost certainly a lone operator, but it was vital groundwork that could not be neglected. The talk of the underworld north of the river, communicated to him in person by a delighted Sam Croker, was that the "nasty" was from "over the water." And Deptford, where he had commenced operations, was said on the grapevine to be not a thousand miles from his home territory, despite the diverging pattern of his later crimes. If the murderer's bolt hole was here, it was even more necessary to cultivate the local villainy. After the pubs closed he wandered along the water's edge and chatted idly to the bargees who maintained a round-the-clock routine at Deptford's wharves. With the help of a bull's-eye lantern, which he had been left by an old City Police colleague who said he had found one of the Ripper's victims by its light, he inspected the spot in Rope Walk where Mr. Henry Antrobus had met his end. There was an elusive familiarity about the place, but he could not recall when he'd been there before.

Each day he spent pursuing his own inquiries into the private lives of the strangler's victims, making copious notes in a large loose-leaf file which he cross-referenced minutely.

In his routine report call to Daubeney on Monday morning he learned that blanks had been drawn all around in the quest for Peterson. The only certain fact was that he had escaped, and how he had done that was a mystery. It seemed that he had managed it without the help of anyone, inside or out. In the morning he was there, in the afternoon he was gone. The most likely theory was that he had buried himself under half a ton of tea slops, potato peelings and other putrid matter on the back of a refuse cart which had visited the prison that day.

"I'd watch my step if I were you," said Daubeney, who, unable to manage the Christian names game, had dropped all forms of address.

"What does that mean?" said Brough.

"Peterson threatened to kill you if he ever got the chance."

"So he did," chuckled Brough. "I'd forgotten. So many villains have threatened to carve me up in my time that it ceased to register after a while. You'll see, the same will happen to you."

"I've had a couple already."

"Take no notice. Windbags most of 'em."

"But not all."

"No, but I doubt if Peterson has much time to think about me."

"Perhaps not, but why else would he be in London?"

"Even though it's full of coppers it's still the best place to hide.

Since he's on his own my guess is that he was at the Beggar's looking for someone who might give him a place to hole up. Some hopes. If Sam Croker had known he was there we'd have had him by now."

"Tell me about him. You knew him better than I did."

"Peterson? Not much to tell really. He's a bungler. Not that he's badly educated. Seems fairly well bred to talk to. But I don't think he's done a single job without messing it up. He's brutal, one of the most savage men I've met and I've met a few. Even so, I believe what his counsel said at the trial. He probably didn't set out to kill those kids. Time ran out, no ransom came, he panicked and killed the poor little devils. When he's under threat he kills."

10

On Monday night Brough was unable to sleep. Something he could not pinpoint was nagging away at the base of his brain. He could not even work out which of his two cases it concerned, if either. He stalked around his bedroom worrying over the events of the past few days, turning over facts and reviving a thousand defunct thought processes. Eventually he went into his living room, brewed himself a mug of coffee and, wrapping his dressing gown around his squat figure, sat down to re-examine in detail all the notes he had made since the first meeting with Daubeney. Not long after three o'clock he closed the file, and with a puzzled frown picked up a single sheet of paper which lay with several others by the bust of Charlie Peace. A deeply thoughtful Brough returned to bed five minutes later.

In the morning he rose early, washed and went out without taking any breakfast. From the post office in Piccadilly he sent a particularly expensive telegram and, walking to Charing Cross, caught a train to Greenwich. He spent the morning with his sister Alice, whom he had rather neglected in recent weeks. Despite the diverging courses their lives had taken, they had remained close friends. As far as both Alice and her husband, the Reverend

Bartholomew Calvin, were concerned, Brough was a welcome visitor anytime.

He returned to Jermyn Street late in the afternoon to find a telegram from Daubeney explaining that the Somerset police had reported the discovery of a Deptford-style strangling the night before. Medical evidence indicated that the murder had taken place some time on Sunday. Hardly raising an eyebrow at the news, Brough put through a call to the Yard for the full details, stoked up the fire and went to sleep until midnight, when he again ventured out into the fog to look up some old contacts in the underworld.

Outside the front door he stumbled across the huddled form of Bruno curled up asleep on the pavement. It was the third time in recent weeks that he had come unexpectedly upon his little friend in places away from the Beggar's. Bruno scrambled to his feet and beamed with imbecile joy.

"I didn't tell the big man, Mr. Brough," said the dwarf, jumping up and down like an excited child. "You're my friend. I didn't tell the big man where you were." And in a flash he had loped off into the mist. It was the third time, too, that he had spoken those same unintelligible words.

Dawn saw Brough climbing the stairs to his rooms once again. He looked cold and exhausted and for once he felt his age. He threw himself into bed fully clothed and slept for eight hours without stirring. He was awakened by a loud knocking on the front door. Descending to the street, he was greeted with a cheery "Aft'noon" from a bandy-legged youth who handed him a telegram.

"Thank you, Rickets," he said to the lad whose deformity had made him a popular hero at the post office. He cut a sadly comic figure pedaling furiously along on his bicycle, but his nickname was as much a part of him as his bowed limbs and his glorious sense of humor, and he reveled in his one means of notoriety.

"There will be no answer," said Brough. He read the brief message as he climbed the stairs.

He sat down and realized he was thoroughly depressed.

11

The telephone rang at three minutes past four on Wednesday afternoon. Slumped in his armchair, his pipe smoke belching up into his eyes and making them water, Brough was not eager to respond. He waited for half a minute hoping the jangling bell would stop. It didn't.

"Persistent blighter," muttered the detective, and stirred from his lethargy.

Nothing in his voice betrayed his mood of misanthropy as he lifted the receiver and said, "Good afternoon, this is Gerard 0734," but a scowl remained on his face.

"Hello? Is that Mr. Brough?" roared the voice of a man who seemed to imagine he had to cover the distance between them with the power of his own lungs.

"It is," said Brough softly.

"Good day to you sir, good day. This is Dr. Orchard."

Brough was reminded of a hearty publican hollering out "Time!" to reluctant regulars.

"Mr. Brough," the voice pressed on, "I am not at all certain that I am doing the correct thing in contacting you, but I would most sincerely welcome the opportunity of a small word with you on a matter of importance."

"Can you give me some idea what about?" asked Brough.

"I fear not on the telephone," replied the doctor. "I might be quite mistaken in my reasoning. I hope I am. But a talk would be most appreciated."

"Of course, Doctor," replied Brough, somewhat recovering his temper. The doctor's reticence imbued the conversation with a dash of that quality Brough loved best. Mystery.

"When do you have in mind?" he asked.

"Would this evening be possible? I have been debating for four days whether or not to speak up. Now that I have decided in the affirmative I must lose no time. I can catch the four forty-five which arrives in town at five-ten. Shall we say in the foyer of the Charing Cross Hotel at five-fifteen?"

Brough's heart sank a rib or two. He had not wanted to stir outside again that day. The last thing he felt like was another dose of London fog.

"Can you not join me here?" he suggested.

"I am sorry, I have a surgery at six-thirty and must be back by then."

Brough toyed with the notion of excusing himself from the proposed meeting, but something made him relent.

"Very well," he said, "I shall be there at five-fifteen. Good day, Dr. Orchard."

But Dr. Orchard had already gone.

12

A party of carol singers was advancing along Jermyn Street from the Haymarket. As they came, half a dozen small boys with tinsel-rimmed buckets were knocking on doors and receiving donations for the poor of the parish. The glow of their lanterns and the strains of "Hark! the Herald Angels Sing" filtered through Brough's window and pierced his aura of gloom. Since returning from his rendezvous with Dr. Orchard he had felt more morose than ever, and even his pipe lay discarded on the hearth.

The jolly wassail floating up from the now snow-laden street restored a fraction of his usual good humor and tempered the misery and confusion that swamped his brain. He loved Christmas, and until this moment he had quite forgotten that it was only a week away. With an effort he climbed out of the armchair and walked to the window. The carolers were now directly beneath and had begun a spirited version of "The Holly and the Ivy" to the accompaniment of a tambourine and a penny whistle. He raised the sash and watched the procession pass by, then he tossed six pennyworth of coppers to one of the pail bearers, who caught it adroitly and rewarded him with a twinkling smile. He was

about to close the window when he spied a dark figure standing in
the shadows on the opposite side of the road. He had just caught
sight of the pallid face staring up at him when the watcher drew
sharply back into a doorway and hid himself from view. Brough
grunted, locked out the night air and drew the curtains.

"Now who is so interested in Reginald Brough that he'd hang
around in weather like this to keep an eye on him?" he mumbled
under his breath. The figure had moved so quickly that he had
been able to obtain only a fleeting impression of a long dark over-
coat, and a heavily bewhiskered face surmounted by a flat cap.
Who the man was he didn't know, but it was certainly the same
figure that he had seen lurking along the street in Church Place
when he had left at five o'clock for his meeting with the doctor.

He sat for a while contemplating the riddle, then decided to
take the initiative and unleash a bit of wind on the doldrums.
Grasping a gnarled beechwood stick which always accompanied
him on his late-night walks, he buttoned himself into his
greatcoat and went out.

Our friend keeps his uncomfortable vigil for one of two reasons,
Brough told himself. Either he plans to follow me for a purpose
as yet uncertain. Or he wants me to go out so that he can enter
my rooms undisturbed.

He inclined toward the latter view because the sentinel had not
followed him on his trip to Charing Cross earlier in the evening.
True, nor had he entered the premises during Brough's absence—
but on that occasion it would have been impossible. Mrs. Canker,
who swept and dusted for him, arrived promptly every Wednes-
day at five, and Brough had let her in moments before leaving.
So, assuming the stranger was waiting for the apartment to be
empty in order to break in, Brough's present stage-managed de-
parture provided the first opportunity.

Downstairs, he turned right and walked toward Regent Street,
keeping close to the wall to avoid the hard patches of ice into
which the snow in the center of the pavement had been trampled.
With apparent nonchalance he ambled along, whistling in time
with the still-audible carol singers. Without looking to right or
left, he sensed the presence of the stranger in the doorway across
the street, but anxious not to arouse his suspicions, he continued
on his way as if he hadn't a care in the world. He turned the

corner into York Street and immediately stopped, concealing himself in the shadow of the corner building. Pressing himself flat against the wall, he hunched forward and peered around into Jermyn Street, aligning his eye with the edge of the wall to provide good vision with the best possible cover. The man was standing by a gas lamp looking up at Brough's window. The detective squinted in order to get a clearer view of him through the falling snow, but before he could do so the stranger turned in Brough's direction, crossed the road and began to follow in his footsteps.

"*In his master's steps he trod where the snow lay dinted.*" The melodic tale of the exploits of good King Wenceslas floated along the frozen street. "*Heat was in the very sod, which the saint had printed.*"

I'm no saint, thought Brough, though this villain would have me one.

He strained again to see his pursuer's face, expecting to recognize one of the old lags he'd had sent down in years past. But he wore his cap so low upon his brow that recognition would have been impossible even in good light. The stranger was now so close that Brough had to push himself from the wall and half run, half skate down the sloping pavement in order to set a credible distance between them. With a modicum of judgment and greater luck than he deserved, he emerged from his acrobatics unscathed. Halfway down the street he pulled himself up sharply and walked the rest of the way into St. James's Square in a manner more befitting a retired gentleman of threescore years and one.

He strolled casually into the gardens in the center of the square and disappeared from view behind a tall privet hedge. Thus concealed, he turned and peered through the foliage at the man who followed him. He had been careful to take the same route he always did when going off to ramble through the city at night, whether on business or pleasure. On such occasions he never returned in less than half an hour, and was usually away considerably longer. He had every confidence that his play-acting would convince the stranger that he was free to set his criminal plans in motion.

The stranger stopped halfway down York Street. He waited a few moments, scanning the snowy gardens for any sign of the detective's reappearance. Concluding with a grim smile of satisfaction that Brough had continued through the square and out into Charles II Street on the east side, he turned on his heels and retraced his steps. As the lean figure vanished back into Jermyn Street, Brough emerged from the bushes and hurried after him.

"The pursuer is now the pursued," he whispered into the frozen air. He stopped again at the corner and there decided he was dealing with an amateur. Anyone remotely proficient in the art of pursuit would have observed the crisscross confusion of Brough's footprints where he had hidden by the wall before. The knowledge of his adversary's inexperience gave him no comfort, however. Amateurs were often more dangerous than professionals. They tended to panic, and if cornered would resort quickly to violence and even murder. Brough realized he did not relish being murdered on such a cold night. He gazed along the deserted street, but his quarry had disappeared from sight. He moved cautiously through the shadows toward his front door. As he had suspected, it was slightly ajar. He crept without a sound up the thinly carpeted staircase, stopping at the top to listen and to allow his eyes to become accustomed to the darkness. After several taut minutes he padded across the landing and through the open door of his sitting room. He could see the silhouette of the stranger standing in the center of the room with his back toward the door. He was searching for something among the books and papers on the table. Brough hesitated, then suddenly stepped forward and jabbed his walking stick into the gap between the intruder's shoulder blades.

"The shotgun which is now some four inches from your heart is fully loaded," he bluffed. "If you decide not to co-operate I shall have to demonstrate its devastating ability."

The man stiffened with the shock of Brough's appearance, but remained silent.

With his right hand Brough turned up the gas mantle near the door. It bathed the room in a shimmering, unreal light.

"Turn toward me," he ordered gruffly. In the warmth of the room his sense of smell was now beginning to thaw out. The burglar turned slowly, his chin sunk upon his chest. In the yellow-green light of the lamp Brough saw a pale face almost wholly hidden beneath a seaman's cap and a massive growth of black whiskers. All at once he heaved an exasperated sigh, threw his stick upon a chair and stalked to the window. The intruder remained immobile, as petrified as if he had come face to face with a gorgon rather than an ex-police inspector.

Standing with his back to the man, Brough said with icy impatience, "I suggest you sit down, remove that ridiculous beard and tell me what this is all about. I must say this is a fine way to treat an uncle and no mistake. What exactly is the meaning of this charade, Nicholas?"

He already knew the meaning of it, but he was hurt, angry, anxious and in no frame of mind to cope with further deceit. Taking the offensive, he reasoned, was now the most productive course open to him.

His nephew turned and, trembling from head to foot, collapsed into a high-backed chair next to the table.

His eyes fast shut, his jaw quivering with emotion, he strove to regain control of himself. Brough walked toward him. Composing himself, Nicholas looked up and said, "How in God's name did you recognize me? I thought my own mother wouldn't be able to see past all this false hair."

"I didn't see past it. You are the only person who has a key to this apartment other than myself. It was of course conceivable that a professional crook could have secured a duplicate, but I had already decided I was not dealing with a professional."

"Thanks," said Nicholas glumly.

"When my nose started to thaw out I relied on that."

"I can only beg you to . . . forgive me," said Nicholas very slowly, as if each word was a struggle to pronounce. "I have been under such tremendous strain that I scarcely know myself. I have even thought I was losing my grip on the real world."

"Perhaps I might help unravel this tangled skein by outlining what I know," said Brough, taking a seat opposite his nephew. "Firstly I must ask if I am right in thinking that you came here tonight to steal the report which you handed me last week?"

"Not to steal it. To replace it with another."

"And that other report varies in certain details with the original?"

"Yes."

"Did it not cross your mind that I might have noticed the switch?"

"It did of course. But I felt desperate. It seemed my only hope."

"It would have been too late, even if you had succeeded in making the swap. I already know what you are trying to conceal."

"I didn't know it myself until Saturday," said Nicholas in desolation.

"It started nagging away at me at the weekend," continued Brough, "but for hours I could not fathom what it was. So I went over every scrap of information I had digested since we met at the Beggar's last week. And what did I find? In your report, as I had requested, you provided me with exact details of a series of murders that took place in Italy in the 1400s. Looking at the facts of that long forgotten case I made a shocking discovery."

He looked searchingly at Nicholas as he spoke. "The interval between each murder and the age and sex of each victim corresponded exactly with the series of killings currently taking place in London. I am correct, am I not, in suggesting that the victims of the Rogano murderer were strangled?"

"Yes," conceded Nicholas with a helpless shrug of his shoulders.

"Yes," echoed Brough quietly. He looked into the fire and thought for several minutes.

"In other words," he said, "it is at least a strong possibility that the Deptford Strangler is emulating a murderer who operated four hundred and fifty years ago in another part of the world."

"Yes," said Nicholas again.

"And the exploits of that first strangler are not recorded in any history book?"

"No."

"Who, apart from you and I, knows of your researches? Or, more importantly, who knew of them at the beginning of November when the strangler first struck?"

"No one."

"Nicholas," said Brough, rising, "I think you had better get some sleep. You look terrible. We can continue this in the morning."

Nicholas rose and made his way toward the spare bedroom.

"And Nicholas," Brough called after him, "don't try to leave."

13

"Drink this," said Brough, handing his nephew a cup of stewed tea laced with rum.

Nicholas sat up in bed, the remnants of his disguise still clinging in isolated wisps of hair to his face. He propped himself against the pillows and received the offering.

"A queer breakfast it might be, but it will give you more strength than bacon and eggs," resumed Brough. He pulled up a wicker chair, sat down and began the elaborate task of lighting his pipe.

"Do you trust me, Nicholas?" he said at length.

"I trust you to be true to your conscience and your duty," he replied.

"But you do not trust me as a friend?"

"Uncle," said Nicholas imploringly, "I hardly know if I can trust myself."

Brough nodded and placed a hand on his nephew's arm. "If there is any hope at all it exists in our trusting each other," he said. "Perhaps we might achieve that by being perfectly frank. I shall begin."

He sat back and puffed with gusto until a thick blue haze hung in the air between them. Even in his despondency Nicholas found his writer's imagination at work—likening his uncle to a comfortable old locomotive getting up steam for a long journey.

"After observing the uncanny connection between the two sets of murders," said Brough, "I charged myself with establishing what it meant. I had to admit the possibility, however slim, of coincidence. If it were truly coincidence then no amount of theorizing would bring us to the solution.

"If, on the other hand, it was not coincidence then a great deal needed to be explained. I am not a great believer in coincidence so I proceeded on the hypothesis that the Deptford killer knew the details of the Rogano murders and for some reason unknown was re-enacting them here in London.

"You had told me at the Beggar's that *only you* knew the facts of that long-forgotten case. Therefore, developing the thesis I had constructed, I had to admit that you, my nephew and my greatest friend, were the prime suspect in a horrible murder inquiry.

"I hardly need describe how I fought against my own ruthless logic, how I searched endlessly for other interpretations, how I prayed that another murder would take place while you were in Germany and clear you of this foul suspicion.

"On Sunday another murder did take place, but by then it was too late. I knew you had not gone to Germany. You see, I visited your mother. She was certain that you received no letter from abroad last week. As a result of what she said I telegraphed the Museum of the Renaissance in Bonn. They confirmed that you had written to them asking for information about papers from the cathedral at Rogano. But they said they had so far not replied, and were most definite that you had not arranged to visit the museum.

"I strove still to find another explanation. Why would you deceive me if you were innocent? And if you were not in Bonn, where were you? Yesterday afternoon I met Dr. Orchard in London."

Nicholas stared into his untasted tea. "Then you know," he said.

"I know that since November you have been suffering from disturbing dreams in which you find yourself engaged in a physical struggle with people you have never before seen. Each time it happens, and it had been five times up to the day you saw the doctor, it is a different person. Against your will you find your fingers tightening around your victim's throat, and despite the pitiful screams for mercy and the agonized spasms of the body, you throttle him. On the last occasion before consulting the doctor your victim was a young girl. Your dream was in the early hours of last Friday. That morning the strangler struck down a nineteen-year-old girl in Piccadilly.

"I know that until the day after you gave me your report you attributed your nightmares to fatigue and lack of food and sleep. You very reasonably thought that they had grown from your day and night preoccupation with the Rogano Strangler."

"You know everything," said Nicholas in a hoarse whisper.

"Not everything, Nicholas, by a long way. When did you begin
to suspect that your dreams were more than the conflict of a tired
mind?"

"About half an hour after leaving Dr. Orchard on Saturday
morning. Now I come to think of it he did look at me rather
oddly, but at the time I imagined he assessed my problem in
much the same way I had done. He gave me some pills and said I
should take at least ten days' complete rest. He recommended a
holiday out of town. As his consulting rooms are close to Green-
wich Station I decided instantly to take his advice and to buy a
ticket to Scotland. I thought a week or so in the hills around
Glencoe would prove an excellent tonic. At the railway station I
bought a copy of the *Telegraph*. It contained a long report on the
search for the Deptford Strangler."

He paused and breathed deeply. "Do you know"—he trembled
—"I had not even heard of the killer before that. I had been so
immersed in my researches that I had not read a newspaper for
months. Reading those ghastly descriptions of the bodies, how the
faces had been purple and the eyes suffused with blood, my
dreams came back to me with a vividness I shudder to recall. Do
you understand? *Before I read that I had no idea how a strangled
person looked.*"

He placed the tips of his fingers gingerly on his forehead.

"But in my dreams I had known. The people I killed in my
nightmares looked just like that. Suddenly the jigsaw seemed to
fall into place. I feared that I had become so obsessed with the
Strangler of Rogano that I was reliving his crimes. Don't you see
why I couldn't tell you? I had been pushing myself so hard in re-
cent weeks that there were times when I honestly could not re-
member where I had been or what I had done."

Brough said, "I learned from your mother that you were away
from home on the three dates the strangler struck before you went
to Florence."

"I have stayed out on several nights when my studies at the Brit-
ish Museum have ended late and I've been too tired to go home. I
have a room in Coptic Street."

"It must also be noted that the strangler did not strike any-
where while you were in Italy, and that he resumed operations the

very night you got back to England. Why did you tell me on Saturday that you were going to Germany?"

"I had to get away from town as the doctor said, and to rest. I couldn't tell you the real reason and I could think of no plausible excuse for taking a holiday just when we were beginning our investigation. A ten-day absence to make some inquiries seemed the only reasonable explanation."

"But you already knew the Rogano victims had been strangled. Why did you lie about that?"

"I admit I suspected they had died by strangling, and when I thought of the killer I automatically imagined a strangler. But I did not know in fact until last Sunday."

"How did you find out?"

Nicholas looked at his uncle beseechingly. "Uncle, before I go on, do you think coincidence is quite out of the question?"

"I don't know, Nicholas. All I know is that the first victim of both murderers was a man aged thirty; that a period of seven days elapsed in both cases before the killer struck again; that both then killed a man aged fifty-nine; a further five days passed in both cases and then each killer strangled a man aged forty-seven."

He pursed his lips, thought for a moment, then pressed on.

"After this intense activity—three murders in twelve days —both killers then stopped for exactly nineteen days. Then, for both, it was back to work with a vengeance. First they each murdered a man aged sixty-three, then two days later a girl of nineteen and three days after that a man aged eighty-three. It stretches coincidence a bit far doesn't it?"

"The truth is worse even than that," said Nicholas. "The dates of the killings are also identical."

"That's not so. The first Rogano murder was on October 30th, and the Deptford Strangler first struck on November 9th. The second killing in Rogano was on November 6th; the present-day strangler went to work for the second time on November 16th. It's been that way all along. Although the intervals between each murder have been identical for both sets, there has been a difference of ten days in actual dates."

"As you've repeatedly pointed out to me, I'm the historian and you're the detective," said Nicholas almost like a jaded pedant chiding a dull pupil. "In 1582 Pope Gregory XIII replaced the old

Julian calendar with his own Gregorian calendar, which we now use. There was ten days difference between the two."

"You mean . . . ?"

"I mean the Rogano murders were committed while the Old Style calendar was operating. Our present murders have been taking place under the New Style. To find the true dates of the Rogano stranglings we must add ten days to each date. That makes them coincide exactly with the days of the year on which the present murderer has struck."

Brough whistled through a gap in his teeth. "I wish to God I could believe in such coincidence," he said gravely, and lapsed into a brooding silence.

After a few moments of moodily puffing away at his pipe he said, "How did you discover the Rogano victims had been strangled?"

"The answer to that one is a mystery in itself," said Nicholas, "and it makes things more bewildering than ever."

14

Nicholas climbed out of bed, pulled on a threadbare dressing gown and began pacing the room. A baker's cart rumbled along the street beneath the window.

"When I got back to the vicarage to pack a case the telephone was ringing. I answered it. It was a dreadfully bad line and I could just about hear a man's voice. It said, '*Good afternoon, Mr. Calvin. Unless I am seriously mistaken you and I shall be meeting very shortly.*' He croaked rather than spoke and at times his voice was hardly distinguishable from the crackling of the telephone line. I said, 'Who is this?' and he said his name was Augustus Carew. He was a painter. I asked him if we had ever met. 'No,' he replied, '*but we shall.*'

"'What makes you so sure?' I inquired. There was something unaccountably disquieting in his manner. '*It is written,*' he said calmly."

"What the devil was that supposed to mean?" said Brough.

"Exactly what I asked him. But he just repeated, '*It is written*,' and gave a nervous little laugh. He sounded as old as God. 'Are you certain it is me and not my father, Mr. Bartholomew Calvin, you wish to speak to?' I asked impatiently. '*It is you*,' he said faintly. I had answered the telephone in a state of extreme tension. In moments this weird stranger had reduced my nerves to shreds. 'Mr. Carew,' I said, 'I don't know you and I don't see why I should agree to meet you. I am extremely busy and you have not even done me the courtesy of telling me who put you in touch with me or what you want.'"

"How did he take that?" asked Brough.

"There was a long pause. Then he said, '*I can tell you about Rogano*.'

"That rattled me. 'Rogano!' I almost shouted. 'What do you mean? What do you or anyone know about Rogano?' I remember thinking as I spoke that I didn't know the sound of my own voice. It was almost a bark. '*I know*,' he said, chary as ever.

"'All right,' I said. 'When can we meet?'

"'*Today*.'

"'Where?'

"'*I live at Allerton Magna in Somerset. If you catch the three-twenty Bath train from Paddington I can meet you at the station at six o'clock*.'

"'Very well,' I said grudgingly. 'How shall I know you?' But he was gone."

Nicholas ceased pacing and sat on a stool by the fireplace. Staring into the empty grate, he went on, "It was a bitterly cold day and even the traveling rug I had taken with me failed to warm me as I sat in an icy little cell that the Great Western Railway Company is pleased to call a passenger compartment. My teeth chattered in time with the clattering of the train and my breath froze as it met the air."

"Should've gone first-class," said Brough.

"It would have been a most wretched journey but for one thing. There was a fellow with tinted spectacles sitting in the opposite corner of the carriage. For most of the way I was able to blot out the misery of the cold and the misery of Rogano by trying to puzzle where I had seen him before."

"Probably an actor," said Brough.

"No, the moment I saw him I knew I had not only seen him before but that I had known him personally. I almost remembered, but as my mind grasped the realization it dissolved. He appeared to have no recollection of me, but that meant nothing. I've always had a good memory for faces and have frequently recognized old acquaintances who have long since forgotten me. I thought at first that the fellow was one of my childhood playmates. He was roughly my own age. Then I abandoned that idea and thought he was someone I had known either at prep school or college. I ransacked my memory as the train lurched through the frozen countryside, but the more I searched the more uncertain I became. I kept willing him to take off his glasses. I was sure that if only I could see his eyes I should know him. Eventually I saw in his face vague reflections of a dozen forgotten acquaintances from my earliest childhood to my days at university. It was a bizarre feeling, I can tell you."

"Why didn't you ask him who he was?"

"I don't know. Something I can't explain held me back. I don't know why, but I felt, somehow, there would be *danger* in my speaking to him."

"Your nerves *were* in a bad state."

"Yes."

"Did you discover who he was?"

"No. By the time I gave up speculating the train was pulling into Swindon. I had to change there and board a little train that steamed around the Wiltshire villages and across the county border into Somerset. My companion also got on the smaller train, but in a carriage farther along toward the engine. The train arrived at Allerton Magna at about ten to six. It was a tiny country station and I was the only person to alight. It was already pitch dark. Carrying my rug and a small overnight case, I walked along the deserted platform to the exit gate. . . ."

Wearily, Nicholas continued his tale.

The ticket collector at Allerton Magna had been a crooked old man with a pointed face and dark bulging eyes, reminding Nicholas of a feeble old hound.

"Mizz'r Caalvin?" he had said with a gruff sort of friendliness.

"Yes. I'm Nicholas Calvin."

The little man scurried to the back of his kennel and returned with a grubby piece of paper.

"Mezzage frum Mizz'r C'roo," he announced, waving the paper aloft.

"Oh?" said Nicholas, fearing that the journey had, after all, been in vain.

"Yaas! Sez as 'ow 'e caan't make it t'meet you 'ere. Aasks will you see 'im at the Old 'Ouse."

"Where is it?" asked Nicholas, relieved that the mysterious Mr. Carew had not cried off altogether.

"Old 'Ouse?" said the ticket collector, sniffing the air. The aroma of fried sausages was wafting in from the scullery of his home, concealed somewhere behind the booking office.

"Yes, the Old House," Nicholas repeated encouragingly. The man described in tortuous detail what proved to be a fairly simple route. Nicholas thanked him, pressed a sixpence into his waiting palm and walked out into the road.

It took Nicholas ten minutes to walk through the village to the home of Mr. Carew. It was nearly all downhill and the way was well lit by the bright electric lights of the community's six pubs.

Just outside the village Nicholas passed an old water pump in a hollow at the edge of the lane. An oil lantern was nailed to a branch of a nearby tree and by its swinging light he could see two farm laborers arguing about some money one said he had lent the other. A third man stood by the tree, directly beneath the lamp. He was better dressed than the other two and took no part in their altercation. He just stood and watched. For one shocking second Nicholas felt sure he was the man who had been opposite him in the train.

Impossible, he thought. After all, he had been the only passenger to get off at Allerton. And yet . . . A moment later the man shifted his position and his face was in shadow. Nicholas, badly shaken, carried on into the country, every few paces stealing nervous glances over his shoulder.

The Old House was aptly named. It was a large, ugly, double-fronted building at least three hundred years old. Half-timbered and with great brick chimneys, it was of a type that Nicholas usually found imposing and attractive.

Funny how vile this one looks, he thought. Probably because it's so run down.

Paint hung off the walls and the gardens were unkempt and overgrown. The building was enclosed in a circle of copper beech trees.

The remarkable thing about the house was its vast number of windows. There were scores of them, in the oddest places and at queer angles. There were little raised sections of roof with leaded lights, a line of tiny square windows beneath the eaves, great casement windows in the main walls and even glazed embrasures cut into sections of wall too narrow for a proper window.

Not particularly pleasant to look at, thought Nicholas, but I suppose they give plenty of light.

He picked his way along the drive, across which a large gas lamp in the porch threw an unsteady light. At one point he had to skirt the drive where a tree had crashed down, blocking the way. Despite the ugliness of the house, it seemed to Nicholas, it did possess a dimension of warmth. Always sensitive to the "atmosphere" of houses, he fancied that the vibrations he received from this one were positive and friendly.

Everything lay under a blanket of snow, enhancing the desolation of the house and giving it the appearance of a ruin. He pulled the bell handle and heard a distant clanging within.

It was fully three minutes before he heard any sounds of life. As he stood before the heavy oak front door the moon appeared from behind a bank of clouds and poured its brightness over the snow and into the glinting windows.

Nicholas looked along the line of the building and back along the drive. The physical attributes of the Old House should have made it an ideal model for a painter wishing to evoke a scene of menace. But as he looked at the house and grounds bathed in the silver-white light of moon and snow, Nicholas realized it could never feel threatening. Something far deeper than its grim façade and ancient trees went to create the aura that surrounded it. Its essential *character* was one of warmth.

At that moment the door opened and he was confronted by a very old man. His garments were shabby and he had few teeth left, but Nicholas realized before he spoke that his host was the

personification of his house. An inner warmth percolated through
the craggy exterior.

"Mr. Calvin," he said, taking Nicholas' hand and encompassing
it with his own. "Please enter."

A blaze of heat engulfed him as he crossed the threshold and
Augustus Carew led him across a wide hall to a chair by a massive
log fire. The light was dim and, apart from the glow of the fire,
was concentrated in a corner to Nicholas' right, where the artist
had his easel and paints. It seemed to Nicholas that the internal
walls of the house had been removed, transforming almost the
whole ground floor into one huge hall. It was uncarpeted and ex-
tremely untidy, but somehow looked neither neglected nor
unloved. A pile of coal occupied one corner and the floor was cov-
ered with books, newspapers and discarded tins of paint. Around
the walls hung portraits and landscapes of an oddly primitive na-
ture, some lacking all perspective. Others depicted scenes of appal-
ling horror with startling realism, and reminded Nicholas of the
works of Hieronymus Bosch or Breughel the Elder. Other paint-
ings, some in enormous gilt frames, stood on the floor and leaned
against armchairs and tables. To the left of the door was a repre-
sentation of Abraham about to sacrifice Isaac that Nicholas could
have sworn was a Rubens. An old straw hat had been thrown
carelessly over one corner of it.

"Welcome to my home," said Augustus Carew. Then, seem-
ingly in answer to Nicholas' thoughts, he said, "The house is built
over a well. That explains its overwhelmingly good vibrations."

"How so?" asked Nicholas with genuine interest.

"It was universally believed by our ancestors that well water
had certain qualities that provided protection against evil spirits.
The old East European belief that vampires were incapable of
crossing running water stemmed from the same idea. The well
upon which this house stands was a holy well and a place of pil-
grimage for a thousand years before the house was built at the end
of the 1500s. I have traced it on ancient maps, and local tradition
has it that some sort of holy place has existed on this site since be-
fore recorded history. If you are interested, as I know you are, I
shall show you the well later on. It remains much as it was, in the
cellar."

"Mr. Carew," said Nicholas, "I am of course fascinated by your story, but of much more immediate concern is what you know of events at Rogano."

He walked across to a side table that had one leg bandaged with a length of sacking, and returned with a carafe of yellow wine.

"I am a direct descendant of the man who built this place," he said, pouring each of them a large glass of the wine. "None of us has been particularly notable in his achievements except old Sir Thomas Carew, who was one of Cromwell's generals. He went over to the Royalists toward the end of the Civil War and spent six years in the Tower for his desertion of the top dog. They let him out eventually and he retired here to write his memoirs. After the Restoration, Charles II gave him a pension and made him an adviser to the Privy Council, with a particular brief to keep a wary eye on the Puritans lest they should conspire to make a comeback."

Nicholas began to wonder if his garrulous old host had reached the threshold of senility. He seemed quite forgetful of the urgency with which he had requested the younger man's visit.

"I haven't forgotten your reason for coming here," he said, again in apparent response to Nicholas' thoughts. "In fact the fortunes of Sir Thomas are closely linked with the mystery of the Rogano Strangler."

"So the victims *were* strangled!" said Nicholas excitedly, momentarily forgetting that he had told no one of his work except Brough.

"Yes they were. But why and by whom I do not know. I know this much only because I have in my possession a document recording the series of crimes, a document you have neither seen nor even found mentioned."

He set his empty glass on the floor and dragged a ramshackle couch toward the fire. He placed it as close to the blaze as he could without the upholstery itself bursting into flames, and sat down upon it. Secreting his slippered feet under one of its cushions, he took a blanket that lay draped over the back of the couch and swathed himself in it. He seemed after a few moments to be sleeping, but when Nicholas shifted his feet an inch or two he realized that he was very much awake and deep in thought.

"What do you know of prophecy, Mr. Calvin?" he said, stirring.

"Nothing," said Nicholas.

"Well," said Carew in the manner of a man about to deliver a lecture. He cleared his throat noisily and said, "I was born a Roman Catholic. I was brought up in the faith and I followed it strictly throughout my early life. But unlike most of my co-religionists I believed that manifestations of supernatural power were more widespread, commonplace even, than orthodox tradition allowed. This brings me to prophecy. I have been absorbed by the subject of precognition since I was a small boy, from the rehearsed ramblings of the fairground gypsy to the divine inspiration of the great prophets like Elijah. I have studied premonitions, dreams, visions. The greatest of all prophets in post-Christian times was a man who has been cursed as a magician. Despite the diatribes hurled against him in the three hundred years since he lived and worked, he was without doubt a man of incredible power and a stunning ability to look into the future. He was called Michel de Nostredame."

"Nostradamus," said Nicholas.

"The very man," said Carew. "He died in 1566 and the first edition of his prophecies was published two years later. He foresaw the French Revolution, the rise of Napoleon and the end of the world at the close of this century."

"But so much of Nostradamus' writings are vague generalizations. They could be made to fit many different events."

"That is true of many of them, and certainly the case with *all* the ones you will have read. Nostradamus also used many metaphors and figures of speech. For instance, he would often personify inanimate objects and where he seemed to be talking of people would in fact be referring to things. But some of his prophecies are so specific that their meaning cannot be in doubt. He described, for instance, the flight of Louis XVI to Varennes, and gave the exact date, month and year, of the treaty between Turkey and Persia in October 1727."

"I didn't know that," said Nicholas.

"Few people do," pursued Carew. "Few people know that while traveling in Italy Nostradamus met a swineherd called Felice Peretti. He immediately fell upon his knees and addressed the peasant as 'Your Holiness.' In 1585, nearly twenty years after Nostradamus' death, that swineherd became Pope Sextus V. On an-

other occasion, while the King and Queen of France were visiting
his house at Salon in Provence, Nostradamus picked out a small
boy in the royal entourage. He said the boy would one day be
King. The prophecy seemed foolish, for the King had two sons of
his own. Strangely, they both died childless and the little boy,
who was Henri of Navarre, became King Henri IV."

Carew rose from the couch, brought a bucket of coal from the
corner and emptied it onto the fire. Once more wrapping himself
in his blanket, he resumed his story.

"Many bogus editions of Nostradamus' predictions have ap-
peared. As early as 1649 the enemies of Cardinal Mazarin pub-
lished an edition containing some fake prophecies condemning
him, dating it 1568. In 1781 the Vatican proscribed the prophe-
cies and thousands of copies all over Europe were burned. It is
now virtually impossible to find a copy of the prophecies pub-
lished before 1781, when Nostradamus was declared apostate. But
even if this holy vandalism had not occurred, the real core of Nos-
tradamus' work would still be unknown. Nostradamus wrote in a
letter that his original manuscripts were burned. This was a ruse
to bewilder the Inquisition, which had him under close observa-
tion.

"All his original handwritten prophecies survived. In his last
years Nostradamus was a hunted man. I have uncovered evidence
to suggest that he renounced his allegiance to the Church of
Rome in the early 1560s. Shortly before he died he handed all his
manuscripts to a man with whom he had evolved a deep friend-
ship. Nostradamus held those who had 'drunk the smoke of the
lamp'—dedicated scholars—in great esteem. This friend was such
a man, and he became like a son to the prophet. Although an
Englishman, he had studied in Paris and Orleans and later be-
came a remarkable administrator. He returned to England in
1566, soon after Nostradamus died. Twenty years later he built
this house. His name was Henry Carew, the grandfather of old
Tommy Carew, whom I mentioned earlier.

"I learned of Henry's exploits when I came to read the un-
published memoirs of Thomas Carew. I re-edited them with foot-
notes, retitled them *Memoirs of a Royalist Puritan* and then
failed miserably to get them published. However, that's by the
bye. Tommy did not know what happened to the papers, or even

their precise contents, but he recalled talk of 'important papers from France' when he was a little boy. It was believed by members of the family then that Henry had been a spy and that he had stolen important state papers from the King of France on behalf of Walsingham, Queen Elizabeth's spymaster. It was thought the papers had been concealed in the house here. As there had been no record since of anything having been found, or indeed of any proper search having been made, I decided to look for myself. That was forty years ago."

He reached for the wine and refilled their glasses.

"As far as I was concerned I was looking for the mysterious purloined state papers of the family legend. I obtained plans of the house and tried to decide where I should hide something if I were in Henry's position. It did not take me long to decide upon the cellars, which not only run under the house but under parts of the grounds as well. The house can boast nothing so picturesque as a secret passage, nor even a modest priest hole.

"After installing gaslight in all the cellars and clearing out the accumulated rubbish of three centuries, sifting each item individually, I concluded that there was no cache in which documents could have been secreted unless they had been built into the wall or floor when the house was constructed. I rejected that notion. A man hiding papers intends them to be retrieved sometime in the future. If he had intended them to be permanently unobtainable he would surely have destroyed them. At last I turned my attention to the well. My suspicions had been aroused when I read in a county history that local legend claimed that any contact between the water of the well and the human body would instantly destroy the well's holy power. In pre-Roman times, it was thought, a shrine had been built over the water to prevent this unhappy pollution taking place. Of course, such an idea was nonsense. Absolutely no basis for it in lore. Simply a local deviation. When I looked into it further I found that the idea was not ancient at all. It had been invented by Henry himself. But such traditions, like those of hauntings and curses, die hard. And this one persisted for centuries. I would not be surprised if the locals hereabouts today give it credence. I decided that a wily old wolf like Henry—at least, that's what his grandson thought of him—that having contrived the legend he would make use of it. I became certain that he would have chosen the well in which to conceal his dangerous treasure. The well is about ten feet across and a good thirty feet deep. I started to examine its inner wall."

Carew startled his visitor by suddenly clambering off the couch.

"Come on," he said. "Let's go down there." He led Nicholas across the bare wooden floor to a large trap door beneath the angle of the staircase.

A system of ropes and pulleys attached to the trap and secured on the underside of the stairs enabled him to lift open the door with comparative ease. Grabbing a lantern from a nearby hook, he lit it with a taper and led the way down a flight of narrow steps into the darkness. At first Nicholas could see nothing except Carew's furrowed face floating in blackness within the rusty corona of the lantern's light. But in a moment the old man had the first gas lamp burning and within a minute the whole place was illuminated. Unlike most cellars Nicholas had been in, it was spotlessly clean and the walls were whitewashed. One wall was stacked with books, another with hundreds of canvases and frames. The ceiling rose above them in great sweeps of vaulted stone, supported on huge pillars. In the center was the mouth of the well, a good ten feet in diameter and bounded by a low wall of stone. Carew set down the lantern and returned to his story.

"With the help of a torch I scrutinized every inch of stone in the well as far down as I could reach. Eventually I could go no deeper without falling headfirst into it, so I tied a rope around my waist, secured it to that pillar over there and climbed slowly down.

"I searched endlessly for loose stones around the walls, but without any success. Eventually I took to combing the floor of the well, which lay beneath three feet of stinking water. Within a quarter of an hour my feet kicked against an object that felt like a long cylindrical stone. It was an earthenware jar. Excitedly I removed it from the water in which it had lain for close on three hundred years. It was no easy task hauling myself to the top one-handed and with my trousers and boots weighed down with water, but I was a good deal stronger in those days and I managed it without losing hold of my prize. In the light of the cellar I could see that furry green algae had grown all over the jar and was in places up to half an inch thick."

He led Nicholas back upstairs and settled himself again beneath his blanket by the fire. His story had kindled a light in his eye but for some minutes he said nothing and made no effort to move. After loudly clearing his throat he went on, "The jar contained a bundle of papers, covered on both sides with minute brown script, wrapped in a larger sheet of parchment. This outer document bore a paragraph of notes by Sir Henry, from which I learned of his relationship with Nostradamus and the true nature of his secret documents."

Once again he stopped. Then, looking Nicholas steadily in the eye, he said, "Imagine my horror and astonishment at finding that the note was addressed to *me*. There had been no Augustus in our family until my father read Gibbon's *Decline and Fall of the Roman Empire* and named me after his current hero. But there, written three hundred years ago by a distant ancestor, was a letter beginning, *To Augustus Carew*, and signed, *Father of your fathers, Henry Carew*. The very thought makes the mind reel, but let us not dwell there.

"In many respects the original manuscript was identical to the published versions of the seer's writings. They were set out in the same order, ten parts, all but one containing a hundred prophecies; each prophecy in the form of a quatrain or four-lined stanza with alternate lines rhyming. Like the published versions, they were in old French. But unlike the published versions they contained prophecies which had never seen the light of day. Each part, containing as it does one hundred quatrains, has become known as a century. But in all published versions to date Century Seven has contained only forty-two quatrains. It has been stated that this century was never completed by Nostradamus. Why this odd omission should have been made no on has explained. In the handwritten version I had before me Century Seven was complete, but quatrains forty-seven to one hundred inclusive had been struck through by the author and were unreadable. That left four quatrains that were completely new."

Stirring from his apparent lethargy once more, Carew got up and dragged the couch clear of the hearth. Grasping a stout poker with both hands, he pried up one of the flagstones in front of the grate. It revealed a hollow about a foot deep and six inches across.

From this he produced a battered metal box that contained the manuscripts.

"As you said, so much of Nostradamus' published work suffers because of its general nature," he said as he took the brittle papers from their box. "But for that we must blame not Nostradamus but a man called Chavigny, who edited the prophecies after the seer's death. He distorted much of Nostradamus' original writing, misunderstood a great deal more and was careless in reproducing the author's original spelling. When you come to study the prophet's own version, with my own translation attached, you will be amazed how accurate he was in predicting the course of world history to date. And you will be horrified at what he predicts in the decades to come."

"Once again, I must say that this is wholly fascinating," said Nicholas. "But how does Rogano fit into it?"

"I am tired, Mr. Calvin," he replied. "Tonight I must sleep. Tomorrow we shall talk again."

Without another word he showed Nicholas into a small antechamber in which stood a solitary bed. It was divided from the main room only by a muslin curtain and as he undressed Nicholas saw Carew return to the couch, drag it to its former position by the fire and lie down to compose himself for sleep.

15

Nicholas rose to his feet and walked to the window. It was now fully light and the daily bustle of life in Jermyn Street was reaching full swing.

Turning to Brough, he said, "You can imagine that the last thing in my mind was sleep. It had been an incredible, disturbing day, and nothing had happened to set my mind at rest about my gnawing suspicion that *I* was the Deptford Strangler. I was physically and emotionally exhausted and the motley images of the day —Rogano, the stranglings in London, Dr. Orchard, Carew and his curious house, Nostradamus and my own recurring nightmare—all coalesced in my tired brain and grew into the most convoluted and distressing night's dreaming I can remember.

"I did not awaken until after one the following afternoon. Dressing quickly, I went into the main room. Carew was not there. I called his name gently but there was no reply. Then I noticed a door leading off toward the back of the house, which must have been closed the night before. I passed through it and along a dim passage. A door to the right led into a kitchen where a pot of stew boiled frantically on an old range. Carew was not there either. I went to the end of the passage and opened the outer door. Two steps led down to a huge garden that had once been exquisitely beautiful. Remnants of the fine Elizabethan landscaping could still be discerned beneath piles of rubble and stacks of timber. The garden was bounded by a semicircle of gaunt and leafless copper beeches. Carew was there hacking away at a log with an ax and replenishing his store of firewood. He turned as I appeared. . . ."

Brough listened wordlessly to his nephew's narrative. These were deeper waters than he had sailed in his life.

"Mr. Calvin!" Carew beamed as Nicholas walked into the garden. "Good morning to you." He buried his ax in the log and gathered an armful of kindling.

A pale light hung in the air and a solitary blackbird trilled somewhere in the snow-covered garden. He ushered Nicholas into the house and sat him down in his chair of the previous night. Banking up the fire and applying the bellows until it raged anew, he withdrew into the kitchen. He returned minutes later with two dauntingly generous bowls of stew and a plate of stale rolls.

Carew saw his guest eying one of his peculiar medieval-style paintings that hung above the pile of coal. It was a representation of a modern port—Nicholas thought Liverpool—but it was painted in a two-dimensional way, without any attempt at perspective, and in stark primary colors. Nicholas thought it had a strange quality of super-reality and an odd kind of beauty.

"You are intrigued by my painting?" he asked. Without awaiting a reply, he continued, "It is a development of the styles that were abandoned when the Renaissance reared its ugly head. It is in fact far more advanced artistically than the pretty pictures of Gainsborough and Renoir which receive such adoration today."

"But it looks so primitive," said Nicholas. "With the dawning of the Renaissance painting took such giant steps forward."

"Giant steps backward," he chided. "By its very nature the Renaissance was a return to styles two and three thousand years old. Those styles had been lost, abandoned, superseded. The period we call the Dark Ages was not a slump into barbarism but the natural progression from the established order of things in Greece and Rome. By reviving Classical tastes in politics, architecture and art, man lost the thread of his intellectual evolution. And we have lost that oneness with nature that gave our distant ancestors such clear insight into the workings of the universe. They knew far more than we, in the same way a newborn baby *knows* much more of the eternal truths of existence than his parents. In growing up the child is conditioned into forgetting his state of knowing. Mankind in the same way, in growing older, has conditioned himself into forgetting what he once knew. My only hope is that the knowledge is not irretrievable. We are still in the depths of the dark age that began with the Renaissance, but the veil might yet lift. There are forces at work in the world of which we have no conception, but the Egyptians and the Druids and the astrologers of old knew. We might yet know again if we only switch ourselves back onto the natural path of evolution."

Nicholas could do nothing but listen. Mr. Carew's views were revolutionary and provoking but he was in no frame of mind for a discussion of any subject but the one which had brought him to Allerton Magna. This stimulating digression was, he hoped, simply to fill the gap while they supped their meal. Mopping up the last of his stew with a hunk of bread, Carew slid his bowl underneath his couch and folded his hands on his chest.

"Mr. Calvin," he began in his usual formal manner, "I realize there are a number of unanswered questions which my intrusion into your life has raised. How for instance did I know of your researches into the murders at Rogano? Why did I bring you here? What has Nostradamus to do with your work? I have left these issues unexplained until this moment because to have announced immediately the facts I have in my hands would have been to invite your ridicule. To make myself credible I had to build up gradually to the crux of my information."

He paused again and returned Nicholas' gaze with a troubled yet somehow elated look on his weather-beaten features.

"This meeting between us was foretold by Nostradamus more than three centuries ago," he said bluntly. He fell silent once more to allow the import of his words to sink into Nicholas' mind.

He reached into the metal box which lay on the couch at his feet and took out a sheet of parchment.

"This is an appendix, written by Nostradamus, to the papers he passed to my ancestor. It is not in his usual strict verse, but as you shall see it is composed in a cryptic form of prose and poetry mixed. Let me read it to you."

He took a pair of horn-rimmed spectacles from his breast pocket and began to read the ancient script, translating as he went.

"*About the time that I shall be conjoined unto VIII, VII and III, the Protestant of Geneva will reappear in name not nature.*"

Carew looked up. "Render those Roman figures as Arabic and you have one, eight, seven and three. Conjoin them as Nostradamus bids and you have 1873, the year of your birth. The Protestant of Geneva was the great reformer John Calvin, a contemporary of Nostradamus. You are Calvin in name though not in nature, as the prediction states. The next part is in verse."

He handed Nicholas his translation of the four-lined rhyme. It said:

> *These my words to C. shall pass*
> *From the upright tunnel in the house of glass.*
> *And the aged man who shows me light*
> *Shall be of the fruit of my English knight.*

When Nicholas had read it Carew said, "Here the seer predicts that his papers will be passed to the man Calvin born in 1873, and that they will be taken from *the upright tunnel in the house of glass*. What can that explicit description refer to if not the well beneath this house? As you have noticed, Old House has a mass of windows. There is glass everywhere. I hasten to add that on a Jacobean map I have found the house is marked as *Ye Glasse House*. It was a favorite joke of my father, who served on Allerton

Parish Council as an alderman, that he was once mildly rebuked
by the mayor for apparent hypocrisy. 'Alderman Carew,' the old
mayor is supposed to have said, 'men who live in glass houses . . .'
and the entire council chamber subsided into laughter. However, I
digress. Nostradamus goes on to say that the person responsible
for bringing his papers to light would be an old man of the same
family as his 'English knight,' which was his nickname for old Sir
Henry Carew. Can there be any doubt that this refers to me?"

"It would seem not," ventured Nicholas. "What does he say
next?"

"Next we turn to the unfinished Century Seven. The first of
the previously unseen prophecies, number forty-three, translates as:
A *puzzle. And a struggle over crimes long dead. The strangling
hands of Rogano kill again and London walks in fear. C. knows
not himself and the terror of the night haunts him.* Exactly what
this passage means you doubtless know better than I."

Nicholas remained silent, stunned by the accuracy of these an-
tique prophecies and the fact that without doubt they referred to
him. At last he said, "Somehow you know already that I have been
researching a series of murders at Rogano in Italy in the 1450s.
When Nostradamus speaks of the Rogano killer striking again in
London he refers to a murderer known at the moment only as the
Deptford Strangler. I learned of this man's crimes myself only yes-
terday morning. But as the prophet stated, London *is* walking in
fear just now."

He paused again, still unable to grasp that a man three cen-
turies dead had foreseen the present state of his, Nicholas', mind.
Then he said, "When he talks of C.—Calvin—me, not knowing
myself, he speaks of my dread that *I* might be the Deptford Stran-
gler. I do *not* know myself. The 'terror of the night' can only refer
to the nightmares in which I have found myself strangling people.
It is those dreams which above all make me think I might be los-
ing my mind."

"I have puzzled over these predictions for years," said Carew,
curiously unmoved by the news that his visitor might be a psycho-
pathic killer. "And still I cannot work out their meaning. I had
hoped your entry into events would elucidate many dark areas. In
fact it has mystified me more."

He became suddenly intense. "What in the world is meant by

The strangling hands of Rogano kill again? Why *again?* Is it met-
aphor? If so, how are we to interpret it?"

"I don't know," confessed Nicholas. They sat turning the riddle
over in their minds for several minutes before Nicholas said,
"How did you know about me and my researches?"

"I have known of your existence for many years," Carew re-
plied. "In fact since shortly after you were born. Did you know that
you were the only Calvin born in this country in 1873? I found
that out from the registers of births and deaths at Somerset House
in London. I did not approach you until now because I had no
way of knowing when the time was right, when my allusion to
Rogano would be meaningful to you. I knew only that it would be
in my old age."

"How did you know that now was the right time?"

"I have a brother, Quentin. At the age of twenty-eight he was
ordained a priest. Unfortunately the rigors of celibacy proved too
much for him and he committed a sin for which he has never for-
given himself. He committed adultery with a woman of his parish.
Afterward he was eaten up with remorse, but he was unable to ex-
punge his sense of sin by confession. He was also powerless to cur-
tail his relationship with the woman, which by all accounts was a
tremendously passionate affair. It continued in secret for six
months. When, through a particularly misguided decision on the
part of his confessor, the chancellor of his diocese discovered his
misdemeanor, Quentin was disciplined and eventually unfrocked.
The Roman Church fancies itself built on divinity. It cannot
countenance human frailty. The shame and misery of it, com-
pounded when only a month later his mistress left him for an-
other, turned poor Quentin's mind. He took to drink. He was ab-
sorbed into the most degraded level of London society and moved
from doss house to seedy doss house. Now he sits at the Beggar's
Alms in Seven Dials drinking from morning to evening. As I
think you know, he overheard your talk with your uncle on Thurs-
day night, and later eavesdropped while you continued your talk
in the upper room and spoke about your investigations into the
Rogano murders. He still doesn't know how you realized he was
outside listening."

The comment was clearly an invitation for Nicholas to en-
lighten him, but he thought the explanation that Brough had

smelled his brother through a wooden door was best left unsaid. After a moment Carew continued.

"Years ago, before Quentin's disgrace, I shared with him my discovery of the Nostradamus manuscript. Since then we have drifted far apart and every attempt I have made to contact him or to bring him home has been met with hostility. But when he heard your conversation three nights ago he was galvanized into action. He knew how important it was to me to contact you and all his old bitterness was momentarily forgotten. He telephoned me on Friday. Then I knew that the long-awaited moment had arrived."

"And now?" asked Nicholas.

"Now, I pass to you the documents which Nostradamus intended you to have. Only you can make use of them. That they have a purpose and a deeply significant one I am in no doubt. Study them carefully, Nicholas, and act as you must. If I can assist you in any way at all I am at your disposal."

Nicholas sighed and looked at Brough. "The whole thing was so unreal, it increased my sense of losing a grip on reality. While I was with Carew the possibility that I was the victim of some unpleasant trick did not cross my mind. Later I could not decide. At that moment I felt I needed a long rest and possibly some psychiatric treatment as well. Nothing made any sense. But what could I do except take Carew's advice? I thanked him as sincerely as I was able in my confused state of mind, I took the bundle of papers he handed me and I left. I spent the next two days in a hotel over at Warminster—do you remember you took me there as a child?—and rested as best I could. I also tried to make sense of the prophecies and notes. They made no sense."

He sighed in despair. "Perhaps they do not apply to me after all. Perhaps that whole experience at Allerton Magna was part of my own fantasy. In any event, I got back to London yesterday and looked more closely at the exploits of the Deptford killer. It was then that I realized that the Rogano killings fitted so exactly with the present series. It was then that I decided I had to retrieve the report of the Rogano killings which I had given you last Friday. I felt sure by then that if you coupled the two sets of murders you could not fail to suspect me."

Brough said nothing. He had allowed Nicholas to tell his story with hardly an interruption. He did not mind admitting to himself that he was as confused as his nephew.

As if suddenly inspired with hope, Nicholas said, "Uncle, you said last night that while I was away the strangler struck again. I can *prove* that I was not responsible. When did the murder take place?"

"On Sunday," said Brough flatly.

"I can prove I was at Allerton Magna on Sunday," said Nicholas with new intensity.

"So was the Deptford Strangler," said Brough.

"What do you mean?"

"At the beginning of the week I received a telegram from the Yard. They had just heard from the Somerset constabulary that an old man called Augustus Carew had been found strangled in the living room of his house."

16

"That's impossible," said Nicholas in token resistance to a notion that he knew despite himself was not only possible but true. Brough fidgeted uneasily in his chair.

"Poor old Carew," pursued Nicholas with a sigh that expressed both bitterness and despair. "Then the case against me seems insurmountable."

Bewilderment struggled with self-pity in his tired, battered mind.

"Did I kill Carew?" he asked aloud, the confusion dilating the pupils of his eyes like an addictive drug. "Did I throttle that old man and *dream* that I left him feeding lettuce to a spider?"

He looked at Brough. "It was one of his hobbies playing about with the appetites of insects and animals. He thought he was doing them a service, that nothing could actually enjoy eating flies."

He smiled wistfully at the old man's antics. "Did I dream all

that?" he repeated, becoming suddenly serious again. "Am I to go
to the gallows for crimes I have no remembrance of committing?
Am I to be incarcerated as a criminal lunatic who knows not what
he does?"

"No one else knows how strong the circumstantial evidence
against you appears," said Brough, steering Nicholas' runaway
emotions onto a more stable course. "You have not been seen
near the scene of any crime, nor has your name been linked with
the murders by anyone but ourselves. There is Dr. Orchard of
course but I am certain he can be trusted to hold his peace."

"Are you saying that because only we know exact details of
what happened at Rogano no one can connect me with the Lon-
don killings?" said Nicholas, rekindling hope.

"I am saying that your exact knowledge of the Rogano case can-
not be brought as evidence against you in the present series of
murders. No prosecution lawyer in his right mind would hang his
case on such a tenuous thread. It would not be difficult for an en-
terprising defense counsel to demonstrate that the Rogano case
was well known to all sorts of people."

"But it isn't."

"Enterprising advocates often prove untruths in British courts
of law, and I frequently thank God they do. Justice would not be
worth a light if you could not employ deception. You can some-
times arrive at a truth only through palpable untruth. A paradox
but there it is. No, your exclusive knowledge of Rogano is not the
evidence that brings you to trial but the evidence that makes you
the prime suspect. There is an awful chasm between suspicion and
arrest, and an even greater one between arrest and trial. Those
gaps are the twin ogres that haunt every copper. It's his job and
his alone to get across. You often have to be a bit of a Blondin to
do it. Your dreams, of course, strengthen the initial suspicion and
confirm that you must be investigated thoroughly. Here we have a
man who has uncovered details about a series of murders,
avowedly the only man to know these facts, dreaming of being a
killer amid a modern series that reproduce that original series
faithfully. Yes, you are the prime suspect, there is no doubt about
it. But even if the Yard were in possession of the facts in our
hands, their investigation would hardly be off the ground. They
have to prove motive, means and opportunity before they can

hope to get the director of public prosecutions to press ahead for a trial. Your presence at Carew's place makes things much stickier of course, but once again only we know about it. At the moment, that is. It won't take them many days to trace the Nicholas Calvin who spoke to the ticket collector at Allerton. As Carew pointed out, there aren't many of you around."

"Aren't we forgetting something? You are in daily contact with the Yard. According to the papers, you have been engaged as a consultant on this very case. You are a policeman to the very marrow. Can you really allow yourself to remain silent in the face of such evidence?"

"The outlook might not be so black," said Brough, staring into space and thinking aloud. "Several points must be considered. Firstly, if you are the Deptford Strangler I am certain that you are unaware of it. You told me of your own volition of your visit to Carew. You had no need even to mention him. You even grasped at your presence in Allerton as an alibi for the latest murder. So, guilty or not, you did not know of Carew's murder until I told you of it a few minutes ago."

"That's so," breathed Nicholas.

"Secondly, your encounter with Carew teaches us that we are *not* the only people who know about Rogano. Carew knew something. His brother Quentin knows what he overheard. Perhaps others know too. If that is so, then you are not the only suspect in sight."

"But the dreams," said Nicholas, far away.

Brough paused and fiddled with a button that was hanging by a thread from his cardigan, allowing his nephew to absorb the fact that above all else he was his friend.

"Thirdly," he said as button and cardigan finally parted company, "we know that the Deptford Strangler—what a stupid name for a man who operates for the most part miles from Deptford—we know that he is conforming absolutely to the pattern set four hundred and fifty years ago by the Rogano killer. Carew's death fits precisely. Remember the old astrologer who lived in the shadow of the campanile? It is therefore reasonable to assume that on the next date which corresponds to a Rogano crime our own friendly neighborhood Jack the Gripper—now there's a name to conjure with—will strike again. If I can keep you with me night and day until after that date has passed, we shall be much wiser. If no murder takes place I shall at least have had an opportunity of observing you during the critical period. If we have blackouts, sleepwalking or other sorts of antisocial behavior then our worst fears might be confirmed. But even that will enable me to testify —God forbid!—to the existence of a side to your nature of which on a conscious level you are oblivious. If on the other hand the strangler does strike while you're under my eye, then we'll have positive evidence of your innocence."

Nicholas listened wordlessly to his uncle's exposition, amused despite his predicament at Brough's evergreen humor, unsinkable even in adversity.

"Lastly," continued the portly detective, "this entire case possesses dimensions of which I never dreamed."

"An unfortunate choice of word," interposed Nicholas in a valiant attempt at matching Brough's humor.

"The entry of Carew and his talk of prophecies, the links between Rogano and the present, make me suspect that we are dealing with something far more mysterious than a berserk historian who relives the past while he's asleep. No, that just won't do. On the whole I'm a canny enough fellow—my mother's grandfather always said he was a direct descendant of Robert the Bruce, the old rascal—and I don't often have reason to consider the *un*-canny. But uncanny this case is. Since my army days in India, when I saw and did things none of your psychiatrists can explain, I've had a healthy respect for the unnatural and I've kept my distance. I've an uncomfortable itching under my skin that makes me think the gap is closing fast."

Nicholas did not begin to understand what his uncle was driving at.

17

After soaking in a tub in front of the fire for an hour, Nicholas felt more refreshed than he had in weeks. The horror of self-doubt still hung over him and images of past and present tumbled in a confused pageant through his aching mind. But at last he felt he was no longer alone, and no matter how the evidence built up against him, logic almost invariably came off worst in its interminable bouts with emotion. Nicholas, siding now with emotion, now with logic, simply could not believe he was a madman. He *felt* sane.

After telephoning his mother to say he would be staying in Jermyn Street for a few days, he and Brough went out for a late breakfast at a coffee room in Bridle Lane, behind Regent Street.

The tables were being set for lunch but Brough managed to get on the right side of a voluptuous lady in a lilac crinoline who supervised the waitresses. A reedlike girl with a voice like a piccolo led them to a corner table behind a bamboo screen where they could talk undisturbed and where their special treatment in the way of menu could not be observed and requested by other clients, who at this transition stage in the day were restricted to coffee and sandwiches. They were soon making an assault on a mountainous fruit hors d'oeuvre, washed down first with orange juice and presently with the incomparable refreshment of the establishment's bottomless coffeepot. The main course was set before them as they chatted inconsequentially about old times, vainly seeking asylum from a hostile present in a comforting past.

"I can't eat this," said Nicholas suddenly, staring at his plate. "I hate meat."

"If you hate meat, why did you order mixed grill?" said Brough in amusement.

"I don't know," snapped Nicholas, who was both dismayed and perplexed by his own incongruous behavior.

Brough pretended not to notice his nephew's agitation. "Oh, I know there's nothing so bad for the arteries as all this fat," he said, attacking a slab of pork, "but I believe the average adult has something like a hundred thousand miles of tubes in his body. By my reckoning it will take more years than I have left to clog that lot up. Besides, I thought you loved meat."

"I do . . . I did," said Nicholas. He was toying with a solitary roast potato in the center of his plate. "Let's change the subject, shall we?" he said at length.

The accommodating lilac lady spirited away the unwanted

viandes and quickly produced a vegetable stew. The two men munched silently for a while like a pair of unrelated ruminants chewing the cud, each deep in his own private reflections.

". . ."

"I'm sorry?" said Brough.

"I said I think I'm going mad."

"Why?"

"The splitting of a mind into two separate personalities," said Nicholas more to himself than his companion. "Schizophrenia isn't it called?"

"Nicholas, if you are dwelling on these murders again . . ."

"What else do you expect me to dwell upon?" he said angrily, and then returning to earth he said dismissively, "I'm not . . . I'm dwelling on meat."

Brough said nothing. He knew that Nicholas needed no encouragement to say what he had to say.

"I like meat but I am revolted by it. Explain that. Tell me how two contradictory urges can exist at once in the human mind. It's nothing to do with concern for my health or any high principles about man's relation to the animal kingdom. It's something unconscious and inexplicable."

"Curious," said Brough. "I've no doubt it stems from your low state of mind."

"My low state of mind stems from *it*," replied Nicholas. "And *it* is something alien that fights against the real me. Oh yes, I know what you'll say. Overwork. Well maybe overwork has brought all this on. Maybe overwork has turned me into a murderer."

"That is exactly what we should know in ten days," said Brough, taking out a notebook.

"Why do I hate my father?" said Nicholas, heedless of Brough's remark.

"I wasn't aware that you did."

"Nor was I until last night. It came to me as I lay in bed. . . . All my life I've had a wonderful relationship with my parents. My father in particular has been a tremendous friend as well as a conscientious mentor. Apart from isolated instances during adolescence I have always been close to him. Now I hate him. Why?"

"Psychiatry isn't my line at all. I am sure Dr. Freud would

delight in weaving some tangled sexual web from your troubles, but I doubt if that need concern us. Until the date of the next murder we are stumbling about in the dark as far as your psyche is concerned. If it helps you to talk by all means do, but I beg you, don't expect any answers yet."

"I don't expect any answers," said Nicholas. His voice had lost its sharp edge and he had subdued his anger. "I am resigned to waiting. It is just that I am unnerved at the changes going on in my personality."

He seemed close to tears and looked away to compose himself.

"I may be a murderer," he said slowly, "but if I am . . . why?" He bit his lip in self-reproach. "I'm sorry," he said. "That's another question." He looked at Brough's notebook. "Let's get down to business."

Brough needed no second invitation to divert his nephew's attention from his morbid self-analysis. He thumbed through the dog-eared pages of the book until he found a page where he had prepared a rough table of events. "Look at this," he said, handing it to Nicholas. In neat script he had written:

ITALY 1454	ENGLAND 1902
Nov. 9 Lorenzo di Corsa (30) murdered.	Nov. 9 Henry Antrobus (30) murdered.
Nov. 16 Pietro Gatta (59) abducted from his house and murdered.	Nov. 16 Colin Manders (59) abducted from his house and murdered.
Nov. 21 Giovanni Crispi (47) found murdered.	Nov. 21 Patrick Lovell (47) found murdered.
Dec. 10 Brother Domenico (63) found murdered.	Dec. 10 Maurice Dakins (63) found murdered.
Dec. 11 Maria Bellini (19) disappears from her bed.	Dec. 11 Jessica Twomey (19) disappears from her bed.
Dec. 12 Maria Bellini found murdered.	Dec. 12 Jessica Twomey found murdered.
Dec. 14 Ruggiero Festa (83) found murdered.	Dec. 14 Augustus Carew (83) found murdered.
Dec. 27 Sister Constanza Ruffo (28) disappears from her bed.	Dec. 27 ?

| Dec. 28 | Mercurio Ferruccio (42) found murdered. | Dec. 28 ? |
| Dec. 30 | Sister Ruffo found murdered. | Dec. 30 ? |

Having given Nicholas time to absorb the data, Brough said, "I have amended the Rogano dates by ten days to fit in with the Gregorian calendar as you said I should. By that reckoning we should expect the strangler to strike again on the twenty-eighth and kill a forty-two-year-old man. Then on the thirtieth the body of a twenty-eight-year-old woman victim is due to be discovered. Before then we have a lot to do. I made some arrangements while you were bathing. We'll take a trip to North Audley Street after we've eaten."

"What's there?"

"The widow of Sir Patrick Lovell, the strangler's third victim. Where are the Nostradamus papers by the way?"

"At my place in Coptic Street."

"We'll collect those later and see what we can make of them."

Snow was still falling as they left the coffee room, and cutting through a network of alleys that took them through Golden Square and Warwick Street, they emerged into Regent Street. Heading for Mayfair, they crossed into Vigo Street. The pavements on either side of the cobbled thoroughfare were under two-feet-deep snowdrifts and pedestrians were forced to walk in the road. The traffic was not heavy and the horses and carts of tradesmen jogged slowly along the icy road, taking care for the most part to avoid those passing by on foot. Someone was moving from a shabby house to their left. Outside, removal men were stacking furniture onto an iron-wheeled cart, between the shafts of which an overweight shire horse gorged the contents of a nose bag and waited patiently for the flick of his master's whip. A butcher's boy carrying a brace of freshly killed pheasants over his shoulder swaggered by like Spring Heeled Jack, whistling his own cacophonous version of a popular music-hall tune. By the corner of Sackville Street a hackney carriage was stuck in a patch of ice and half a dozen burly men had their shoulders to the back of the vehicle trying to heave it clear. A horse-drawn van was parked outside a chandler's shop in which lights blazed in merry defiance of the gloomy weather and in which men and women lounged around gossiping. On the backboard of the van three men in mufflers and dungarees stood with their eyes upraised. Brough and Nicholas looked up and saw an enormous packing case swinging slowly down on a rope from the open doors of a warehouse on the top floor of the building.

"Take it *slowly!*" bawled the tallest of the three men on the wagon, a grizzled fellow with muttonchop whiskers and a greenspotted handkerchief knotted around his neck. From his imperious manner it was evident that he was the foreman.

"Just the sort of man who'd never stop telling you how he's pulled himself up from the gutter by his boot straps," chuckled Brough as they passed under the precariously swinging load. Touching Nicholas' arm to indicate his intention, Brough stepped into a cubbyhole between two shops which was occupied by an old woman who sold tobacco.

"'Allo, Mr. Brough," squeaked the woman, whose dark and wrinkled face reminded Nicholas of a walnut. She was so tiny that he at first thought she was sitting down behind her overladen counter.

"How are things with you, Kitty?" asked Brough as she weighed and wrapped an ounce of his favorite shag.

"Not so dusty, Mr. Brough," she said as she darted from scales to cash box. "Still got me own teeth." She cackled uproariously. Brough paid her the compliments of the season and followed his nephew into the street. The hoarse man on the back of the wagon was still involved in his heated altercation with his invisible minion in the warehouse above.

"Let it down s-l-o-w-l-y!" he shouted impatiently.

"That little ha'p'orth is a hundred and six," said Brough as they passed through the slush. Nicholas whistled.

"Old Carew was all set for the century," he said. "He looked as fit as a fiddle. Who'd want to kill a harmless old boy like that?"

Every conversation Brough engineered to take Nicholas' mind away from its constant brooding seemed instead to lead directly back to it. It was foolish, he concluded, to expect his nephew to be concerned with anything but the strange events in which he was enmeshed. He decided to abandon his diversionary tactics. Before he could reply, a shrill cry rang out behind them. They spun around in time to see the three navvies jumping from their wagon, and a young well-dressed man apparently rooted to the footpath. The packing case hung twenty feet above him by a single strand of rope.

"Clear out of the way, the rope's breaking," shouted the man who had done all the shouting before. But the young man stood perfectly still, his eye never straying for a moment from the deadly pendulum that creaked menacingly over his head. In another second the tired cord broke in two and its load hurtled to the ground. Brough and Nicholas had instinctively started to run toward the man the moment they had realized his danger. In the last moment before the plunging crate crushed him beneath its weight the man turned with what seemed almost casualness toward the running men, and looked deliberately into Nicholas' face. Nicholas grabbed a gas lamp for support while Brough arrested his own momentum just in time to prevent himself being injured from the debris that flew in all directions. As dust and confusion subsided together, onlookers saw that one side of the crate had splintered and heavy machine parts spilled onto the footpath. The excited shouts which had filled every mouth during the descent of the crate ceased instantly. Death exacted its tithe of silence. The crowd gathered about the damaged packing case and its victim, whose shattered corpse was hidden from the waist upward.

The first man to regain his composure was the vociferous foreman. He bawled an order to his man above, who stared down with terrified eyes, and the rope was lowered to street level. Hacking off the frayed section of rope, the man secured the undamaged part to an iron hoop on top of the case. At the same time he ordered his two cronies to join the man upstairs in hauling the crate upward. A silent signal passed between both parties when the men reached their post and the rope was pulled taut. After some moments the crate began to creak and groan. Its complaints lasted a full two minutes but then it began to rise laboriously into the air. With the help of men in the crowd the foreman swung it clear of the body and at a second signal it was lowered safely into the road. Those who now looked upon the young man turned quickly away.

"Why didn't the damn fool move? He had time," whined the foreman, whose belligerence had evaporated with the realization

that vengeful relatives might hold him responsible for the acci-
dent.

"He just stood there," said a voice from behind.

"As if he *wanted* it to fall on him," said another.

"Don't talk ridiculous," said an angry woman. " 'E couldn't
move becourse 'e was too scared."

"He didn't look scared to me," said a swarthy knife sharpener
who had been closest to the dead man at the moment of impact.

"Nor me," said another, and the sentiment was taken up by a
dozen or more witnesses.

The conversation rumbled on in dry, deadpan tones. Fatuous
comment followed fatuous comment until the arrival of a young
police constable, ruddy-cheeked and out of breath.

Probably his first week on the beat, thought Brough, noting the
vein of exhilaration that underlay the P.C.'s show of authority.
Poor beggar. He'll be sick of corpses before the month's out.

Enough witnesses were forthcoming to enable Brough and his
nephew to pass on without the tedious rigmarole of making state-
ments. As they turned into New Bond Street, Nicholas said, "Did
you see his face?"

"Who, the dead man?"

"Yes."

"I got a good look at him as he looked at you. He had odd eyes
—one brown, one blue."

"He did want to die, didn't he?"

"I think he did. He was too relaxed, pleased even, for one who
was too petrified to move. Haphazard way to commit suicide
though."

They walked on without speaking until they reached a covered
passage that led through to Berkeley Square.

"Do you remember those nightmares I used to have when I was
a child? When I used to wake up screaming?" said Nicholas.

"Yes, now you come to mention it, I do. I'd quite forgotten all
that."

"So had I. Until today." He paused. "Do you remember the
great bogey of those dreams, how I used to describe the devil that
haunted me every night?"

It all came flooding back. "The Man with Odd Eyes!" said
Brough quickly.

"Yes," said Nicholas. "The Man with Odd Eyes. I was afraid to go to bed every night because I knew the moment I fell asleep he would be there."

"You had everybody very worried for a long time over those dreams."

"The Man with Odd Eyes has now stepped out of dreams and into reality," said Nicholas. "That was him."

"I can understand your sudden recollection of those times with the appalling horror of this incident, but having odd eyes isn't that uncommon a trait."

"I tell you, Uncle, it is the *same man*," said Nicholas coldly. "And what is worse, it was the man I saw on the train on the way to see Carew. Only then he had dark glasses on, do you remember? No wonder I thought I knew him."

"Are you sure?" asked Brough.

"I was studying that man's face for over an hour. It was him. And I am now certain that the man by the water pump at Allerton was him too. I know logic says he couldn't be there if he were still on the train, but I don't care. It was the same man."

Brough said nothing.

18

Lady Jennifer Lovell, the widow of the strangler's third victim, was remarkably composed. She received them in the drawing room of her home in North Audley Street and answered Brough's tactful questions calmly and with thought. She was a beautiful woman, at least twenty years younger than her husband. The first bloom of youth had gone but it had been replaced with a more mature beauty, finer and of more substance. She sat, pale with grief but not crushed by it. A modest blue dress advertised her much publicized refusal to don widow's weeds.

"Patrick and I were married for seven years," she had told a journalist who had commented upon her rejection of conventional mourning. "In that time we were profoundly happy. We both abhorred the tribal customs that have clung to our dealing with the dead. I have no wish to wear black and wander in misery for months feeling sorry for myself. I want to remember Patrick as he was, as we were together, and to do him the honor of conducting myself as he would have wished."

Neither she nor her companion had anticipated the storm of self-righteous condemnation which her comments had provoked. Letters on the subject were to be read daily in the press, and cranks had now begun to deluge the Lovell home with venomous missives that castigated, abused and on occasion threatened violence.

"Such appalling disrespect as yours," glowered one anonymous correspondent, "deserves and will surely earn the wrath of our most merciful Lord God. Only the flames of eternal damnation can purge you of your blasphemy."

As a result, Lady Lovell was preparing to leave London as soon as the adjourned inquest on her husband was over.

"Lady Lovell," said Brough, "I know you have been questioned endlessly by my colleagues at Scotland Yard and I do not wish to burden you by going over facts already covered. I should like to ask you just two questions. Have you any idea why your husband was murdered? And do you have any knowledge of the work he was engaged upon when he died?"

"In answer to your first question, no I have no glimmer of an idea why anyone should want to kill him," said Lady Lovell softly. "In answer to your second question, yes my husband was working on plans for an expedition to Palestine. He was very excited about it. He believed he was on the brink of a major discovery that would shed new light on biblical studies."

"What sort of discovery?"

"I know no more than I have told you. He said it was so important he did not want to discuss it even with me until he had more concrete evidence."

"And his papers?"

"He took them with him on the night he died. They have not been recovered."

"And you do not know where he was going that night?"

"No. As I told Inspector Daubeney, he received a telephone call at about six-thirty and said he had to go out to meet someone.

He did not say who." Her eyes filled with tears. "That was the last time I saw him."

Brough waited until Lady Lovell recovered herself.

"Might I ask one more thing?" he said. "I should like if I may to examine your husband's study and the papers he has left. It is just possible that they contain a clue."

"Of course," she said, and led them silently across the wide vestibule with its curving staircase into her husband's meticulously tidy workroom. In the detective's minute examination of the room only one item seemed to interest him deeply—a blank note pad next to the telephone. The little white pad of square paper seemed both to puzzle and disturb him.

Half an hour later they thanked Lady Lovell for her indulgence, bade her good-bye and moved to the front door. As she stood aside to let them through, Brough said, "Lady Lovell, has your husband's workroom been used by anyone since his death?"

"No," she replied. "It has been locked ever since. I have not even been in there myself."

"Any clues?" asked Nicholas when they were out of earshot.

"Very possibly," said Brough. "Very possibly."

19

Something in the way the early afternoon sun glinted upon the frosted glass of an antique-shop door struck a forgotten chord in Nicholas' mind. He looked up at the street nameplate on the blue-washed wall of a stockbroker's office.

"Half Moon Street," he said, speaking his thoughts aloud, "I've been here before."

"When?" said Brough in desultory fashion, still wrestling in his mind not only with the evidence of Lady Lovell but with the strange incident of the man with odd eyes. Was that grotesque episode in some way bound up with all the other perplexing goings-on? Or had the young man's death been absorbed by Nicholas' convoluted mind into some inexplicable fantasy that involved the London stranglings, the Rogano murders and the whole sinister imbroglio of events in which they were now entangled? The detective was already doubting the wisdom of his earlier decision not to consult a psychiatrist: his nephew's behavior was becoming more erratic by the minute.

"In my childhood I suppose," said Nicholas, allowing his eyes to rove from building to building in search of more tangible memories. "Whenever it was, it was long, long ago. Perhaps it was only in a dream."

Brough stumbled and caught hold of Nicholas to prevent himself falling. "Sod these laces," he said in a rare descent into profanity, and stooped to retie them. Nicholas walked slowly on, his wandering eye scrutinizing each landmark and delving for its double in his memory. He had walked about twelve paces from where Brough crouched to attend his delinquent laces when he brought himself to a sharp halt outside a large house with three steps leading up to its front door. The door was open.

"I know this place," he murmured to himself. He looked in vain for the customary brass plate, but there was none. All the curtains were drawn and mud from passing traffic dappled the lower windows. Then he saw a painted sign on the door. It stated in unpretentious half-inch letters "Mayfair Gentlemen's Club."

"When have I been here?" he repeated, cudgeling his tired memory. In his impatience Brough had broken one of his laces, and was still engrossed in his work out of earshot. An inner door opened and closed with a bang and a gangling fellow with a dark mane and red whiskers emerged from the hallway of the house. He wore a gray tweed suit of faded stripes and sorry-looking spats worn purely as a token concession to convention. For in seeming contradiction to these conservative garments he wore a red rose in full bloom. And he wore it, curiously, in his hair. Fully absorbed trying to remember the items of a shopping list that vanity precluded him from committing to paper, he gave Nicholas one glancing look and brushed past. He stopped almost immediately, screwed up his face in frustration or pain—Nicholas could not decide which—and turned back to the open door.

"What was it at the butcher's?" he called.

"Four lamp chops!" screamed a shrew from within.

"Four lamb chops," said the man mildly. He shrugged and

turned again. In so doing he obtained a clearer impression of Nicholas than on his first harassed passing, and a look of uncertain recognition lit his uneven features.

"Mr. . . . Calvin. So nice to see you again," he said obsequiously.

"You . . . you know me?" asked Nicholas in surprise.

"It is the pride of our establishment that we always remember our clients and their particular requirements," said the other. Nicholas felt that his manner was supercilious rather than deferential. Was there, too, a hint of malice?

"When did we meet?" asked Nicholas.

"Why Mr. Calvin, sir," said the singular fellow in mock surprise, "have you forgotten us already?"

Nicholas felt a sudden urge to strike the man.

"Forgotten who already?" Each word, clipped and harsh, told of his antipathy.

"Oh Mr. Calvin," said the fellow, "I am disappointed. And you one of our star turns as well."

Nicholas now observed a hint of rouge on the man's cheeks, a touch of vermilion on his lips and a subtle shading over his eyes.

"What precisely are you trying to say?" he said, realizing all too well what the euphemistic "Mayfair Gentlemen's Club" really meant.

"Don't let it concern you, Mr. Calvin," said the man, his feigned servility now giving way to undisguised insolence. "Some of our clients do prefer to forget in the warm light of day the facilities and services extended to them by our house. They don't find our ever-open door so uninviting when darkness falls and loneliness and cold slither hand in hand into their sterile bachelor apartments. Good cheer, human comfort and relief for a soul in need we provide then, don't we?"

Brough had by this time arrived and was standing behind Nicholas listening to the curious dialogue.

"Nathaniel Potts," said Brough. The man looked up, startled.

"Brough," he said, a note of hostility taking his voice up half an octave. "What trouble have you come to stir up?"

"Trouble?" said Brough. "Now when was I ever anything but a good friend to you?" Potts was a man he could happily have throttled.

"Prick," said Potts.

"Potts, I don't care how you and your kind sport yourselves. Law or no law, I think you should be left to follow whatever path you choose, providing it's in private and doesn't harm anyone else. That's how I was content to leave it. Your morals didn't interest me."

"Hoppit."

"It was you who introduced little boys into your odious cabaret, and you who bear the sole responsibility for the retribution that followed."

"Retribution, my tits," said Potts, now openly hostile. "I did two years for you and your William Wilberforce act. Don't talk to me about morals."

"Shall we go, Nicholas?" said Brough.

"So you two know each other? Now isn't that a thing?" pursued the bitter Potts. "I'd have thought you'd have more sympathy now you've got yourself a girl friend too," he said to Brough. "Helps you wile away the long winter hours, does she?" Without another word he strolled off with his nose in the air.

"Nicholas?" said Brough.

"Who was that man?" was the reply. "I've never seen him in my life before."

"But he knew you."

"So it seems, though God knows how."

"You've never been here before?"

"No . . . Well—yes," he stammered, confusion rising and flooding his mind once more. "Yes, I told you. I *have* been here before. It all seems so familiar, like something glimpsed in a dream. But it has associations with a past so dim it must have been way back in my early childhood."

A rushing of feet along the hall of the establishment interrupted them. In a moment an enormous woman in a mass of red- and white-check cambric and an ill-fitting wig emerged into the street.

"Nathaniel," she bellowed to the retreating Potts, who turned nonchalantly around to face her from the end of the street. "What is it, old woman?" he shouted contemptuously.

"Get some tallow from Fatty Richardson!"

"All right, Flabby Flo," said Potts, taking venomous delight in reminding her that Mr. Richardson was not the only example of obesity in the neighborhood.

"Aaach!" she spat, and shook an oversize fist at him. Potts stepped lightly on his way. As she turned to go back indoors, Flo's moist eyes alighted on the two companions.

"Why, Mr. Calvin, sir, you've brought a friend along," she beamed, her manner switching from belligerence to false bonhomie with disarming speed.

"You know me too?" said Nicholas.

Her bulbous nose twitched and she frowned almost imperceptibly.

"Know you, Mr. Calvin?" she said, and the words dripped like syrup from a broken jar. "*Know* is hardly the word for it, would you say?"

"Exactly when am I supposed to have been to this Godforsaken place?" cried Nicholas, exploding.

"Come in, Mr. C., and I'll give it to you chapter and verse. Bring in your lady friend too."

Brough winced and exchanged a silent glance with Nicholas. Nicholas, his gorge rising, followed the great beast up the steps into her lair, while Brough brought up the rear. The air inside the house smelled dank, and mildew painted a mad pattern on the walls. In stark and inexplicable contrast, purple hangings adorned the windows and the moldings on the doors were picked out in gold. The gargantuan harlot vanished into a room on the left and reappeared moments later with a small tin box, which she placed on a side table.

"No skin off my nose if your memory's troubling you," she said, opening the box. "And if you really want to know I'll tell you exactly when you were here."

She shuffled through a wad of promissory notes and checks until she found the one she wanted. "Here it is," she said. "Last time you settled up was on the twenty-first of last month."

"Show me that," said Nicholas, striding toward her and snatching the check. He read it. He reread it. He stared at it uncomprehendingly. At last he handed it to Brough.

"God help me, it's true," he whispered.

"I'll leave you to it," said the puzzled woman, retrieving the check and stuffing it back into its box. "If you want me I'll be in the back. If you decide you want your usual, Conrad's in the Saffron Room, first floor." She bustled off.

"Something else you didn't know about?" said Brough with ill-concealed skepticism.

"I have no memory of all this," said Nicholas. "The very thought of what goes on here revolts me."

A veil seemed to descend in front of Nicholas' eyes and he seemed incapable of looking directly at his uncle. The detective could not decide whether the apparent furtiveness meant Nicholas was deceiving him, or whether his behavior stemmed from the fear that he would be judged a liar, or worse. Without a word, Nicholas walked out into the street.

"The blackouts you mentioned to Dr. Orchard," said Brough when they were outside and walking toward Piccadilly. "On what dates did they occur?"

"I let the first few pass, thinking they were a temporary thing," said Nicholas, beads of sweat breaking out on his forehead. "The rest of them I marked down." He took out his diary and handed it to Brough. As he had suspected, November 21st was marked as his nephew's most recent memory lapse.

Woke up at 10:20 P.M., he read. *Don't know where I've been or what doing since lunchtime. Must see the doctor.*

The detective made a mental note that Sir Patrick Lovell had met the strangler on the same day.

"You didn't see Dr. Orchard until December 14th," said Brough.

"No," said Nicholas, but he was no longer aware of Brough's presence. Images began to cross and recross in his mind in a dreadful nightmare procession. He began to sway on his feet and he grasped some railings for support.

Strangling fingers—love—hate—perversion—death—fire burning —torture racking—father—mother—death—hate—Rogano—Deptford—murder—hate, hate, hate—*the man with odd eyes!*

Brough was not quick enough to save him as he fell senseless to the ground.

20

The fall had given Nicholas a nasty graze on his forehead, and as he stirred into consciousness his head was throbbing with pain. He sat up and looked about him. It was late afternoon and the sun was setting. He rose unsteadily to his feet and dusted himself down, surprised that Brough was no longer at his side. Wondering in which direction he should go, he surveyed the darkening landscape. Behind, the ground rose steeply to a wide plateau. Beyond that Monte Arretto and the smaller but no less formidable Monte Bellanone reared up at the head of the great army of peaks that formed the Brenta Dolomites. The mountains on the opposite side of the valley, at least eight miles away, were ranged almost parallel to those upon whose slopes he stood. Looking across at the squatter peaks, Nicholas felt he was between two opposing legions that only awaited the signal of their commanders to rush headlong into bloody battle at the valley bottom. Glancing back over his shoulder at the majestic bulk of Monte Arretto, he was in no doubt as to the leader of the nearer army. The sinking sun had splashed Arretto's summit with liquid fire and the glaciers glinting on its eastern face were no longer white but a dazzling shade of pink. The wooded foothills, by contrast, were looking dark and forbidding as the sunlight climbed slowly out of the valley. To his right, the land sloped away to one of the cascading mountain streams that fed the Pergino River, which he could see winding through the valley far beneath him. It would eventually flow into the Lago di Garda near Verona and on, by way of the River Mincio, to the Adriatic. Hundreds of feet below, and at least five miles along the valley at a point where the river took a sudden turn to the east and then curved dramatically back on its original course, he could see Rogano.

It lay under a mantle of snow, the elegant spires of the cathedral pointing heavenward like the beringed fingers of the sybarite cardinal who had erected them in the twelfth century as a lasting monument to himself. Cardinal Montenigro's fingers, thought Nicholas, not realizing how he knew the traditional local name for the spires. Much of the rest of Rogano was rambling and medieval and sprawled higgledy-piggledy about the central mound on which the cathedral was built. The outer areas were more modern and the new classical architecture of the Renaissance, with its fluted ceilings, its pediments and its Corinthian columns, encircled the old city and hemmed it in. Rogano had long ago broken out of its ancient walls, but the heritage-conscious chief architect of the town had constructed two magnificent gates at the eastern and western extremities that he bragged emulated the gates of ancient Rome. They were a costly piece of affectation, for almost nobody traveled by road to Rogano, except those from other communities within the valley. Those from farther off came by river. Nor had the architect neglected the water-borne visitors. Almost an island, situated as it was within the horseshoe curl of the river, Rogano possessed many places suitable for use as landing points. Indeed, for hundreds of years almost the entire perimeter of the city had been one long unbroken wharf. With the rise to eminence of Pietro Gatta as chief architect he resolved to build a properly equipped harbor at the zenith of the river's curl. Not only had he persuaded the city elders to raise taxes in order that a harbor could be constructed, he had appealed to their rediscovered love of aesthetic beauty and he had created a harbor that he believed would earn for his city the name Ephesus of the North.

The peal of a great bell began to resound along the valley. It was the early summons, for the benefit of the peasants in the outlying villages of the valley, to vespers at the cathedral. By the time they reached the town, by donkey, by foot or by the portable coracles peculiar to the region, the bell would be thundering out its more urgent reminder to the inhabitants of Rogano itself. Few dared ignore its call, even the old and sick. The taint of heresy was nigh impossible to expunge. Nicholas guessed that Brough had gone into Rogano to find help. He started the long downward trek.

It must have been a trick of the light, but however far he walked, he seemed no nearer his destination. After half an hour the main buildings of Rogano, their windows now illuminated with

flickering yellow candlelight, seemed as aloof and unattainable as
when he had started. By now quite tired, the muscles in his calves
aching through the unaccustomed exertion of the downward
climb, his progress was becoming slower. At least the crisp moun-
tain air had begun to clear his head. The shadow of the moun-
tains crept imperceptibly across the valley to meet the unmoving
shadow of the dark Forest of Amprizio that clung to the foot of
the mountains on the other side. In the last light of day Nicholas
now saw for the first time the magnificent spectacle of the abbey,
rearing up on its great natural foundation and looking more like
an ogre's castle than a house of God. With its four round towers
and its high crenelated walls, it looked impregnable. It clearly
wasn't, mused Nicholas, and the Rogano murderer had proven it.
As darkness enclosed the abbey, Nicholas saw its enormous draw-
bridge rising slowly upward, cutting off the sole link with the out-
side world, and leaving a fifty-foot chasm at the end of the dusty
road that meandered up from Rogano.

An alarm bell began to shrill beneath the now muted pain in
Nicholas' head. Something was wrong. Something . . . something
. . . was . . . out of place. He searched his mind tensely but could
not isolate the gnawing doubt. Where was Brough? Why had he
deserted him? He had last seen him . . . where? Something
clicked in his memory. But it was like a forgotten name salvaged
from the depths of the mind, rising swiftly to the surface and then
sinking like a stone as one reached out to grasp it. Just as he
reached the point of remembering the place he had last seen his
uncle, the memory slipped through his fingers and sank into the
unplumbed depths of his subconscious. As compensation, his
mind replaced the lost truth with an assumption based on logic,
which his mind instantly accepted as fact: he had last seen
Brough as they climbed under the lee of Monte Arretto. Then he
had stumbled on a stone. Fallen. Blacked out. It was true, he
knew it was true, but the answer did not satisfy him. Something
. . . terrible . . . was . . . wrong. He stumbled on, the barren soil
of the foothills now giving way to the fertile, rolling lands closer
to the valley bottom. Though he couldn't see the grass under his
feet, he could feel its springy softness as he trod. It told him he
had reached the slanting meadows carpeted in spring in bright-
blue gentians and pink dwarf rhododendrons, which he had seen

from above when twilight illumined the valley. Beneath him, he knew, were the highest of the sloping vineyards that covered hundreds of acres of lowland around Rogano. He remembered playing hide and seek here as a child; secreting himself in a patch of lush soft turf in an indented part of the hillside while Giuseppe searched vainly below. *Giuseppe?* Doubt engulfed him once again. *Who is Giuseppe?* Almost before the question formed in his brain it was answered. *Giuseppe, my brother.* Colorful, flamboyant Giuseppe, the blue of the flowers and the brown of the mountains. Strong, beloved Giuseppe.

Mist was beginning to rise from the river, and with it swarms of mosquitoes. Climbing back up the hill in the hope of rising above the mist, he found himself on an overgrown track, long disused, that ran around the hill parallel to the path he normally used.

"The specter of the Santine Hill holds no terror for you, signore?" a voice said in Italian from somewhere in a clump of pine trees to his left.

"Who's there?" called Nicholas in alarm. To his surprise, he spoke in English, a language unknown to him.

"It is only I, signore, I—Alessandro of Porfino." As he spoke, the owner of the voice shambled, as if from nowhere, into view. He stood, barely visible, in the undergrowth of mushrooms and creepers at the edge of the path. He was an old man. Lank greasy locks fell onto his narrow shoulders and a wispy white beard tumbled down his chest. He was dressed in a coarse smock and a mangy dog yelped and frisked at his feet.

It is the old herdsman who saw the lights and the men on the hill, thought Nicholas. Then he remembered the tale of the ghost of the Santine Hill with which he had so mercilessly ragged Giuseppe in childhood. *Giuseppe.* Now the story of the malevolent shade, said endlessly to haunt the cave where in life it had summoned the devil to turn rocks into gold, returned to mock him. *The cave.* Nicholas had quite forgotten. The cave. The epicenter of the mystery. The lair of the Rogano Strangler. There lay salvation . . . it must be close by.

"Where is the cave?" he said suddenly to the herdsman.

"There, signore," said Alessandro, pointing the gnarled finger of retribution along the path into the wood. He looked, thought Nicholas, like a man defeated by life. Sad, exhausted, he shrugged his bony shoulders and turned away. He trudged off into the darkness. As he vanished to God alone knew what miserable hideaway, Nicholas heard him muttering to himself like one delirious. "Beware." He was repeating over and over, "Beware the ghost of the Santine Hill." In a moment even the sound of his voice died away and Nicholas was alone on the whispering hillside.

Panic suddenly seized him. Where was he to go? Why had he been abandoned? Why could he not reach the safety, the warmth, of Rogano?

"Nich-o-l-a-s!" That was Brough's voice!

"Uncle!" he called. "Uncle!" And he began running toward the voice.

"Where are you?" called Brough.

"I'm over here," shouted Nicholas in relief.

"Where?" cried his uncle, more distant than before.

"Through the trees!" he yelled back, uncertain now in which direction to run. A second later he heard the sound of Brough's footsteps breaking on the twigs that were strewn over the forest floor.

"Over here by this plane tree!" called Nicholas again.

It was then that he saw his uncle's portly figure taking shape in the darkness thirty feet away to his right. Nicholas ran into the trees toward him, feeling like a lost child found at last. Before he had covered half the distance the cheerful figure was again obscured, this time by the mist that had followed him up the hill. Nicholas stopped a moment, waiting for it to clear. As Brough appeared once again from the swirling fog, the gloom and the mist played tricks on Nicholas' senses. Surely, it was Giuseppe. It was a momentary aberration. In a second Brough was there, smiling as before, only a dozen feet away.

"Uncle," Nicholas called again in final, utter relief, but the rest of his greeting remained unspoken. Where Brough had stood an instant before he now saw . . . *the Man with Odd Eyes!* Nicholas screamed. As he did so, the scene dissolved. Mind and body whirled in spangled vacuum. Then he was falling, falling, and the sound of his own cries—distant, unconnected with him—filled his ears. A blaze of light, real light, the light of twentieth-century London, hit him like a physical force, and he lay still, gasping for breath but safe. His eyes flickered open. Brough was seated by the bedside, a comforting hand on his arm.

"Where am I?" he said.

"Back in Jermyn Street," said the familiar voice. "I got an ambulance to bring you back. Dr. Orchard came into town and had a look at you and he says you'll be all right. You have slight concussion from your fall—you hit your head on the railings—and you've had a bit of a breakdown. But rest should do wonders."

"I was dreaming."

Brough smiled. "You were tossing around as if all the devils in hell were after you."

"They were," said Nicholas, dimly aware of the sound of the crackling fire and the warmth of the water bottle on his feet. "What time is it?" he asked.

"Nearly seven," said Brough. "Would you like some hot milk?"

Nicholas looked directly at his uncle for the first time since awakening. No reply came from his lips. His jaw sagged open and his eyes bulged in amazement. In turning to Brough he had caught sight of another figure standing moodily looking out of the window. Dead but not dead. The Man with Odd Eyes.

21

"I refuse to say that you are dead," said Nicholas, "in case you tell me that I am too."

Faced at last with the object of his dread, he was surprised to discover that he felt no fear, only numbness. The Man with Odd Eyes moved gently toward his bedside. The eyes had the disconcerting effect of those with a squint: whichever one Nicholas focused upon, he found his gaze irresistibly drawn by the other. Brough did nothing and said nothing.

"You are not dead, Mr. Calvin, and neither am I. Nor am I the devil come to claim you. Your uncle has told me of the fearful part I have played in your nightmares. Had I known I should never have practiced my perhaps vulgar deception."

"Who are you?" Nicholas demanded curtly.

"My name is Rudolf van Galen. I am from Osterode in the Harz Mountains."

"A Prussian?"

"A German."

"You are doubtless the twin brother of the man we saw crushed to death this morning," said Nicholas aggressively. His mood had changed again and he was on his best-defense-is-belligerence tack once more.

"No. I have no brother."

Nicholas looked away. He had expected that reply. The conversation seemed unreal, far less sensible than the dream from which he had lately emerged, yet at the same time it was predictable. *As if it had happened before.*

"Then it was you." There was no upward inflection on the last word; it came as a statement rather than a question.

"In a manner of speaking it was I," said the stranger. "I must apologize for my display of pyrotechnics. It was not pure conceit, but to you it must seem so."

What is he talking about?

"Are you saying that whole thing was a trick? I can't believe it."

"I am not saying it was a trick, Mr. Calvin. It happened as you saw it. But you did not see what you think you saw."

"Uncle," said Nicholas, appealing to Brough, "I don't like this man. I'd rather you asked him to leave. Let him take his riddles elsewhere."

"Herr van Galen," began Brough quietly, "I think we should try to explain your story from the beginning. We must remember, my nephew has not been well, and your sudden appearance before him must have been as unnerving as when I opened the front door to you earlier today."

"Of course. Forgive me," said Galen. There was just the slightest trace of the guttural Teutonic accent. "It is not easy to explain the experiences of a lifetime in a few minutes."

"Riddles again," said Nicholas unsympathetically. "Forget the experiences of a lifetime. Just tell me whether it was you or whether it was not you whom we saw crushed beneath that crate."

"It was a part of me. Me but not me so to sp . . ."

"In hell's name!" interrupted Nicholas, shooting another glance at his uncle. Brough placed a finger on his lips and nodded gently to indicate that all was well.

Nicholas looked at Galen. The German was thinking how best to continue in the light of Nicholas' distress. Nicholas guessed he was about his own age, although he looked older. A tall, spare man in a suit of shark's-tooth tweed and a blue cravat. The same suit he had been wearing on the train. Apart from those queer unmatched eyes, a very ordinary-looking man. The eyes were everything. The energy of his soul burned in them. One as brown as the earth, the other as blue as the sea.

Mountains and flowers.

"Do you ever read Hoffman or Heinrich Heine?" asked Galen.

Nicholas decided to co-operate. "I have glanced through Hoffman's *Kater Murr*, but I haven't read it," he replied.

"You have not looked, for instance, at Heine's poem *Der Doppelgänger?* It was set to music by Schubert."

"The Doppelgänger," said Nicholas, sinking back into his pillows. "I have not read the poem you mention, nor have I heard the musical version as far as I remember. But I think I know about the Doppelgänger."

"Please go on," said Galen.

"It means double walker. It's the German word for the old belief that the human soul can take visible form."

"Not only visible, but *physical* form," said Galen.

"We have similar beliefs in this country," interposed Brough eagerly, as if they were all three engaged in learned but abstract discussion on folklore.

"Yes," said Galen mildly, "in Great Britain you have the fetch, the fye and the task. Like the *fylgja* of Norse folk belief, they are all variations of the Doppelgänger concept. According to Norse lore, every person had a fylgja. This was said to be a soul or spirit as mortal and physical as the body itself. It emerged into the world clinging to the foetus, and dissolved into nothingness when its original died. From this ancient belief spring all later variations. The idea of the fetch, once prevalent in Great Britain, is revived every time we read newspaper reports of ghosts of the living appearing at the moment of death to relatives or dear friends. In Ireland the fetch is often thought to haunt its own human double. This is absurd. So too is the Haitian heresy that the dead can be transformed into zombies, or mindless undead. And the notion that it is dangerous to awaken a sleeper lest his wandering spirit cannot return to his body is demonstrably untrue.

"While much folklore surrounding the fylgja is the product of overactive imaginations, it is nevertheless certain that there is a central core of truth—the truth our distant ancestors knew and which has since been buried beneath centuries of embellishment."

He paused.

"All ideas of ghosts, ghouls and zombies, while themselves untrue, spring from the central truth that the spirit exists and that it is distinct from the body. Knowledge of the fylgja is not a belief or a religion, but a science. The existence of the soul is scientific fact, and ideally should be studied scientifically. The training that enables the student to isolate and control his own fylgja is merely the beginning. That isolation opens the door to an entirely new world of learning that few people today even suspect exists. The opening of the door turns man's formulated laws of the universe upside down."

Galen stopped speaking. He had been pacing back and forth, talking in a voice so measured and low-pitched that Nicholas had to strain to hear.

"You are saying . . . what?" said Nicholas.

"That it was not me you saw this morning but—"

"Your fetch, your fylgja, your bloody Doppelgänger, is that it?" cried Nicholas almost hysterically.

"I prefer to use the word 'soul,'" said Galen. "It was my soul you saw this morning. For a specific purpose I commanded my soul to go forth in emulation of my physical self and to appear to be destroyed. The method I had in mind was beneath the wheels of a coach. The fortuitous weakness of the rope that held the crate in Vigo Street provided a far more spectacular, and I think more convincing, 'death.'"

Nicholas looked away. Despite his apologies Galen looked as if he enjoyed the effect he was having. Tears began to well up inside him. The past weeks, he told himself, had been enough to fray the nerves of the strongest man. The whole catalogue of misfortune reeled endlessly before his eyes once again. He sank his teeth into his lower lip and gripped the bed sheets with a neurotic strength in order to regain control of himself.

"Why?" he said desperately to the man with odd eyes.

"I had to prove to you that the soul genuinely exists as an entity separate from the body. Christians speak blandly of man being a spiritual creature, and we are taught from the kindergarten onward that the essence of man is an immortal soul. How many of us accept that unequivocally? What *proof* is there that man has a soul? For most of us there is none, just a certain amount of circumstantial evidence that can be interpreted in many ways. We accept the word of the scriptures that we are spiritual beings and we take it on trust that the lower animals are soulless and entirely mortal. Yet conventional science, apparently the only constant and the only security for the open, questioning mind, indicates that our single advantage over other animals is higher intelligence.

"But conventional science is not the only recourse. There is another science, which has existed for centuries, for the most part in secret. In provable ways this science can unlock some of the doors to greater understanding of our existence."

He paused again to allow the significance of his words to become apparent.

"It has many branches, this science. And slowly, cautiously, it is integrating its findings with those of conventional science. In general it will not overturn, but will rather extend and explain much of what conventional scientists know. It will also open up whole new areas of thought. How, you will ask, has this movement managed to achieve so much more than ordinary science? I answer— one, because it has had access to the best brains in the world; two, because it took as its starting point the knowledge of the Old Ones, that great body of scientific fact dismissed as hocus-pocus by the post-Renaissance thinkers; and three, because it has not allowed itself to be tied by inflexible rules and preconceptions. It has regarded facts as more sacred than security. Modern scientists cling to the security that comes from feeling they have solved the major problems of the universe. Sadly, they have not even managed yet to bring the real universe into focus.

"One of our members, a young and brilliant man from Ulm in Germany, will soon be ready to show conventional scientists how little they know by imparting a section of our knowledge. It is our intention that he should receive sole credit for the work of many, that it should be thought he has achieved alone what in fact has taken scores of thinkers over eighty years. But this is how we increase mankind's knowledge of universal truths, and every so often edge him gently in the right direction. Other approaches might bring abuse. Conventional science has to be allowed to think that it alone is responsible for all new discoveries. You have not heard of Albert Einstein?"

"No."

"There is no reason why you should. But within five years, possibly less, his name and that of 'his' theory of relativity will be on every lip. Thus we achieve our aims.

"The section of our movement in which I have been most closely involved has been the study of the soul. It was inspired by a personal preoccupation, and my private studies have continued in parallel with my 'official' ones. Over the years, the two have become inextricably linked. It became imperative that you, Mr. Calvin, be given incontrovertible proof that man has a soul. What I earlier described as my vulgar deception was designed to give you that proof."

"Why do you tell us all this if your movement is so secret?" demanded Nicholas aggressively. "Aren't you worried that we might betray your secret?"

"No," said Galen. "For the simple reason that no one would believe you."

"Uncle?" said Nicholas helplessly. His head was pounding once again.

"I telephoned the mortuary when Herr van Galen first told me his story," said Brough. "The body of the man killed this morning vanished from a locked room while the attendant was at lunch between half-past one and two o'clock."

"Do you *believe* him?" said Nicholas incredulously.

"I am inured against shock in such cases," replied Brough, postponing absolute commitment. "I have told you already that I was in India for four years. The great lesson I learned there from firsthand experience was that almost anything is possible. I think it is important not to dismiss Herr van Galen's story out of hand."

"But it's monstrous!" said Nicholas.

"Why?" asked Brough and Galen in unison. Brough continued, "Herr van Galen has only demonstrated what you say you have believed all your life, what Christians have taught for nineteen hundred years. Man has a soul. What's so monstrous about that? Your father would be shocked if he thought you doubted it. But faced with proof in that belief you shy like a frightened horse."

"My father would shy too at the suggestion that man can *control* his soul and send it out on errands. It's witchcraft! Hundreds of harmless old women were hanged in England in the seventeenth century for sending out their souls to commit murder and blight crops. Now we live in more enlightened times. We condemn such beliefs and such tribal justice as primitive and appalling."

"That is so," said Galen. "And that so-called justice was primitive and appalling. It was born of hysteria and I would guess that virtually all of the victims of the witch-finder general and his revolting crew were innocent. But that does not disprove the concept of the fylgja any more than it disproves the concept of murder. Many people may be executed for murders of which they are innocent. But murder still exists. As you now know from personal experience, the fylgja exists too."

"Is there no other way the body could have disappeared from the mortuary?" said Nicholas, consciously striving to block Galen from his thoughts and directing his question at Brough.

"None that I can imagine," said Brough. "I have known the attendant there for twenty years. He's one hundred per cent reliable. He locked that door, as he has done every day since he took the job, at one-thirty sharp. He has the only key. When he left, the corpse of the man killed this morning was on the dissecting table. It had been examined by a Dr. Barter, pronounced dead and its injuries noted. The attendant, a man called Rolt, had undressed the body ready for washing down in the afternoon. When he returned at two o'clock the door was still securely fastened, but the body had gone. According to a plumber repairing some burst water pipes in the passage and a pathologist in an office near the outside door, no one passed in or out of the building in those thirty minutes. Even so, it might be argued that such an incident could be capable of a rational explanation. What makes me certain is that I saw the face of the dead man in the moment before the crate struck. Who could forget a single detail of that relaxed, even amused, countenance? No identical twin ever resembled his brother as closely as Herr van Galen does that corpse. I *know* it was he."

Behind Nicholas' glazed eyes emotion battled again with logic. He strove to dismiss Brough's words as absurd, and absurd indeed they were. But Nicholas too had seen that face. He knew every detail of it, far better than Brough. It had been with him for years. Absurd yes, but also true. He closed his eyes and nodded a painful acquiescence.

"Lastly," said Brough more gently, "Herr van Galen's story is the only explanation I can yet imagine for the strangest thing I have ever encountered. Never in my life before have I met with a person totally lacking in scent. But that young man crushed to death this morning was devoid of smell, even after the smashing of his body. That is an impossibility in normal scientific terms."

He looked kindly at his nephew. "The study of man's astral spirit, as the English philosophers tend to call the soul, is by no means so disreputable as you seem to think. Many well-respected public figures have consented to take part in experiments sponsored by the Theosophical Society. I myself had a sort of out-of-the-body experience while I was in India. It was nothing dramatic, but according to the yogi teacher in charge of the demonstration, my spirit left my body and experienced in reality what I took to be just a dream. It was a rudimentary enough experience, but it certainly opens your eyes to something of man's potential."

Stirring after several minutes of tense, therapeutic reverie, Nicholas looked at Galen and whispered, "Why was it vital that I accept the existence of the soul?"

"Because without that acceptance you were unlikely to believe in the concept of reincarnation."

"Go on."

"Having established that human beings possess a soul that lives on after the body dies, it is natural to ask what happens to this soul after death. And where is it before birth?"

"The ultimate riddle," breathed Nicholas.

"Not the ultimate, but those not yet set out on the path to Knowledge might be forgiven for seeing it as such. The simplest explanation of reincarnation is that a single soul is born again and again in a succession of earthly lives or incarnations, separated by many years from each other. Once again I am not speaking abstractly. All this has been proven scientifically."

Nicholas made no attempt to argue, so Galen proceeded in a flat, matter-of-fact manner.

"Rarely does any memory of our past lives filter through into the conscious mind of our present existence. But occasionally we experience what is known as *déjà vu*—an unaccountable certainty that we have been somewhere or done something before, although we know in this life we never have. These are fragments of knowledge from a past life."

"I am familiar with the basic outline of belief in reincarnation," said Nicholas, "and I have to say that I find it one of the more logical attempts at explaining existence."

"That is gratifying," said Galen. "But if you are to study the subject with any hope of success you must realize that your present viewpoint is also illogical. Your first reaction was to reject the concept of the fylgja, yet you find it easier to accept the vastly more complex system of reincarnation which is based upon it. Both reactions are emotional, and as the only real way to truth is by scientific investigation I urge you to be dispassionate if you possibly can."

"I'll try," said Nicholas, and he smiled weakly. "I have read that in certain circumstances it might be possible to identify one's previous incarnations."

"Once again, the only literature available on reincarnation is philosophical rather than scientific, but occasionally the philosophers do hit upon a scientifically provable truth. Yes, with proper guidance and training it is possible. I have traced three previous lives, the earliest of which was in the fifteenth century."

He paused like an actor in rehearsal calculating the precise moment to deliver a dramatic line. "I am the reincarnation of Giuseppe Aquilina, the younger of the two brothers executed by the Inquisition for the Rogano murders," he said.

Nicholas stared at Galen. "That explains your interest in me," he began, "but it hardly explains your conduct. If you . . ."

He stopped abruptly, his intended comment disintegrating as it collided with a new, shocking thought that reared up in his mind.

"Uncle," he said excitedly, turning to Brough and pointing a trembling finger at Galen. He stumbled over his words, hardly able to speak at all for the great waves of elation and relief that swept over him. "Uncle, don't you see the significance of all this?"

Brough frowned, but Nicholas hurried on. "We have a murderer in London conforming exactly to the pattern set in Rogano. And here is a man admitting he has the soul of one of the men executed for those crimes!"

Brough shifted uneasily in his chair but said nothing.

Galen, unflurried, said, "Your reasoning discounts one essential point. A few moments ago I think you were about to question my having followed you in the past days."

"Yes," said Nicholas, momentarily deflected from his course, "you or your damned fylgja have been dogging me everywhere."

"I had to be certain," said Galen, "that you were who I thought you were. Since last week I have been sure. You are the reincarnation of Antonio, the elder of the brothers Aquilina."

"So you must understand, Nicholas," said Brough, breaking his silence at last. "We are faced with the same problem the Inquisition had on its hands in 1454. One of you two has the soul of a murderer. One of you is the reincarnation of the man who was the Rogano murderer. That one of you is also, I am sure, the Deptford Strangler."

22

Numbness suffused Nicholas' mind. He slipped away from the cold light of the room in Jermyn Street and slid down a steep, winding tunnel of consciousness that led to his forgotten past.

"My brother," he whispered reverently. And instantly he knew that everything Galen had said was true.

He was seven years old. The Man with Odd Eyes stared at him out of the blackness of a dream, pursued him endlessly night after night as he tossed fretfully in his cot and struggled to wake up.

The autumn of 1880. Summer lasted long into October. Mother took him to the zoo. And there had been a memorable trip to Box Hill for a picnic. His best friend had broken his leg jumping from the window of the school dormitory in an overoptimistic leap toward the upper branches of a cherry tree. For five weeks the dreams stopped. An all too brief respite. November limped in, turning October's fallen leaves to muck and the golden sunlight to lead. Winter and his dreams returned together.

But now they were different. The Man with Odd Eyes was no longer an anonymous devil come to claim his soul but . . . but . . . come to claim his soul but . . . his soul but . . . his *brother*.

"*I have no brother!*" the boy Nicholas shrieked in the thick-walled silence of his dream. The contradiction wrung droplets of blood from his raging brain and somehow . . . somehow *taking physical form* . . . that palpable contradiction gyrated and piped like a crazed hobgoblin. Even as he dreamed he knew he slept at home in the narrow box above his father's study, but the knowledge gave him no comfort. For now the startling world of sleep was real and the ordered pattern of waking a fable.

Months passed. At length his whirling odyssey back through his own childhood brought him, gaunt and staring, to eleven: the final frightful nightmare that for eighteen years would erase all memory of the Man with Odd Eyes.

He was tied to a rough stake. Flames engulfed his twisting body. The skin cracked and belched open. Through the stinking smoke that was his own vaporized flesh he suddenly saw another victim writhing in an identical inferno not ten yards away. The face of his fellow sufferer turned toward him beseechingly just before it burst and disintegrated in the fire. *Himself*. No, too much like himself but not he. His brother. The Man with Odd Eyes.

Then blackness, and the horrible screams that brought his parents rushing to his bedside.

He looked with the eyes of an old, old man at his uncle and the mysterious Galen.

"So that was why I became so suddenly and so deeply obsessed with discovering the truth of the Rogano case," he said without expression. "A part of my brain knew of my former existence and urged me on to find the truth."

"A very reasonable assessment," ventured Galen quietly.

"If this hidden part of my mind knew that much, why did it not know the truth about the murders automatically?" he asked.

"The full story of our past lives is locked in the cells of our subconscious minds. Each cell contains a fragment of the truth, and the cells are scattered like pebbles in the desert. Billions of them. Lost in an endless landscape. The part of you that retains the misty outline of your incarnation as Antonio is divided by a seemingly impassable gulf from the part that encapsulates the data on the murders. And every other aspect of your former existence is likewise shattered and dispersed. Imagine this desert of the subconscious like a wasteland under the sea. Many of the pebbles of knowledge lie not only beneath the sea, but are embedded deep in the desert soil beneath that. Locating the constituent parts of the truth and bringing them together in any order is out of the question in any medicinal or surgical sense. Drugs have proved useless. A certain drug, a variety of mescaline, was developed that could root out millions of the particles in question. But it was mindless, uncontrolled, and created such chaotic patterns of memory that insanity was more than once the result. Brain surgery was as futile."

"What is my own state of mind if not insanity?" asked Nicholas. "What were the mad dreams of my childhood but manifestations of my own peculiar lunacy?"

"Your childhood dreams were memories of a former life, subtly distorted as a prism distorts light, to fit your current consciousness of yourself. In other words, you in the person of Nicholas were reliving the experiences of Antonio."

"And you? Your odd eyes became the core of my horrible fantasy."

"It often happens that a physical attribute is repeated in a later incarnation. We have so far not discovered the reason. Giuseppe Aquilina had odd eyes, one brown, one blue. It was this fact that gave me my first positive indication of my past life. In fact the characteristic has reappeared in all three of my incarnations since Giuseppe."

"Was Antonio a . . . homosexual?" asked Nicholas after a long pause.

"A homosexual and a vegetarian," nodded Galen with a reflective smile. The subject, so sickening to Nicholas, did not seem to disturb the German. "Your uncle has told me of your unpleasant encounter with Mr. Nathaniel Potts. Unlike the color of my eyes, which has come down to me from previous incarnations as a definite part of my present self, the traits of Antonio which you manifest seem more fluctuating, more tenuous. Rather like your fragmented dreams.

"You have periods of memory loss in which you somehow slip back temporarily into Antonio's mold. Your disquieting visits to Mr. Potts's establishment are part of this. An Antonio trait that is completely alien to Nicholas Calvin takes command. I believe your exploits as the Deptford Strangler are exactly similar acts committed while the character of your former incarnation is uppermost."

"You have no doubt then that I am the murderer?"

"There is no certainty. All is doubt. I *believe* you are he. I believe it on logical grounds. But it would be unscientific and obstructive to pretend that emotion does not enter into my belief. The emotional side of my nature wants desperately to be exonerated from this murder charge. I *want* you to be the guilty one. This need must inevitably color my judgment, however dispassionate I try to be."

He looked deeply into Nicholas' eyes for the first time. Piercingly. Boring to the nethermost regions of his awareness.

"Whichever of us has been responsible for these two series of crimes has more to concern him than the mere earthbound wickedness of a single incarnation. It is possible he has the *soul* of a murderer."

"I see," said Nicholas, barely audible.

"It might seem cruel, but in fairness to us all I must point out that unlike you, I have not dreamed in the last weeks of being a strangler."

The silence stretched on interminably.

Wordlessly, Brough got up and went to each gas mantle in turn, adjusting the erratic, dancing light they were giving out.

Nicholas tugged nervously at a lock of hair behind his ear. Galen minutely examined his fingernails.

At last the German ruffled the bizarre atmosphere that had descended upon them, and spoke again.

"You have experienced aspects of Antonio not only in dreams and blackouts," he said. "There are sides of him which have made themselves apparent to your conscious self."

Nicholas raised a questioning eyebrow.

"The sudden inexplicable hatred of meat," said Galen in reply to the gesture, "and the more gradual but equally mysterious hatred of your father. I have already said that Antonio was a vegetarian. How or why this came about I don't know. He also entertained a violent loathing for his father, who had no time for him but lavished all his affection on Giuseppe. I have discovered a diary penned by the youthful Antonio which makes his feelings about his father abundantly clear. Your suddenly discovered hatred is not of Nicholas Calvin's father but of the abstract notion 'father.' In your everyday understanding your only possible interpretation of such an abstraction—with no other knowledge to guide you—has been to despise the father of your present existence."

Nicholas looked across at Brough, who observed an attentive silence.

"So you see, the traits that come to us not through the genes but by way of our souls from previous incarnations are manifested in many different ways. The traits can be physical, emotional, mental or spiritual. They can be odd-colored eyes like mine, your own abstract loathing of a parent or the brilliant creativity of the young Mozart, who wrote a symphony at the age of four."

"Or a predilection for murder," said Nicholas.

After a moment he said, "I have heard that much of what is put down to reincarnation is in fact attributable to race memory."

"Race memory." Galen laughed aloud. "The notion that abilities appearing at a prodigiously young age, or memories of the past, have been passed through the genes from physical ancestors. Yes, I have even heard it said that the well-documented precocity of Blüber Søgrens, who was holding rudimentary conversations with his mother within an hour of his birth, was attributable to race memory."

He sat back in his chair, straightened his spine and breathed deeply twice.

"No," he resumed, "it just won't do. That argument relies on each of us being lineally descended from those whose lives we can recall. Exhaustive researches have shown that time after time a person remembering a former identifiable existence in tremendous detail was not a descendant in any physical sense of that earlier individual. And even if you and I were lineally descended

from Giuseppe and Antonio, there is no way we could have in-
herited the memory of their deaths. They could hardly have con-
ceived any children after being burned at the stake."

"What are we going to do?" asked Nicholas hopelessly.

"That has yet to be decided," said Brough.

"How long before the next murder is due?"

"Ten days."

"We can't just sit around until then. If only we could identify
the next victim and forestall events. Two innocent lives might yet
be saved. Is there nothing we can do to get the investigation fur-
ther forward?"

"I still have to interview the relatives of some of the strangler's
victims," said Brough. "I think we should get down to that first
thing tomorrow."

"Queer business taking the murderer to visit his victims' loved
ones," responded Nicholas gravely.

"Yes," said Brough, making patterns in the dust on the side-
board, which momentarily made the present horror dissolve and
his mind revert to the behavior of his erratic charwoman. Mrs.
Canker will *have* to go, he thought incongruously.

"And if we find nothing to help us?" asked Galen.

Brough was instantly back in the present. "We wait for the
twenty-eighth," he said. "Then I keep both of you under my eye
twenty-four hours a day. As I suggested to Nicholas, the behavior
of the guilty man on the day the next murder is due should tell us
pretty quickly what we want to know."

"You will keep us locked up?" said Galen.

"No," said Brough. "If anything odd starts happening to one of
you, the unaffected one and I should be able to restrain him."

They lapsed into silence. Outside, it had started to rain and
thunder rumbled uneasily a long way off.

"Wait a *minute!*" cried Nicholas, lurching forward on the bed.
"Aren't we forgetting something just a tiny bit important?"

Bewildered, the others looked at him expectantly.

"This wonderful plan to sit around looking at each other
watching for suspicious signs, this elaborate 'Spot the Murderer'
charade. We could both be sitting here looking perfectly normal—
*and Galen's soul might be out there strangling some poor wretch,
with us two none the wiser.*"

"I must point out that I would not be looking perfectly normal at such a time," said Galen. "When my soul is separate from my body I am in a deep state of unconsciousness. It is the same with everyone in all out-of-the-body experiences."

"There should be no need for us to sit around here waiting for events," said Brough. "I still have investigations to conduct in London, people to interview, facts to check. But the greatest obstacle facing us in this case is the total obscurity of the motive. Whichever of you is the Deptford Strangler, he is not killing for logical, calculated reasons, but for some dark purpose embedded deep in a past incarnation. On any normal level of inquiry that makes the Deptford stranglings insoluble. The key to the present mystery is the solution of the Rogano murders. If we solve those, we shall know the answer to the current riddle."

"Therefore we must go to Italy?" said Nicholas.

"After the groundwork here is accomplished there will be more than enough work to keep us fully occupied in Rogano."

"I am in agreeance," said Galen.

"-ment," said Brough.

"I'm sorry?"

"Agree*ment*, not agree*ance*."

"Ah," said Galen, "I agree."

"Another point which has just struck me," said Brough, raking out the bowl of his pipe with an old pencil, "is that if we are in Italy we can avoid the inevitable, break the pattern. If we are safely ensconced in Rogano, neither of you can commit the next murder due in London."

He blew along the stem of his pipe, making a thin honking sound, and knocked out the debris into the coal scuttle.

"I am nevertheless sure," he said, "that the behavior of the guilty party on the day of the twenty-eighth will be decisive. A speedy departure from London in the next day or so might at least save one life."

Someone hammered on the front door and Brough walked down. "I don't know why I'm doing all the running about," he called over his shoulder with a grin. "With two unpaying guests you'd think an old fellow would get a bit of help." He had an ingenious knack of dispelling the tension from the most fraught situation.

"Rickets," he said to the impeccably dressed and beaming post-office boy. The lad handed him a telegram.

"This come across from the depot over the water," he said. "People at the address on the envelope reckon Mr. Calvin is stayin' wiv you."

"Yes," said Brough, glancing at his sister and brother-in-law's address at Greenwich. "It's my nephew. He's upstairs."

"Foreign 'un so they tell me."

"What, my nephew?"

"No!" said Rickets with a giggle. "Bleedin' telegram." And in a moment he was off down the road on his bicycle, looking for all the world like a pair of living calipers.

As he closed the door, the detective caught a fleeting glimpse of a tiny, broken figure retreating along Church Place toward Piccadilly.

Bruno.

I didn't tell the big man, Mr. Brough. You're my friend. The dwarf's words began to echo in Brough's mind once again as he ascended the stairs. What in heaven's name was the little beggar up to?

Nicholas wasted no time in ripping open the buff envelope containing the telegram.

"It's from Bonn!" he said jubilantly. Then, slightly shamefaced at the memory of his earlier deception: "No tricks this time, Uncle. It's from Albrecht Wehrner, superintendent of the museum's department of Italian manuscripts. Hold on."

He scanned the message, and as he did so his face clouded.

"Impossible," he breathed.

"What is it?" asked Brough and Galen together. Brough smiled at the German. "We're becoming like the Cheeryble brothers," he said.

"They have a whole repository of relics from Rogano, brought there when the ruins of the cathedral were excavated fifty years or so after the 1781 fire," said Nicholas. "They have them all, properly catalogued and indexed, from the twelfth century to the year of the inferno."

"Wonderful!" said Brough.

"Terrible!" corrected Nicholas. "Out of all those thousands of documents, covering six hundred years, there is just one batch missing. Those for the period October 1454 to February 1455 have simply vanished. And there's no question of them having been mislaid by the museum. They have a note in their files that the very papers we want must have been removed from the vaults before the cathedral burned down."

"Curiouser and curiouser," said Brough.

23

"One vital link has been slipping our minds in the hours since Herr van Galen entered the case," said Brough over breakfast next day. "We really must examine those prophecies passed on to Nicholas by Carew. It's conceivable they have no value, but it will be unthinkable to ignore them."

Nicholas languidly dangled his knife and fork an inch or so above his empty plate and deliberately let them drop with a clatter.

"That's another part of the case that points to Galen's guilt as much as it points to mine," he said, cupping his chin in his hands and gazing into his coffee. "*He* was in Allerton last week too. Remember the figure at the water pump?"

"My soul," corrected Galen. "*I* was deeply asleep on that chugging little country train from which you rightly observed I did not disembark."

"Either way," said Nicholas, "you—your physical self *or* your soul—might have killed the old boy."

"We must not rule out any possibility," said Galen a trifle grudgingly, "but I think we are agreed that whichever of us committed these crimes, his conscious self is unaware of it. I have already explained my presence in Allerton. I was finally confirming my identification of you with Antonio, and watching, by observing your behavior, for signs of guilt."

"That explains nothing," said Nicholas, shaking his head. "How did following me confirm your identification?"

"There is much you do not yet know," said Galen. "Although I have not been prey to dreams of the past to quite the same extent as you, I too have returned to Rogano in my mind. I too suffered childhood dreams of burning at the stake. You, exactly as you look now, writhed in agony in front of me. I knew what Antonio would be like."

He paused, straightened his back and breathed deeply twice in exactly the way he had before.

"I told you last night that drugs and surgery have been useless in helping us back to a proper awareness of our past lives," he said. "What I did not tell you is that there *is* a method that in certain circumstances will succeed."

"I am all ears," said Nicholas. Brough chewed attentively at a finger of yolk-coated toast.

"The method takes years of training to perfect, and I am far from perfect, but it is allied to the ability to manifest the soul physically. As I have said, sending out the soul involves descending to the profoundest depths of unconsciousness. This voluntary coma can be achieved by a kind of self-induced trance, rather like a cataleptic fit brought on deliberately."

He looked from Nicholas to Brough to ensure that his explanation was making sense.

"Having cultivated the ability to enter such trances, one can pass through the various levels of consciousness until one reaches former incarnations. It is then a matter of passing over the stepping stones of intervening incarnations and, by a tremendous effort of will, reaching not only the desired incarnation but the correct period within it. Failure is frequent, but when I have succeeded I have found myself looking through the eyes of Giuseppe, thinking with his brain, yet all the time detached and entirely myself. One is also fully able to remember the experience on waking."

"If only we could both go back in such a way," said Nicholas. "It might be the surest way of assessing the personalities of the two brothers."

"That might not be out of the question," said Galen. "You were telling me before breakfast of the tremendously vivid dream of Rogano you had while you were unconscious after your fall. In many ways, Antonio is a more powerful part of your present incarnation than Giuseppe is of mine. It seems likely that you are one of the fortunate few for whom 'regression,' as we call it, comes automatically. Lack of sleep might achieve for you what for another would require years of intense work and self-study. Given the right ambience, and I can think of none better than Rogano itself, we might both be able to return in our minds to the fifteenth century and solve this riddle once and for all."

"What are the dangers?"

"The chief one is being unable to return through the levels of consciousness to the present. In other words, being perpetual prisoners in the minds of our former incarnations. To outsiders that would look like an interminable cataleptic fit."

"How likely is that to happen?"

"I have no way of knowing. It would be very likely indeed if we were disturbed during our regression."

"Perhaps, then, it is a bridge we might cross when we come to it."

"Nicholas," said Galen, "I want us both to be certain that we are not enemies. Clearly we each want the other to be the guilty party. That is natural self-preservation, it needn't create enmity."

He's right, thought Nicholas, realizing with surprise that he felt no dislike for Galen. Although they knew almost nothing about their visitor, both Nicholas and Brough felt instinctively that he could be trusted.

"It is our duty to report any point which seems to throw light where there is darkness," Galen continued. "I feel no animosity that you pointed out my presence in Allerton as a possible indication of my guilt. In the same way, I must record that Greenwich, where you were living when the Deptford Strangler first struck, is only a mile or so from Deptford. To review the state of the case to date, the balance is still, I think, in my favor."

He looked at Brough for confirmation.

"It would be foolish to deny that Nicholas remains the prime suspect," he said simply and sadly, licking butter from each finger in turn.

"But this is such an incredible case one would hardly be surprised if apparently transparent clues meant something far removed from the obvious," said Nicholas.

"Quite," said Brough, and switched the conversation back to

the subject he had introduced at the outset. "Can we pick up the Nostradamus papers today?"

"Why not?" said Nicholas with a shrug.

"I've already arranged to call on the mother of Henry Antrobus, the strangler's first victim, at ten-thirty. We can go to your room in Coptic Street afterward."

Last night's rain had done little to wash away the snow that had blanketed London since Tuesday, and any slush that had been created by the sporadic downpours had now been refrozen and covered by fresh snowfalls in the early hours. As they cleared away the breakfast things, an uncertain sunlight began to filter through the dark banks of cloud that had lowered upon the city for weeks, and by the time they were ready to leave, the sun's diluted warmth had started to break up the clouds.

"It's going to be a bright day," said Brough cheerfully, noting the scattered patches of clear blue sky gradually being unveiled by the parting nimbus. "Let's take the omnibus."

Wrapped in overcoats, scarves and mittens, the three men went downstairs and ventured into the street.

Outside Freybourg and Treyer, the eighteenth-century tobacco and cigar shop in the Haymarket, they caught a horse-drawn omnibus and at Galen's suggestion climbed to the open upper deck. Despite the disarray of his emotions, the tourist in him struggled to the surface and for the duration of the bracing trip down to Pall Mall, left into Trafalgar Square, past St. Martin's-in-the-Fields and so into West Strand, his blacker thoughts were submerged. The omnibus drew up outside the dark and shuttered Lyceum Theatre, where the thirty-one-year reign of the world's greatest actor had ended only five months before. A torn poster, with the words *Irving, Terry* and *Merchant of Venice* now barely readable, was peeling from the wall.

They cut through the back streets behind the Aldwych to Wild Court, a brick-built tenement building off Drury Lane. Finding themselves in a tiny rectangular courtyard bounded by a high wall on three sides and iron railings on the fourth, they made their way to a stone stairwell that led to the six upper floors. The mingled smells of last night's cooking from the dozen or so apartments on each story still hung about on the landings, trapped in the brick of the cold but seemingly airless staircase. By the time they reached the fourth floor, Nicholas and Galen were markedly shorter of breath than their older companion, whose lungs and muscles seemed unperturbed by the exertion.

"Gilbert might well have been right in putting down a policeman's lot as not an 'appy one," panted Nicholas in what these days was a rare foray into humor, "but whatever way you look at it, the bobby's life is an 'ealthy one."

D'Oyly Carte comic operas had barely penetrated Galen's Wagnerian homeland so Brough's amusement at the remark left him baffled. Nevertheless, he smiled politely. Brough chuckled warmly, and scraped his hand along the black dado of the wall to rid himself of a sticky cobweb he had acquired from a banister lower down.

"Exercise and energetic relaxation," he said. "That's something else I learned in India. Does wonders in staving off old age."

He buried his face more deeply into his scarf to dilute the stink of stale cabbage that hung in the muggy air of the landing.

In contrast to Lady Lovell, Mrs. Clara Louise Antrobus seemed desolated by her bereavement. Henry had been her only son and, never having married, had continued to live at home long beyond the age when many children have uprooted themselves and drifted away into lives of their own. Since she had been widowed seven years before, the dependence she had always reposed in Henry had become still more intense.

"Come in," she whimpered when Brough had introduced himself, and presented Nicholas and Galen as his two assistants. Her red-rimmed eyes told of the volumes of tears she had shed in the five weeks since her son's disappearance and murder.

In the five weeks since he met Galen or me, suffered Nicholas inwardly. God, is it possible that I wrung the life out of this poor woman's son?

His earlier reserves of optimism had decayed.

The poky little apartment, with its neatly arranged trinkets, its aspidistra and its tapestry antimacassars, exuded an air of genteel poverty.

Once again Brough apologized for seeming to duplicate the work of Daubeney and his men, and promised to be as brief as he could.

"Your son was a master at a private school, I believe?" he probed gently.

"He had been attached to the Frognal Academy for Young Ladies in Hampstead for six years."

"Was he a conscientious teacher?"

Brough was well aware of the answer before it came. His ploy was to draw Mrs. Antrobus out of her grieving introspection in the hope that some detail previously missed might emerge.

"None more so, I can assure you," she said somewhat tight-lipped.

"And his subjects were . . . ?" interposed Galen.

"European history and religious studies. He specialized in the political struggles between France and Italy in the Middle Ages and was a recognized authority on the early spread of the Church."

"The name Henry Antrobus is linked on the highest levels with European studies," said Brough tentatively. "I am surprised he did not scale greater academic heights."

"Our family has been poor, Mr. Brough," said Mrs. Antrobus, fussing around her tiny, cluttered scullery and brewing them tea in a brown earthenware pot. "Without money, connections, and with the need to support me when his father died, Henry was denied the chance of a university education that his talent and singleness of purpose so richly deserved."

"So he pursued a course of self-education?"

"Just so. His evenings for the past nine years have been spent in the reading room and the manuscripts department of the British Museum, or home here studying. The number of hours in all that time he has taken off to refresh himself and rest has been pitifully small. He has spent all his vacations on study trips abroad, financed by the pittance he received from giving extracurricular tuition on Sunday afternoons."

She stopped talking just long enough to pour each of them a cup of watery tea, and to add a trowel full of coal dust to the kitchen range.

"He never stopped working, Mr. Brough," she said with a wretched shake of her head, bitterness rising in her almost as if it had been overwork that had killed her son. "I feared so much for his health. His eyesight was congenitally weak and his furious study did nothing to improve it. But he was as stubborn as he was gifted. Nothing I could say or do would dissuade him from his chosen course. Eventually he lost the sight in his left eye."

"And he intended by his own independent labors to sit for—what?—his Bachelor of Arts degree?"

"*Bachelor* of Arts? He had already achieved that distinction by the time he was twenty-five, despite all the obstacles in his path. In another three years he had his master's degree."

She became reflective as her grief welled anew. "At the time of his death he was working on his doctorate of philosophy."

"Yet he chose to remain at the Frognal Academy? Surely he could long ago have become attached in a professional capacity to one of our leading universities?"

"He was anxious in no way to abandon me here in London. And though I loved him so, I really could not uproot myself and undergo all the strain of moving to a strange town. Henry understood that. Also, I know he felt that he was more at liberty in his independent capacity to follow the course he had chosen."

"Which was?"

Mrs. Antrobus looked blankly across the green and brown paisley tablecloth at a fading sepia studio photograph of the infant Henry with his bespectacled and respectable father. Respectability oozed from the picture. Henry, aged about three, looking more like a girl, with fair ringlets and masses of white frills; his father looking the typical insurance clerk he was, gray suit under brown Chesterfield overcoat, buttoned right up to the stiff choker collar, and just the right width of cuff showing at each sleeve.

"I'm sorry?" said Mrs. Antrobus, shaking herself from her tearful reverie.

"Henry's thesis for his Ph.D.?"

"That was something he would never tell me," she said, and the shadow of a frown passed across her face at the memory. "Before that he shared all his studies with me, and although I was in no way able to make constructive comments—his field of learning was far too complicated for me to do that—yet he always used me as a willing ear, as an experimental audience if you will. It seemed to help him clarify his own thoughts. But with his Ph.D. he became strangely secretive and told me nothing, even becoming quite defensive when I asked one or two innocent questions. But he was obviously very excited about it. It crossed my mind that he might have relinquished his customary solitude and started working with someone else. There certainly *was* someone very interested in his work in the last weeks. He would go out late at night and see this man. . . ."

Nicholas blanched at the memory of his own late-night blackouts. His palms were sweating and he found himself unable to swallow.

". . . I know this because of something he once let slip," Mrs. Antrobus was saying in her dry monotone, "and whenever he went out he took his books and papers with him."

"As he did on the night he died?"

"Yes. He took everything with him that night and the police told me there was no sign of any papers on his body when it was found."

"Yes, that is so, Mrs. Antrobus," said Brough kindly.

"I discovered only one thing which might be of some use, although Inspector Daubeney did not seem to attach much importance to it."

Already her painful reminiscences had given Brough three clues that he regarded as vital, and an added vague suspicion that might just be capable of verification. Daubeney could hardly be blamed for dismissing or misunderstanding points that to Brough were critical. After all, Brough knew about Rogano, Daubeney didn't.

"Oh?" he said quickly to Mrs. Antrobus' disclosure.

"Henry had obviously gathered his things together very hurriedly on the night he left to meet his murderer. I found this on the floor of his room by his bureau."

She walked across to the mantelpiece over the kitchen range and took a folded sheet of notepaper from beneath a chipped marble clock. She handed it to Brough.

"It bears some kind of serial number," said the detective. "I take it this is your son's handwriting?"

She nodded.

"HM 27145 f.22," mumbled Brough under his breath. "May I keep this, Mrs. Antrobus?"

"Of course, if you find it helpful in any way, although I would like it back when you have done with it. There is so very little of him left to remind me."

He nodded and gently patted her hands as they nervously twisted at her apron.

"What was your son's date of birth?" he asked casually.

"August the nineteenth, 1872," she replied.

"Finally, do you know how your son was contacted by his killer on the night he arranged to meet him in Deptford?"

"I know only that a note was pushed through our letter box at about half-past nine that night. Henry opened it. He seemed somehow both elated and agitated but would not say why. Shortly afterward he left, taking his documents with him."

"It goes without saying that the note has not been seen since?"

She nodded absently and bit her bottom lip to stave off returning tears. "After that I never saw him again."

24

Their next stop was Nicholas' cramped room above a pawnbroker's shop in Coptic Street, five hundred yards from where Antrobus had lived. They ascended a rickety set of steps that ran up the outside wall of the corner building to a solitary wooden door. Nicholas fumbled in his pocket for a key and let them in. It was a grimy box less than eight feet by six. A sagging bed occupied more than half the floor space; there was a rattan table littered with papers and an old wicker chair. A slow but steady drip from a leak in the roof had been dealt with by the beneficent landlord by placing a small pail on the floor. Even this breath-taking ingenuity had not solved the problem because he never came to empty it. Nicholas had not been to the room for some days and the bucket was now overflowing. When the entry of the three men bathed the room in the uncertain light of day, there was a rapid exodus in all directions of wood lice and silverfish that had found sanctuary in the sodden coconut mat beneath the pail. The only light source in the room, apart from a guttered tallow candle hanging in a rusty sconce over the table, was a grease-spattered quarter light in a bashed-out panel of the door. With the door closed and the candle unlit, the place was in almost total darkness.

"Not much to write home about," snorted Nicholas, striking a match and lighting the swaying candle.

"I daresay it serves its purpose," said Brough. "What's all the paper work?"

"Mainly my scribblings about Rogano. All the important stuff is stowed away at Greenwich. This is the inevitable build-up of dross that any researcher has to contend with. It has no intrinsic value but I am loath to part with it."

"Are the Nostradamus papers here?"

Nicholas shifted a bundle of newspapers beneath the bed and extracted the documents passed to him by Carew. They were still enclosed in the brittle parchment tied with string that Nicholas had described.

"These will have to be examined word by word," ventured Galen. "Where their significance lies I cannot imagine, but significant they must be."

"Well they beat me," said Nicholas. "As a study of the real Nostradamus they make incredible reading, and they must be worth thousands in terms of historical value. But what relevance they have to me or the solution of the case I can't begin to think. You and Uncle can make of them what you will."

Brough had been shuffling through the litter on the table.

"What's this?" he exclaimed suddenly. Galen and Nicholas turned. He was holding a tattered piece of paper evidently torn from a note pad. He handed it to his nephew. "Is it yours?"

"Yes of course it's mine."

"What is it?"

Nicholas read out the words on the paper: "*NB Get HM 27145 f.22 from BM.*"

At the same moment Brough retrieved from his waistcoat pocket the paper Mrs. Antrobus had given him.

"*HM 27145 f.22,*" he read. "Strange coincidence, don't you think?"

"Was *that* the paper found in Antrobus' study?" asked Nicholas, who had previously not known what it contained. Brough nodded briefly.

"Coincidence is beginning to harrow me. This is a catalogue

number from the British Museum Department of Manuscripts. *HM* signifies the Harley-Manvell Collection of Historical Documents. *27145* is a thick handwritten document in Italian called *History of the Dukes of Rogano,* collected from contemporary records. *Folio 22* is a life of Lorenzo, the second duke, written by the Grand Inquisitor who prosecuted the case against the two brothers. It was later printed as a pamphlet and distributed all over Italy."

"Why would Antrobus be interested in Lorenzo?" asked Galen.

"I have my thoughts," said Brough pensively.

Nicholas said, "The report goes on to justify the execution of the brothers, further vilify the heretical Gormini sect and rounds off with a fanatical reaffirmation of the supremacy and the infallibility of the Roman Church."

"How long have you known about the Grand Inquisitor's document?" asked Brough.

"About six weeks," said Nicholas. "I came across it quite by accident in a mass of other stuff about the north Italian dukedoms. I also have a transcript of the printed version which appeared about the time of the brothers' execution."

"Surely it must have been much later," said Galen. "I know Gutenberg devised a sort of printing press at—where?—Mainz I think, in about 1450 or '51. But I am sure printing never reached Italy until much later in the century."

"Presumably the Vatican made sure it was in on the act of all new inventions as soon as it had the chance," said Nicholas with a shrug of his shoulders. "Whatever the explanation, I'm sure that pamphlet was in circulation by early 1455."

"Fascinating," said Galen.

"Does the paper contain anything startling?" asked Brough.

"Nothing I've not already told you. It catalogues Lorenzo's life, sums up his character and achievements, goes into blood-curdling detail about his murder, and that's it. Real Inquisition propaganda."

"Does it mention the strange mood of blasphemy and misanthropy that overtook Lorenzo in his last year on earth?"

"Well, actually . . . no."

"An odd omission in a biography, don't you think?"

"It is hardly a biography in the strict sense."

"But an account of such an eminent man's life, whatever its strict definition, is strangely lacking in not even mentioning the inexplicable decline that almost led to his overthrow."

Nicholas was compelled to agree.

There was a long pause, the silence broken only by the raucous calls of a costermonger who had his barrow pitched on the corner of Bedford Place and Bloomsbury Square, and the clatter of iron-wheeled vehicles trundling over the cobbles of Great Russell Street.

"Who was this Grand Inquisitor? He seems to have been quite a man," said Brough at last.

"There I can help you," put in Galen. "His name, as I think you already know, was Vincenzo Palestrina. He was a ruthless exponent of the Vatican's edicts, a merciless inquisitor and a founder of the dreaded Order of St. Jerome, which did more to foment terror and keep the north Italian peasants under the thumb of the Church than any other branch of the Inquisition. It was he who headed the investigation into the Rogano stranglings, he who championed the cause of the citizen who accused the Aquilina brothers and he whose machinations brought their appalling deaths. Though technically inferior in rank to the Bishop of Rogano, his political influence was immense. And although he paid lip service to the ailing bishop, he really took his instructions directly from Rome."

He paused a moment or two. "It is gratifying that our independent inquiries into events at Rogano are proving rather to complement each other than cause useless duplication," he said to Nicholas. The comment was accompanied by a light in his eye that Nicholas saw as the first dawning of friendship.

Is it *possible* for us to be friends? Nicholas asked himself, but in the tortured labyrinth of his mind he could find no answer.

"So this Grand Inquisitor was policeman, prosecutor, chief witness and, if the bishop really was so effete, in effect judge and jury as well," said Brough. He followed the observation with a low whistle.

"Certainly without his powerful influence on events, things might have turned out very differently," said Galen.

"I am puzzled how a man of such power and prestige could narrow his inquiry down to only two suspects," said Nicholas. "What was the great hurry? Why couldn't they keep both of them . . . Antonio and Giuseppe . . . safely behind bars and pursue their inquiries until more definite evidence was obtained to implicate the guilty one?"

"We mustn't forget the mood of the townsfolk," said Galen. "Not only Rogano but the whole of the Cavenna Valley and beyond were in a frenzy, almost frothing at the mouth for revenge. They were in no frame of mind to dally perhaps months with an evil killer in their midst. Let's not forget the nature of that killer's crimes, or the unspeakable fear in which everybody had lived. The Grand Inquisitor's solution of executing both men satisfied this lust for vengeance. Rough justice, yes. But delay might have brought the wrath of the reviled Gormini upon the town. It seemed by no means out of the question that the confederates of the guilty brother, from their lair in the hills, were plotting to rescue him and wreak further terror on the people."

"And tribal justice triumphed again," said Nicholas with a grimace. "At least now we might be able to redress the balance of that awful crime committed in the name of Right and discover the true perpetrator of the murders."

It was so easy to think in terms of Antonio and Giuseppe divorced from Nicholas and Galen, so tempting to overlook the London killings and dwell just on Rogano. The realization of the inescapable oneness of the two courses of events now forced itself upon him in a further ruthless assault on his reason. He felt his eyes going out of focus as his pupils dilated with the panic of self-doubt. He turned to the table and feigned preoccupation with some irrelevant press cutting, which in his plight he was unable to read or even identify, but the ruse successfully concealed his crisis from his companions.

"The pattern of connections between the two cases is becoming more tangible all the time," said Galen, dwelling again on the catalogue number from Antrobus' study, and he repeated his former question, this time each word interspersed by a silent beat: "Why was Henry Antrobus interested in the life of Lorenzo di Corsa?"

"Because," said Brough, "he was the reincarnation of Lorenzo di Corsa."

25

He sat on the edge of Nicholas' iron bed and savored for an instant the surprise he had sprung upon them.

"Oh yes, Henry Antrobus was the reincarnation of Lorenzo all right," he said, staring into a dusty corner and chewing his thumbnail. "My only real doubt is whether he knew it himself. Or was he responding to some *subconscious* knowledge when he started digging into the duke's life?"

He thrust his hands deeply into his greatcoat pockets and hunched himself up. It was bitterly cold in the room and their breath was pumping out of them like jets of steam.

"The first thing that started me thinking after Herr van Galen introduced the facet of reincarnation into the case was that Lorenzo was found dead by one of his servants, as it happened an elderly dwarf. So was Antrobus. He was discovered by my crazy little friend Bruno, that aging circus midget who spends his life at the Beggar's."

"Really? I didn't know that," said Nicholas.

"No, few people do. It wasn't in the papers. Next, as I elicited from Antrobus' mother, he was the same age to the day as Lorenzo when he died. Thirdly, he lost the sight in his left eye, just as Lorenzo did after the falconry accident. And of course, both Antrobus and Lorenzo were the first victims of the respective stranglers."

He got up and began to pace back and forth along the length of the room, hoping the limited exercise in the tiny chamber would revive his flagging circulation and begin to thaw his frozen limbs. Nicholas and Galen, apparently not quite so incapacitated by the temperature, remained immobile and listened.

"The hypothesis was clinched for me when I learned that he was researching the life of Lorenzo, who can be described at best as an obscure north Italian duke who in most biographical works gets four lines or nothing. There was also the more tenuous connection between the two that they were both highly studious

men. Now that could have been a trait passed on from one exist-
ence to another, as Herr van Galen has said is often the case, or it
could have been meaningless coincidence. Combined with the
other points, I do not believe it was coincidence.

"I am pleased to report that I learned a great deal more from
Mrs. Antrobus than the former existence of her son," he contin-
ued, "but at the moment my thoughts are in a state of flux. The
disparate facts we have gleaned must be allowed to come together
into a meaningful whole before I say more."

He saw in a flash the look of disappointment on Nicholas' face.
He wanted to offer him encouragement, but in his inimitable,
enigmatic way he set his nephew wondering even further when he
said, "I have discovered so far that four of the Deptford
Strangler's victims had one major thing in common. I shall be
looking for it when we investigate Professor Dakins and the girl
Jessica Twomey."

"I am sure your ideas about Antrobus are correct," said Galen.
"It is one of the unfathomable yet immutable laws of reincar-
nation that exactly the same length of time elapses between each
existence. I, for instance, was born precisely four hundred and
forty-seven years after Giuseppe Aquilina. You may recall I told
you that since Giuseppe, my soul has been reborn three times.
The other two birth dates have been in 1576 and 1725. I have no
wish to cloud an already complicated issue by going into details of
those intervening existences, but you will see that we are reborn
every one hundred and forty-nine years. We do not yet know the
significance of this period of time on the cosmic plane. The
length of our earthly lives has no bearing on this unchanging in-
terval."

"So however clever the quacks become, they'll never be able to
extend man's life expectancy beyond a hundred and forty-nine
years?" said Brough.

"Never," said Galen.

"I wonder . . ."

"At the beginning of my search for Nicholas, the only informa-
tion I had was the exact birth date of Antonio," continued Galen.
"I even knew from the Aquilina family journal the exact moment
in the day that Antonio had been born. That told me I was look-
ing for someone born at twenty minutes past four on the morning

of May twenty-fifth, 1873. How do you track down all the people born on a certain date? I did not know in which country, or even which continent, I should be searching. I have grave doubts that I should ever have found you, but for an astonishing accident.

"I had come to London in search of certain papers connected with Rogano which from my researches I had reason to believe were deposited in the Public Record Office. That was last October. When I applied for the papers in question I was told they were in the hands of another reader.

"I inquired with some surprise who that reader was. Who else in the world could be interested in the statements of witnesses at the trial of the two brothers in Rogano? You were pointed out to me. That was my first view of you, and in a rush the dreams of my childhood returned. You looked, as you sat there absorbed in those dusty scrolls, just as you had in my nightmares.

"Hurried checks on you at Somerset House—I got your name from the Record Office attendant—confirmed that you were born on the exact day the reincarnated Antonio should have appeared."

"Coincidence after coincidence," said Nicholas. "The odds against a chance encounter like that must be billions to one. It's all too much to take in . . . and so many threads seem to lead back through the maze to the Beggar's. Bruno—Carew's brother—it was there that I first told you about Rogano, Uncle. One almost begins to believe in fate."

"Somehow I think fate *is* at work here," said Brough. "Fate, destiny, call it what you will, something has decreed that those embroiled in the Rogano nightmare are to become entangled together once again. For what purpose we have yet to discover. As Herr van Galen has told us, and as I think we both now admit—you perhaps more reluctantly than I—there are laws in the universe of which man so far has no conception. Carew on the other hand told you he thought man had once been in possession of this knowledge but had, through the process of civilization, forgotten it. Whatever the truth, there might yet be some sound scientific explanation for this emotive word *fate.*"

"I have been blind!" exclaimed Galen with a suddenness that startled his friends. "Something you said a moment ago . . . *those embroiled in the Rogano nightmare are to become entangled to-*

gether once again . . . it all makes so much sense, and the evidence has been there from the beginning."

He paused, astonished that they could not see what he was about to say. "*All* the victims of the present murderer are reincarnations of the Rogano victims!"

His fiery odd eyes darted from one to the other as his thoughts outpaced his words, which then began tumbling out one upon the other: "The ages and sexes have reproduced themselves exactly each time. Why couldn't I see the significance of that? Why should I think Nicholas and I were the only two trapped in this incredible web whose former existences had been at Rogano? Look at the fourth victim of the Rogano killer, eighty-three-year-old Ruggiero Festa, described as a dabbler in astrology and predictions. That description could fit no one more closely than the Deptford Strangler's fourth victim, Augustus Carew."

"Then it is no joke at all," said Nicholas, "to say that Bruno is probably the reincarnation of the Sicilian dwarf who found the dead Lorenzo."

26

"This could take us years," said Nicholas, poring over a bundle of the Nostradamus manuscripts. He was sitting with Galen and Brough at the table in the detective's living room. Charlie Peace and the clutter that usually obscured the table's fine rosewood inlay had been consigned to a deep armchair. It was already dark outside and from the muted sounds filtering up to the little room it seemed the returning foul weather had chased most people indoors. They had divided the papers into three roughly equal piles and had been studying them for an hour. Carew's translation of each quatrain was set out in his neat notation on a separate sheet attached to each of the original pages. Even though Nicholas knew Latin and Galen was no mean hand at medieval French, they had made little headway in prying any new interpretations from the prophecies so far examined. That afternoon Brough had bought an inexpensive edition of the *Centuries*, published in Edinburgh the previous year, from an occult bookshop a stone's throw from Nicholas' room.

"One thing is crystal clear," Brough said out of the blue. "Carew was not mistaken when he said many of the original quatrains have been woefully distorted through ignorance, carelessness and deliberate misrepresentation. Some of them are identical with the originals, but others are wildly out."

He pressed open the cheaply produced volume they had obtained that day at page fifty-seven.

"Listen to this," he said. "Century Two, quatrain twenty-four. This is the version readers have been fed for the past three hundred and forty years."

He cleared his throat and in his own quaint version of a French accent, he read the following lines:

> Bestes farouches de faim fleuves tranner,
> Plus part du champ encontre Hifter sera.
> En caige de fer le grand fera treisner,
> Quand rien enfant de Germain observera.

With a brief apologetic smile for his comic accent, he said, "As with almost all the other printed prophecies that is a vague, undated spiel. It concerns ravenous wild beasts swimming across rivers, a battlefield and a cage of iron, and some mysterious German who 'observes no law.' Then there is the baffling proper noun *Hifter*. What is that supposed to mean? According to the commentary in the book, it refers to the River Danube, the Latin name for which was Ister. All in all it doesn't make a lot of sense. But look now at Nostradamus' original unadulterated quatrain. I'll not bother you with the French, but listen to Carew's translation. It's not, of course, in verse: *The wild beast Hitler, the mad leader of Germany who recognizes no law, crosses the Rhine with his armies in their iron tanks in the third year of the thirty-eighth decade after my death. The countries of the West combine to defeat the tyrant."*

There was a strained silence. "That," said Brough at last, "is a whole different kettle of fish. The real prophecy gives us an actual year. Nostradamus died in 1566, so the thirty-eighth decade after his death would start in"—he made a rapid computation on a scrap of paper—"in 1936. Add three to that and you're in 1939, thirty-seven years from now. It's so clear and detailed it's almost a report of what's to be. The hitherto misspelled *Hifter* we can now see has nothing to do with the River Danube, but refers to some insane German leader, presumably a future Kaiser, called Hitler —though thinking about it, I can't imagine that rascal Kaiser Wilhelm giving any of his sons such an unlikely name. None of it is much use as we've no way of knowing even if this demonic Kaiser is ever likely to exist. And I'm puzzled too by the word *tank*. How do you cross a river in a tank? You're surely more likely to fill a tank from a river than travel in it. However, that by the way. What this quatrain does show us is that Nostradamus has been poorly treated by his publishers and commentators."

He slid his fingers up under his half-moon reading glasses and covered his eyes, thinking deeply. With a glum twist of his mouth, he slumped back in his chair.

"What we need," he said with a sigh that mingled tiredness and bewilderment, "is a quatrain in that sort of detail that tells us something we know to be true—something that's already happened. So many of the predictions *are* vague. Then we come across one like this, which is so precise it could prove or disprove Nostradamus' abilities once and for all, and damn it, it refers to the *future*."

They again fell to studying the hundreds of prophecies before them.

"Dreyfus!" cried Nicholas after a moment, snatching Brough's pile of papers from him and frantically turning back through the pages.

"I remember it was one of the earliest of the quatrains," continued Nicholas heatedly, "and I really was impressed by its total accuracy. How could you have missed it, Uncle?"

In an instant he had found the verse he was seeking—Century One, quatrain seven.

"Listen," he said, smoothing the papers out before him and glancing with impatience at the printed version in Brough's book. "Forget that tripe," he said with a dismissive gesture toward the open book, "and listen to Carew's translation of the real thing. *Six years are still to pass before the end of the century numbered nineteen. Dreyfuss is innocent but condemnation follows. The Is-*

*land of the Devil has him four years because evidence arrives too
late. The enemy Rousseau presides and blames him again.* If that
does not convince us once and for all that Nostradamus had some
fantastic means of seeing into the future, nothing will!"

"Truly amazing," said Brough.

"Do pardon my ignorance," said Galen, "but would one of you
enlighten me?"

"Dreyfus!" said Nicholas in exasperation.

"Dreyfus," said Galen, nodding sagely as if the mere repetition
of the word had explained all. "Hmm."

He paused.

"What is Dreyfus?" he said with a frown.

"Oh come on, Galen. Alfred Dreyfus is a Jewish French soldier
who was unjustly convicted of selling military secrets to Germany
in 1894. It's an unusual name to say the least, but Nostradamus
had it almost exactly right—just an extra 's.' The dating too is pre-
cise. Six years before the end of the century numbered nineteen
can only mean 1894."

"And the rest?" said Galen. "The Island of the Devil and the
enemy Rousseau?"

"Dreyfus was transported to Devil's Island, the French penal
colony, where he languished for four years until he was returned
to France for a retrial. One of his bitter opponents, a government
minister called Waldeck Rousseau, presided at the new hearing
and found him guilty a second time. As Nostradamus points out
so clearly, the reason he was convicted to begin with was that evi-
dence of his innocence arrived too late."

Brough gave a long, low whistle. "Even the prophecy that
seemed to mention Nicholas did not totally convince me," he
said. "But this . . ." He beat a spirited tattoo on the tabletop
with his knuckles. "Our exercise has served its purpose," he pro-
nounced with finality. "We can be left in little doubt as to
Nostradamus' incredible powers of precognition."

Nicholas and Galen nodded.

"That faith established, then, we must search for what he had
to say about Rogano. Where is the one that Carew read you
about the strangling hands of Rogano striking again in London?"

"Wasn't it where there are some extra quatrains tacked on at
the end of the Century that was never finished?" said Nicholas in

genuine confusion. "My mind is so disordered I can't remember facts from one day to the next anymore."

They all began shuffling through their papers once again until Galen said, "Here, I have it! The unfinished Century is number seven. How many quatrains does that Century contain in your book?"

"Forty-two," said Brough after a quick consultation.

"Ah yes," said Galen. "Forty-three reads, *A puzzle. And a struggle over crimes long dead. The strangling hands of Rogano kill again and London walks in fear. C. knows not himself and the terror of the night haunts him.*"

"I've looked at the quatrains that follow that one," said Nicholas, "and though they are obviously concerned with Rogano I can't make any sense of them."

"Read number forty-four," said Brough.

Galen looked again at Carew's minute script.

"*Beware the son of Peter. Lorenzo and his confederates meet him and they die. Their design is ill advised. One of the children of Peter is true and one is false.*"

"That's not even a prophecy," said Nicholas despondently. "It's clearly linked with the Rogano murders because of the reference to Lorenzo—but they took place before Nostradamus was born."

"For some unknown reason, certain of his predictions are retroactive," said Brough. "It says so in the introduction to the book. Following on from the verse about the Rogano Strangler and mentioning Lorenzo, there can be no doubt of its connection with Rogano. But it has a lot more to it than that."

He took the manuscript from Galen and read it again. "*Beware the son of Peter,*" he repeated. "Does it actually say Peter in the original French?"

He cast his eye over Nostradamus' own winding brown writing.

"No, there it's rendered as the French equivalent, Pierre. Who was the son of Peter?"

"One of us," said Galen. "Antonio or Giuseppe. Their father's first name was Pietro. Pietro—Pierre—Peter. Even the prophet, it seems, didn't know which of us was true and which false."

"But there's more," said Brough quickly, countering the pessimism. "This describes the victims of the Rogano Strangler as 'Lorenzo and his confederates.' Can that mean that the victims of the Rogano Strangler were all known personally to Lorenzo? If so, that puts an entirely new slant on things."

"*Their design is ill advised*," repeated Galen. "What design?"

"That's the vital clue," said Brough, "I can feel it in my bones."

"What about quatrain forty-five?" said Nicholas.

"It's a continuation of the one before," said Brough. "*The son of Peter reappears and kills again. He must be destroyed or great misery will follow. The great untruth of Eusebius must be preserved. It will die a natural death.*"

"There he goes again," said Nicholas, "telling us what we know already. The killer is Peter's son. We *know* that. Why can't he tell us *which* of Peter's sons is the killer?"

"*He must be destroyed or great misery will follow*," said Galen, visibly trembling. "Until now the whole nightmare has been to discover which of us is the strangler. The thought of what must follow the discovery of the guilty one has eluded us. *He must be destroyed . . .*" And his voice trailed off into silence.

"Eusebius is a new name to the case," said Brough. "There must be a clue in that, too. If we can find out this great untruth that according to the prophet must be preserved until it dies naturally, we might just be making some progress.

"There is one last quatrain before the seer decided to obliterate all further predictions in Century Seven. You read it to us, Nicholas."

He handed his nephew the manuscript.

Nicholas read aloud, "*The pious lady knows but cannot tell. The citadel holds their secret. Behind the altar the true son of Peter is concealed . . .*" He broke off suddenly and consulted the original French. "The last line is in capital letters and is a repeat of what appeared in the quatrain before. HE MUST BE DESTROYED OR GREAT MISERY WILL FOLLOW."

Nicholas put down the papers and stood up. Walking across to the fire blazing in its black-iron grate, he said, "As I told you before, it beats me."

"*Il,*" said Brough, more to himself than his companions.

"What?" said Nicholas.

"*Il.* The French for *he* and *it.*"

"What about it?"

"I'm not sure."

"I have a theory," said Galen, "which might explain the ambiguities contained in this last clue left us by Nostradamus. I think 'the pious lady' was the mother superior at the great abbey above Rogano. I think 'the citadel' means the abbey, which as we know had been built as a fortress. Is it not possible that Mother Maria d'Aprillia knew who the Rogano Strangler was? If the killer had confessed to her after securing her promise not to betray him, she might have felt compelled to keep silent—thus 'the pious lady knows but cannot tell.' I can't think how the line about the true son of Peter being hidden behind the altar fits in. There was no time for either of the brothers to escape and go into hiding, because they were arrested in the cathedral immediately after being denounced by the bishop. That line is very puzzling."

"We're running ahead of ourselves," said Brough. "Nicholas, will you hand me volume four of my encyclopedia from the bookcase?"

Turning the pages of the volume, Brough said, "*The great untruth of Eusebius.* That sounds like a Latin name to me . . . *Eurystheus, Euschemonidae, Eusden* . . . ah, here we arc, *Eusebius.*"

He read in silence for several minutes. "How interesting," he said at length. "Well, my friends, in the opinion of the compilers of this encyclopedia there have been only three people in history called Eusebius who are worthy of mention. Funnily enough, they were all around at the same time, the beginning of the fourth century."

"What sort of men were they?"

"All religious, strange as it might seem. Two bishops and a pope. Both the bishops were involved in the Council of Nicaea, set up by the Emperor Constantime the Great in 325 to determine the true nature of Jesus Christ."

"Hang on," said Nicholas, "wasn't Colin Manders writing a book about Constantine the Great?"

"Yes," said Brough. "Interesting, don't you think?"

"Tell us about these men," said Galen.

"Not much to say about the Pope—oh, he was a saint as well, by the way—born in Greece, died in Sicily. He was pontiff for about four months. Must have been a *raging* success. As for the others . . . well . . ."

He continued to run his eye down the page.

". . . after a bit of opposition to start with, Eusebius of Cae-sarea eventually decided to toe the official line set down by the Council of Nicaea, which was basically that Jesus was divine and an equal of God the Father and the Holy Ghost. The council ratified the tradition of the virgin birth and the Resurrection, which had by no means been universally accepted until then. Eusebius later wrote a history of the first three hundred years of Christianity which is regarded as one of the most important eccle-siastical works. Apparently, there are no copies of the gospels that predate those produced by Eusebius in his role as official church historian.

"Eusebius of Nicomedia, on the other hand, was the exact op-posite. He was one of the leading advocates of the Arian heresy that said Christ was *not* divine and not eternal, but human. He later became the leader of a heretical sect called the Eusebians, which preached the Arian viewpoint. Until the council made its decision about Christ's divinity it was apparently up to each bishop to make his own mind up and teach his own interpretation of the scriptures to his flock. After 325 the universal view held today was adopted all over Christendom and enforced with the threat of torture and crucifixion for dissenters."

"The *Arian* heresy!" interjected Nicholas. "My God, *he* must be the man Nostradamus was referring to. Eusebius of Nicome-dia. The heretics of Rogano based their precepts on Arianism, but took the belief much further than the Eusebians. The Grand In-quisitor referred to the Gormini as latter-day Arians in that report I spoke of."

"The gaps are filling in!" said Galen. "If you are right, 'the great untruth of Eusebius' was the sinister Arian heresy resur-rected and expanded by the Gormini. Nostradamus said that if it was left alone it would disappear naturally. Certainly this seems to have been the view of the Inquisition, for in all my researches I have been unable to find any further record of the sect after the execution of the brothers."

"It just fizzled out," said Nicholas.

"So it would seem," said Galen. "As Nostradamus said it would."

"Muffins! Hot muf-fins!" sang a merry peddler in Piccadilly, just yards away through Church Place. Maimed at the beginning of the Boer War, poor old Percy Gilpin had sat in his ramshackle booth by the church railings summer and winter for the past four years. In warm weather he sold beer, mainly to off-duty cabbies who sauntered across from the cab rank near the Royal Academy, and in cold weather he sold muffins and chestnuts. All year round he supplemented his meager income by selling newspapers as well.

"Nip across and buy us some muffins, Nicholas," said Brough, looking curiously pleased with himself. "They'll go down a treat with piping hot cocoa."

"What happened to the plan for us all to stick together twenty-four hours a day?" replied his nephew.

"The next murder is not due until the twenty-eighth," said Brough, the intriguing smile still lighting his face. "Until then we have nothing to fear."

While Nicholas tramped off through the snow on his errand, Brough brewed the cocoa in a saucepan over the fire.

"You know, Herr van Galen," he said, pouring the drink into three half-pint mugs, "I think you're right about the last quatrain. Nostradamus would have made a great copper."

27

Ridiculous as it seemed, getting out of bed in winter was one of the hardest tasks Reginald Brough had to face in life. It hadn't always been like that. And even now, in summer, he was up and ambling about the city with the first rays of morning sunshine. But at this time of year, forsaking the enveloping warmth of his woolen blankets for the penetrating coldness of the bedroom air took just about as much determination as he could summon before the fortification of breakfast. The old blood must be thinning out, he thought, nestling farther into the womb of his heavy eiderdown and watching the hands of the clock climb with irritating haste toward nine o'clock.

Even though it was barely light, the carol singers were already out and their melodious rendering of "Once in Royal David's City" mingled with the yells of barrow boys who wandered up and down peddling sweetmeats, nuts and fresh turkeys.

To expedite the trio's departure for Rogano, it had been decided the night before that Brough would try to conclude his interviews with the closest relatives of the Deptford Strangler's victims while Nicholas and Galen would spend the day making ready for the journey.

Professor Maurice Dakins, Brough was now convinced, had been the reincarnation of Brother Domenico, the monk found strangled in the cloisters of the monastery at Rogano. And Jessica Twomey had been the latest existence of the merchant's daughter Maria Bellini, whose body had been discovered in the foundations of a partly built house.

According to Daubeney, Jessica's mother had died of consumption two years previously, and since then the girl had lived with an elderly aunt and uncle and a cousin, Meg, in a large villa in the Essex parish of Leytonstone. That imposing residence was to be his first objective: he had no wish still to be out in the snowy suburbs on the edge of Epping Forest when darkness fell in less than six hours. Dakins, who had at least been living in London, would have to wait until his return.

He decided that only by a supreme effort of will would he conquer the overwhelming desire to snuggle all day in the warm cocoon of bedclothes. He began to count slowly to fifty, intent on heaving himself out into the icy room the instant he reached that magic number. Neither Nicholas nor Galen had yet risen so there was not a fire going in the place. A crystallized pattern of frost had formed on the inside of the window, and the sudden sight of that in the midst of his intrepid counting rather blunted his determination, so he had reached seventy before finally throwing back the covers and diving into his dressing gown.

The carol singers were closer at hand when he reached the arctic wastes of the living room, and scraping away a rough square of frost from the window with the carving knife that Kate Webster had used to dismember her mistress back in '79, he looked along the pure white ribbon of Jermyn Street. By now "O Little Town of Bethlehem" was winding to its low, gentle close, and the animated chords of "Good King Wenceslas" were beginning, recalling to Brough's mind the sinister evening of Nicholas' return. Only three nights ago, but with all the harrowing, inexplicable events since, it seemed weeks. The voices, mainly the sweet harmony of children, but accompanied by one or two adults— presumably the vicar of St. James's and a parent or two, swelled as the joyous tale of the benevolent king unfolded once again.

> ". . . through the rude wind's wild lament,
> And the winter wea-ea-ther . . ."

Snowflakes as big as florins floated down upon the singers, as if summoned by the incantation of their song.

The detective decided to eat out rather than spend a minute longer than necessary in his icy rooms. He dressed quickly after reluctantly doffing his heavy dressing gown—that took a count of ten—and was out in the street by twenty past nine. His friends still slept on.

After sausages, eggs, bacon and lashings of hot coffee in a cozy restaurant at Piccadilly Circus, he walked a little way along Shaftesbury Avenue and caught a cab.

"British Museum Underground Station," he said to the cabby. He always enjoyed a ride on the new Central London Railway.

I could have walked it in less time, he grumbled in his thoughts ten minutes later as the cabby found street after street choked with tradesmen's carts.

It was the cold, too, that kept Nicholas and Galen in bed until after their host had left. For them the day ahead was to hold packing of trunks, a visit to the main office of Cook's Tours to book their passage and after lunch a trip down to Greenwich to pick up Nicholas' research notes and papers on Rogano. Galen also wanted to stop off at the Bloomsbury boarding house which had been his base from the day he had arrived in London to the morning he had so dramatically engineered the crossing of his own path with that of Nicholas and Brough. All his own notes on Rogano were contained in a single thick notebook bound in quarter leather with hand-marbled boards, and opulently blocked in gold with his initials. It was the first and last sign of anything that seemed to conflict with Galen's natural sobriety that Nicholas and Brough were to see, and Brough concluded that it had been a gift. After copying the vital quatrains of Nostradamus' predictions into the book, they were also to deposit the priceless originals with Brough's bank in Regent Street.

From the very first that morning, Galen thought Nicholas' behavior odd and preoccupied. By the time his uncle had breakfasted, Nicholas had completed his share of the packing. To Galen's surprise he suddenly said there was something important he had to do, and suggested Galen go off to Cook's alone. The German was puzzled by Nicholas' secrecy about the errand, but reassured by Brough's assertion that they had nothing to fear until the twenty-eighth, he agreed.

A few minutes later, Nicholas was in a hansom clip-clopping along toward British Museum Station.

At British Museum, Brough bought a ticket for Bank, the end of the line. From there, it would be a short walk to Liverpool Street main-line terminus, from which the Great Eastern Railway would bear him overland to Leytonstone.

The mass of workers having been at their labors since eight o'clock, many since seven or earlier, the platform at British Museum was almost deserted. A knot of about six people at the farther end, and a straggling line of four or five women, one with a whining child, halfway along, were the only travelers awaiting the eastbound train when Brough reached the platform. He took up a lone position close to the mouth of the tunnel where the train would emerge at something like twenty-five miles per hour and where the rear carriage would come to a standstill. At that moment, forty feet above his head, his nephew was being deposited at the station entrance by a gruff cabby. Brough had to wait no more than three minutes for the train. He could feel the wind on his face as it surged forward through the tunnel even before he could hear its echoing clatter and the rhythmic tattoo of its wheels passing over the bolted joints of the rails.

He smelled him an instant before the train hurtled into the station, but he did not get a chance to turn around. A savage kick in the back of the legs accompanied by a double-handed blow in the small of the back sent him reeling forward, over the edge of the platform and into the path of the train. So timed was the attack that the driver of the train did not register that he had passed over someone until the locomotive was halfway along the platform. He applied his brakes and brought the six-coach train to a shuddering halt, the rear carriage still inside the tunnel.

"Bloody Christ in heaven," he blasphemed as he scrambled from his cab and raced back to where Brough had pitched forward. Other passengers, quickly made aware of the tragedy, were soon milling about the spot and bending down, trying to peer through the inky gap between the bottom of the train and the edge of the platform, striving to get a glimpse of the mangled horror that must lie beneath.

No one seemed to have witnessed the incident except one of the women along the platform, who had turned in Brough's direction just as he plunged into the path of the engine. She had seen a man in a long black overcoat running back up the sloping foot tunnel toward the station exit, but she would be unable, she was positive, to recognize him again.

"How did he fall?" asked one of a score of passengers who had leaped from the five carriages in the station, and who now swelled the awe-struck throng jostling each other for a glimpse into the darkness beneath the train.

"'E was pushed," said the woman who had seen the retreating assailant. She was a garrulous, scrawny creature in a faded bonnet. "And I'm not so sure I couldn't identify the feller wot done it after all."

"Deliberate?" inquired a pudgy little fellow in a checked waistcoat and a floppy hat.

"Sure as I'm standin' 'ere," affirmed the woman, who was already on tiptoe and straining over the shoulders of the crowd for signs of the police and the men of the press.

"What am I going to do?" panicked the driver in a shrill treble.

"Might I suggest moving the train forward," said a voice barbed with impatience.

Everyone looked down.

"Move the train forward and I can climb out," continued Brough's voice from beneath the fifth carriage, as if explaining the simplest of acts to a backward child.

"You *alive* down there?" shouted the driver.

"Do I really need to answer that?" Brough called back.

"You just stay there," said the driver, as if Brough had any choice in the matter. "I'll pull right up to the other end of the platform. Clear out of the way everyone!" And he lumbered back to his cab.

The train eased forward with painful slowness, the quaking driver trembling from head to toe as the shock of what had happened began its delayed effect.

Any faster than a snail, he thought, and I might knock the poor bastard out with the undercarriage or drag him onto the live rail. Inch by inch the engine dragged its carriages forward over the prostrate Brough. The end of the fifth carriage, then the beginning of the sixth, appeared, and at last the whole train was out of the tunnel and crawling along the platform. As the back of the last coach passed over him, the detective was revealed to the gaping crowd lying on his side fully stretched out in the narrow trough that ran beneath the rails for almost the entire length of the station. He raised himself on his hands, taking care to avoid the electrified rail. In a trice he was standing upright on the concrete floor of the trough, and grasping two of the two dozen arms stretching out from the crowd of onlookers, he clambered onto the platform in two awkward movements.

By now the guard of the train, trapped inside until it had moved out of the tunnel, was on the scene.

"All right, sir?" he asked anxiously.

"I'm bruised," said Brough. "I have a grazed hand and what feels like a sprained ankle. But yes, thank you, I'm all right."

"You're lucky it happened here is all I can say," said the guard. "Not all the Central stations have got these safety troughs, and none of the Metropolitan stations have 'em."

"Fortunate indeed," said Brough. "Is there a telephone I can use?"

"'Scuse me, sir," said the woman who had seen Brough's assailant making his escape. She pushed forward through the crowd of bystanders. "I saw it all with me own eyes. I saw who pushed you and I reckon I'd know 'im again anywhere."

"That's not what you said before," said a mildly spoken man with a waxed mustache and curly brimmed bowler who had heard every new variation of the publicity seeker's account.

"Never you mind what I said before," was the angry retort. "I know what I saw."

Brough, gentleman even in adversity, came to her rescue: "I am grateful for your concern, madam, but do not upset yourself. I know only too well who the man was."

Inside the station master's white-tiled office a crepe bandage was applied to Brough's ankle while he telephoned Daubeney at the Yard.

"Ambrose? It's Brough. I'm at British Museum tube station. Peterson tried to kill me here less than ten minutes ago. Pushed me in front of a train. . . . What? . . . No doubts whatever. He's not only still in London, he's within ten minutes of where I'm sitting. . . . I'll be fine, just a bit shaken up . . . I tell you the man's a bungler. No discipline. He has a completely irrational violence in him. He had me right where he wanted me, and instead of just a good push at the right moment, he bashes me in between the shoulder blades and boots me in the back of the shins at the same time. Of course, my legs went from under me and I slid neatly into the safety trough a second before the train went over the top. Thank the Lord it's winter and I'm wearing all these heavy clothes, or I'd have been black and blue. . . . No, I can't pretend I'm not badly shocked. In fact it's just beginning to hit me now. . . . No, don't worry, I'll be all right. These fine people are brewing me a good strong cup of sweet tea right at this moment. That'll work wonders. . . . I'm on my way to see the relatives of the Twomey girl. . . . Fine. I'll ring you tonight."

Once fortified with the said beverage, and free of the Central London Railway Company's agitated ministering angels, Brough resumed his journey.

At Liverpool Street he caught the 11:45 from Platform Two and settled back in his seat for the short journey to the country. Bishopsgate—Shoreditch—Bethnal Green Junction—Coborn— the great dirty steam locomotive charged onward, passing Stratford New Town and High Meads on the right and the flat, white expanse of Hackney Marshes and the Lea Valley on the left. All the way he was troubled by Peterson's sudden reappearance. *Why now?* He had been out for more than six weeks. If he wanted to do away with Brough, why wait all this time to make his first attempt? There was something, too, about the killer's name. What was it? It had never worried him before, but now it seemed to have some significance. If he could only pinpoint it. Peterson, Peterson, Peterson. The name wound around and around in his mind until he could hear it in the steady, repetitive tempo of the train clattering over the tracks. Peter-son, Peter-son, Peter-son. Still he could make nothing of it, but then, being pushed in front of a train and barely escaping with your life was not the best formula for clear, logical thinking. But at least he knew now the meaning of little Bruno following him around and telling him that he hadn't told "the Big Man" where Brough was. Peterson, intent on getting even with his old enemy, must have interrogated the dwarf about him when he went to the Beggar's.

The track took a wide sweep around the belching chimneys and new factories of Stratford Works, and after suffering a minor delay at Loughton Junction, the train was speeding past row upon row of identical brick dwellings with postage-stamp rear yards backing on to the railway. Suddenly, after passing through Leyton Station without stopping, they were in the country.

"Epping Forest, London's Health Resort, Begins at Leytonstone" Brough learned from a sign at the end of the platform when he reached his destination. Indeed, the station seemed to be enclosed on both sides of the track by woodland. The carved wooden canopy and seats had all been recently painted in a rich brown.

Limping slightly from his injured ankle, the detective made his way through the barrier and out into the street. Once in the road, it struck Brough that the proud words of the sign might soon have to be erased. New roads were being cut through the trees and there was a proliferation of signs offering parcels of "Prime Building Land for Sale by Auction." The Great Forest of Epping was being chased farther and farther back, and rural Leytonstone was fast becoming the outer edge of London's growing urbanization. For the past thirty years its broad tree-lined roads with well-spaced mansions had been attracting the City merchants who had once lived at Stepney Green and Bow. Now the migration was becoming something of an exodus.

Brough asked a postman, shambling toward him on two left feet, where he might find Hainault Road. The directions were simple enough, and after a brisk ten-minute walk he found himself outside a big semidetached house of yellow stock bricks, set well back from the road opposite an old church. Etched into a limestone plaque on the front of the bay was "Dunrobin Villa, 1876."

A scullery maid in a frilly cap answered his knock on the door. "Mr. Brough, sir?" she said. "Miss Meg is expecting you."

He was shown into a large room on the right with a fire blazing beneath a massive mid-Victorian mantelpiece in dark marble.

"Miss Meg won't be a minute, sir," said the maid, who curtsied briefly and darted away along the broad, high-ceilinged hallway.

When she appeared, Meg Brandon proved to be a tall, striking woman of the sort Brough always dubbed "comely." He set her age at between twenty-eight and thirty. Her fair oval face was set with two of the saddest eyes he had ever seen, and surmounted by Titian hair swept up into a becoming "cottage loaf" style that accorded well with her aura of subdued grace.

"Please sit down, Inspector," she said, indicating a leather sofa. She sat opposite him on the very edge of an elegant spoon-back armchair. A low table strewn with papers stood between them.

"I cannot apologize enough for trespassing upon your privacy and your grief," he began. "Especially so soon after your cousin's funeral. You were, I think, Jessica's closest friend and companion?"

"We were like sisters," said Miss Brandon softly. "There would be no point in your troubling my parents. Not even they knew Jessica as I did."

"But even you did not know where she was going on the night she was . . . on the night she disappeared?"

"Inspector, I am going to tell you something of which I have so far breathed not one word to anyone. It is something I should have told Mr. Daubeney when he came here last week. But his visit was only a few hours after the terrible news was broken to us, and to say I was not myself is, believe me, an understatement. Later I determined to telephone him at Scotland Yard, but when I heard you wished to see me I thought it best to leave it until we met."

She lowered her gaze.

"I believe that my cousin was losing her mind," she said.

An unpleasant twingeing sensation had started to make itself felt in Brough's twisted ankle, but he contrived to dismiss it from his mind. He looked at Miss Brandon inquiringly.

"She was not herself for the last five or six weeks of her life. Strangely enough, her trouble began the day we read in *The Times* an account of this dreadful strangler's first murder. That very night she began to suffer nightmares which persisted to the day she died. What I find so unnerving is that she became convinced from these horrid dreams that she herself would become a victim of this strangler."

"How did she explain her belief?"

"I don't know if you are familiar with the philosophy of reincarnation, Inspector, but after her dreams began Jessica became *obsessed* with it. None of the things she valued in life were of any consequence to her after that. All her thoughts became centered on the mad certainty that she had lived before."

"Did she go into detail?"

"Oh yes. She even wrote a letter on the subject of reincarnation to the *Pall Mall Gazette*, which was published about a fortnight before she died. She said that in a former life she had been murdered, and that she would be murdered in this one too."

She sorted through the papers on the table between them, and withdrew the printed copy of the letter. It was headed I WILL BE STRANGLER'S FIFTH VICTIM.

"I firmly believe that by writing that letter Jessica brought about her own death, that the Deptford Strangler read the letter and in his mania decided to make the prediction come true."

Brough read the letter carefully. As he took all the main London papers, including the *Gazette*, regularly and scanned their columns religiously, he wondered how he had missed it. The letter took the form of a general discussion of the concept of reincarnation followed by the statement that Jessica herself had lived a previous life, and culminating in the prediction upon which the *Gazette* subeditor had chosen his headline.

"Did she tell you about the previous life she thought she had lived?" he asked.

"Inspector, you sound as if you take it seriously."

"I am only trying to obtain a clear idea of Jessica's state of mind, which you so wisely decided to tell us about," he replied, realizing her trust in him would be irreparably damaged if he even hinted at his true thoughts on the subject.

"Yes, she told me *everything* about it," said Miss Brandon, mollified. "She spoke of nothing else for five weeks. She said she had lived in Italy in the Middle Ages in a city called . . . what? . . . Ruffino, Roffano—something like that."

"Rogano?" asked Brough.

"Yes, Rogano it was!" she exclaimed. "How did you know?"

"Coincidence," he lied. "I passed through Rogano last year on a trip to Venice."

"It does exist then," she said. "I even had my doubts about that."

"Oh yes, Rogano exists all right."

"Well, Jessica was convinced she had been the daughter of a merchant of this town. Her name had been Maria Bellini. It really is all so romantic and ridiculous. It's like some badly written novel."

"Please go on," said Brough gently.

With a sigh of impatience, Miss Brandon said, "Jessica believed that in this previous life she had been the mistress of the duke of this place—Rogano—after his wife had fled from the town and returned to her family in Florence."

Miss Brandon blushed and averted her gaze. "She went into rather intimate detail about her love affair with this nobleman, which it is hardly proper for me to repeat."

"Of course."

"She was introduced by this Lorenzo—oh! I never ceased hearing about beautiful, one-eyed Lorenzo—she was introduced by him to a group of his friends, seven in number, some of whom had studied with him at university. Others had accompanied him on a pilgrimage to the Holy Land and during that great adventure their friendship had begun. It was always dark when they met, and in the strictest secrecy. They had made a fearful discovery and Lorenzo promised to make her party to it. The trouble was, the dreams were not in any chronological order and Jessica never actually learned what the secret was, except that it was something to do with a cave and a man whose name was Aquilina. Then she dreamed she was abducted by a mad killer who was terrorizing the city, that she was strangled and her body thrown into the basement of an unfinished building."

She suddenly broke off. "That's all," she said, and to conceal her tears she rose and walked to the right of the fireplace, where

she tugged the sally of a wire bell pull to sound a tinkling sum-
mons in the scullery at the rear of the house. While she awaited
the appearance of the maid, Miss Brandon stood by the tall win-
dows and looked at the snow now falling faster than ever upon
two slender silver birches in the front garden. From an icicle-hung
perch on a low branch a robin sang. Brough's footprints, deeply
imprinted on the garden path when he arrived, were now com-
pletely covered. A milkman's horse had come to grief on the slip-
pery road outside the house and his master, incensed at having his
delivery delayed, was laying into him with an empty bottle as the
poor horse struggled to stand up.

Unembarrassed by the silence, Brough cast his eye slowly
around the room and eagerly awaited the warming cup of tea
which he felt sure Miss Brandon would order when the maid re-
sponded to the summons. His gaze drifted from the crystal chan-
delier to the mantelpiece with its silver-framed family photo-
graphs and its black-marble clock; from the mantelpiece to the
crackling fire; and from the fire across the richly carpeted floor to
the low table in front of him. Among the disordered pile of news-
papers and letters of condolence his attention was caught by one
particular sheet of paper, half obscured by a torn lilac envelope
that had been cast carelessly on top of it. It had been many years
since he had perfected the art of reading upside down, and now
he read with ease the four lines of blue copperplate that were
visible:

> *Deep inside the mind of Man*
> *Beyond the reach of thought*
> *Past untold byways in his brain*
> *In regions still unsought . . .*

Oh God, he thought. Nicholas' poem.

28

As the final, crushing blow was dealt to his feeble hope that
Nicholas might, after all, be innocent, the maid entered the room.

He hardly noticed her presence, and the dialogue that followed between her and Miss Brandon was a meaningless hum in the background as he stared unblinkingly at the first direct and concrete link between Nicholas and a victim of the strangler. Events had prevented him mentioning to Nicholas the finding of the poem among the pages of his report on the Rogano murders. That copy, he now realized, must have been the first rough draft. The one on the table before him was clearly the finished version, beautifully inscribed.

". . . or China, Mr. Brough?"

"I'm sorry," said the detective, stirring from his rumination. "Were you speaking to me?"

"I said would you like India or China tea?" she said softly.

"Oh, India for me please," he said, still distracted by the poem. He thought China tasted like perfume.

The maid disappeared.

"This poem," he said, picking it up and deciding to come straight to the point, "whose is it?"

"Why, it's mine," she replied, stepping forward and taking it from him. "It is extremely personal. Why do you ask?" There was more than a hint of asperity in her voice.

"Who wrote it?" asked Brough, ignoring her own question.

"Inspector Brough, this is too much!" she said angrily. "Your visit here is to inquire into matters which might in some way bear upon my cousin's death. That does not give you liberty to pry into my most personal affairs."

"This might seem hard to understand, but this poem could well have a bearing upon your cousin's death."

She glared at him, her cheeks flushed with anger. "This poem, which I have said twice is of the most personal nature, was written to me by the gentleman to whom I am engaged to be married. Does that satisfy your most unwelcome curiosity?"

Was it possible? Was this thing they had decided to call Fate again playing mad tricks with coincidence?

"Forgive me," said Brough. "The last thing I wish is to add to your misery. But I must know, who is this gentleman?"

"His name," she said with the sigh of one defeated, "is Nicholas Calvin."

Was it then, after all, a direct link between Nicholas and the murdered girl? Yes, Nicholas must have known Jessica if he was intimate with Miss Brandon. If so, why had he not said so? Was he, despite everything, fully aware of his guilt and concealing it?

"Miss Brandon," said Brough, trying to choose his words carefully and in the event blurting it straight out, "Nicholas Calvin is my nephew."

She stared.

"*You* are Uncle Reginald?" she said in astonishment.

He nodded.

It took a moment to sink in. "Nicholas has spoken so much about you. I had no idea when you telephoned and introduced yourself that Inspector Brough and Nicholas' uncle were one and the same."

"How long have you known each other?"

"Just a year. We are planning to marry next autumn."

"Until a week ago I had not seen Nicholas for close on two years. I must confess he has been most secretive about you. But then he has had an awful lot on his mind, as doubtless you already know."

"Indeed I do know how absorbed he has been in his latest research work. So absorbed in fact that what with his travels hither and thither I have not seen him for some weeks. I got a letter from him when he was in Florence in which he promised to tell me all about his work when he got back. He did telephone me once last week a few hours after he reached London, but so far we haven't seen each other."

"You obviously don't know, then, the subject of his present research, or that in fact he is staying with me at the moment?"

"No."

"Did Nicholas know Jessica?"

"He met her several times."

She looked at him with a sudden light of understanding in her exquisite eyes.

"Something has just come to me. In the moments I have had to myself in the past week I have been troubled by the fact that Nicholas has not been in touch since Jessica's death. But do you know, I doubt if he realizes that Jessica my cousin was the Jessica Twomey who was murdered. I don't think I ever told him her surname. For some reason she was rather embarrassed about it. I introduced her to everyone simply as my cousin Jessica."

"I am sure that must be the reason for his not contacting you," said Brough.

A knocking on the front door curtailed the conversation, as did the entrance a second later of the maid with the tea. She set the tray down on a side table and went out to answer the door. When she came back into the room she whispered something to Miss Brandon.

"Why, show him in," said Miss Brandon. Nicholas appeared a moment later.

The color drained from his face when he saw Brough.

"Uncle!" he said. "What in the name of heaven are you doing here? You were supposed to be out interviewing the relatives today."

He looked from one to the other of them in perplexity. The maid discreetly withdrew.

"I am," said Brough.

Nicholas stared at him uncomprehendingly. Then he looked at his fiancée, took in her mourning clothes, her distress, and understood in a moment.

"Jessica," he whispered, and a chill ran through his entire body.

"Yes, Nicholas, Jessica," said Miss Brandon, breaking down at last. She ran to him sobbing and threw her arms about his neck.

"I expect I'm right in thinking you've come to tell Meg all that's happened since your return from Florence," said Brough, "in which case I shall intrude no further on your privacy. Miss Brandon—Meg—please accept my sincerest condolences, and forgive my intrusion into your grief."

She offered Brough her hand, but said nothing.

"I'll see you back in Jermyn Street later this afternoon, Nicholas," said Brough. "Don't keep me waiting."

29

"How much did you tell Meg?" asked Brough when Nicholas got back to Jermyn Street about five o'clock. The detective was unusually distracted and seemed hardly to listen to his nephew's reply.

"Everything," said Nicholas, collapsing with exhaustion both physical and mental into the armchair opposite Brough's. He placed his head in his hands and heaved a sigh of misery. Wrapped in his own desperate isolation, he was unaware of Brough's preoccupation or the fact that the old man sat staring with a glassy, faraway look at his photographs of London murder sites on the wall above his nephew's head.

This is the final blow, thought Brough. After all my prayers, it is Nicholas after all. . . .

"Needless to say," said Nicholas, "she was staggered. What I told her about Rogano fitted precisely with what Jessica had been telling her for weeks. Just as I did, she fought with all the logic she could summon against the idea of the Rogano Strangler being reincarnated here in London. When I told her I could be the killer she broke down completely. . . ."

Nicholas after all . . . Brough could hardly grasp the enormity of the thought. It resounded again and again in his mind, compelling his attention, until the real words spoken by Nicholas became little more for him than a muffled sound in the background.

". . . Later . . ." Nicholas was saying, "we spent hours going over and over every single detail, as I have been doing interminably in my own mind since this horror began. We searched and searched for a natural explanation—something, just a detail—to indicate my innocence. But in the end she had to face the inescapable fact that we are entangled in a web of unnatural events."

He stopped talking, his face still hidden in the dim refuge of his hands, which shut out the cruelty of the real world as uncertainly as they shut the light from his eyes.

"After everything," he said, "she still had faith in me. Even though I might be her cousin's murderer she swore her love for me and repeated her conviction that I was innocent. I fear she is going to be sadly disillusioned."

He sank deeper into the chair and began to sob, quietly but uncontrollably. Brough, oblivious still, gazed as if mesmerized at the photographs on the wall. Even when he roused himself and stood up, he remained heedless of his nephew's distress. His thoughts far away, he went to the kitchen to throw together a quick meal. He had not eaten since breakfast but he felt in no condition for imaginative cooking.

When Nicholas had not returned from his mysterious errand by lunchtime, Galen—who had already obtained their travel documents from Cook's—had left a note on the living-room table and gone alone both to Greenwich and his own lodgings to pick up all the research material they needed. So far he had not reappeared.

Brough found a cold chicken leg in the pantry, and with that and a little wooden bowl of cheese, beetroot and cucumber, he came back to the living room, still looking as if he were in a dream.

By what seemed to him an enormous exertion of will, Nicholas had recovered sufficiently to notice his uncle's limp.

"What happened?" he asked. His question seemed to break the spell, and Brough, returning in a flash to the present, said, "Peterson pushed me in front of a train."

"*Good God!* When?"

"This morning."

"Peterson," said Nicholas with awe. Realization quickly dawned. "At British Museum!" he said.

"Yes," said Brough.

"It must have happened just about the time I got there. I bought my ticket and was just about to make my way down to the platform when the barrier was put across the stairs. A porter told us there had been an accident down below and we'd have to wait for the line to be cleared. But people coming up from the platform soon put it about that a man had been pushed onto the track. Never for a moment did I imagine it could be you. That's why I was so late arriving at Meg's. How did you get out alive?"

Brough recounted the story of his survival in much the same way as he had given it to Daubeney on the telephone.

"Did they get him?"

"Peterson? No. I was speaking to Ambrose Daubeney at the Yard just before you came back. By the time they managed to get anyone on the scene he was long gone. Hardly surprising. But at least we know he's still in London."

"Think he'll try again?"

"When he learns this attempt didn't work he'll want to, but by then I'll be out of the country. Let's hope they've managed to nab him by the time I get back."

"Did you see the relatives of Professor Dakins?"

"He was a bachelor, living alone, with no known family. But I got to see a close colleague of his, another professor from Magdalene College. He said Dakins lived in the country outside Cambridge at a place called Girton, but that he'd been down in London for about five weeks doing research for a massive book he was writing. The subject was the Inquisition. Have you noticed that apart from Jessica and Carew, all the strangler's victims have been learned men?"

"And each of them was digging into the past."

"Even Jessica, with her dreams of her previous life, and Carew with his lifelong study of Nostradamus, were doing that."

"Coincidence again?"

"No," said Brough, solemnly shaking his head, "the pattern is too strong for coincidence." He was observing his nephew closely for signs of conscious guilt.

"Pattern?"

"Yes, a pattern of links with Rogano. Antrobus was an expert on Italy in the Middle Ages and was working on a biography of Lorenzo. Professor Dakins was investigating the Inquisition. Sir Patrick Lovell was about to embark upon an expedition to the Holy Land—just as Lorenzo and virtually all the able-bodied men in Rogano had done about a year before the murders. The link between Manders and Rogano seems more tenuous, but it isn't. He was writing a book on Constantine the Great. Two of the most influential figures in Constantine's life were the bishops called Eusebius. And according to Nostradamus, Eusebius—whichever one it was—is centrally connected with the Rogano mystery. On top of that, Daubeney has found out that Manders was about to leave for Italy to research his book, and he wasn't going to Rome as you might expect, but to Rogano. The final two victims, Carew and Jessica, have connections with Rogano we have already discussed. As I have said all along, the answer to the entire mystery lies in Rogano still."

"I'm still not sure what you're getting at. We know the present victims are the reincarnations of the first set of victims, so *of course* they are linked with Rogano."

"But they didn't *have* to be."

"What do you mean?"

"There didn't *have* to be links apparent in their present lives. The big doubt in my mind was whether the four men *knew* they had lived before, whether they possessed any conscious knowledge about their earlier lives in Rogano or whether it simply lay dormant and unknown inside them.

"From the nature of their work in this life I now think that Antrobus, Manders, Lovell and Dakins did have some knowledge of their past existences. Just how detailed, it's impossible to say. I don't know about Carew."

"The papers and research notes of the four victims actively investigating the past were all stolen by the killer," said Nicholas.

"Quite so. It seems they had each discovered something, or were on the point of discovering facts crucial to the Rogano case. As far as we know, Jessica was not doing any actual study, but her dreams were providing her with vital, detailed information about Rogano. She knew that as Maria Bellini she had been strangled and thrown into that unfinished building. That means she knew who the Rogano Strangler was. Before she could reveal it, she was silenced by his reincarnation, the Deptford Strangler."

"You mean . . . ?"

"I mean that Antrobus, Manders, Lovell and Dakins were all murdered because they were about to discover *why* the Rogano killings were committed. As I have said all along, finding the motive will lead to the killer. Identifying the fifteenth-century killer will tell us who the current strangler is."

"But how did the present-day murderer know what work each of his victims was engaged upon?"

"I have been checking the correspondence columns of *The Times* over the last two months. In the space of a few weeks, Antrobus, Manders and Dakins had all written letters discussing aspects of their work. On November fourth there was a story in

Reynolds News about Patrick Lovell's proposed trip to the Holy Land. While refusing to disclose details of the expedition, he did correct one or two errors that had appeared in the newspapers about his recent activities."

Brough's eyes strayed again to the photographs above Nicholas' head, but he forced his attention back to his nephew.

"The story contained one item," he said, "which from my reading of it looked as though it had been given in confidence. You know as well as I how the hacks at *Reynolds* regard confidences."

"What was it?"

"That the starting point of his latest project was an archaeological expedition to northern Italy which he completed last summer."

"Rogano?"

"No, but not far away. Bolzano. It's my belief that Lovell learned of his previous incarnation during that expedition, and that whatever plans he had on foot when he died resulted directly from the discovery that in the 1400s he had been Giovanni Crispi."

He paused.

"That explains how the murderer knew about the work of four of the victims," he said. "And he discovered about Jessica's former life from her letter in the *Pall Mall Gazette*."

"What about Carew?"

"I wondered for a time how he'd known about Carew," said Brough. "Certainly there has been no newspaper story that I can find about the old man. Then I remembered his drunken brother Quentin. He has often burst into alcoholic tirades at the Beggar's, in which he has rambled on for hours about seemingly unconnected subjects. I remembered after you had told me about Carew how once Quentin was ranting for over an hour about 'Nostradamus,' 'Brother Augustus,' 'supercilious bastard,' 'Old House,' 'Allerton Magna,' 'Rogano.' In among all the other rubbish he has spouted over the years I had forgotten it all, but anyone listening carefully to him would doubtless have been able to piece together a reasonably connected story. And if he has shot his mouth off in a similar way on other occasions, it might well have reached the Strangler's ears and enabled him to realize Carew's role in the drama."

"And I am far more likely than Galen to have heard his story," said Nicholas. Brough did not reply.

After a moment, Nicholas said, "The publication of the facts about the first five victims, and Quentin's drunken ramblings about Carew, might well explain how the murderer was first alerted. But to have identified them positively as the reincarnations of the Rogano victims, he would have to be aware of his own former existence. If that is so, it rules me out. I didn't know of my past life until Galen brought the glad tidings."

"He would not necessarily have to be aware all the time," said Brough, "just at moments when the murderer in him takes over. At other times he might well be unconscious of his knowledge."

"You are thinking of my blackouts," said Nicholas.

Again Brough did not reply. He was looking once more at the photographs on the opposite wall.

"But the same could apply to Galen when he is asleep and his soul becomes active," continued Nicholas, realizing only too well that his harping on the possibility of Galen's guilt lacked all credibility.

"Going back to what you said about the 'reason' for the murders in Rogano," he said. "Surely the Rogano killer selected his victims at random. He—Antonio or Giuseppe—killed because he was a member of this ghastly Gormini sect, and murder was part of the heretics' evil search for 'power'?"

"That has been your assumption all along. But from what you and Herr van Galen have found out, it is by no means fanciful to suggest that the Gormini had a specific motive for eliminating these individuals."

Nicholas sat forward in his chair.

"In quatrain forty-four of the unfinished Century," said Brough, "Nostradamus speaks of 'Lorenzo and his confederates' encountering Peter's son and dying as a result. He speaks of the group's 'design.' Jessica in her dreams was introduced to seven of Lorenzo's friends who always met in secret and who had made some shocking discovery.

"It does not require a great leap from this point to deduce that all the Rogano Strangler's victims were known to each other and that they possessed some secret which led to their murder. If we knew what that secret was, we should be close to a solution."

"Perhaps they knew the identity of the leader of the heretics?" hazarded Nicholas.

"Possibly," said Brough noncommittally. "I think—"

A gentle rat-tat on the door knocker cut him off in midsentence. He went downstairs. It was Galen, carrying his own and Nicholas' research notes, carefully wrapped in brown paper and reposing in the crook of his arm.

"Hello," said Brough. Then, softly so that Nicholas could not hear, he said, "I'd like to talk to you in private as soon as possible."

Galen glanced up the stairs to the room where Nicholas sat, and nodded to Brough.

Once he had removed his heavy outer clothing and warmed himself in front of the fire, Galen reported that all preparations were now made and that they could leave by the 10:40 boat train that night. He was then given a rundown on the events of the day from Brough and Nicholas in turn.

"I think I'll get an hour's rest," said Nicholas at the end of it. "We'll probably not get a lot of sleep while we're traveling." He went into the spare bedroom and closed the door behind him.

Brough picked up the food that had remained untouched during his talk with his nephew and moved to the table, indicating with a toss of his head that Galen should join him.

"Herr van Galen," he whispered, "I am now almost certain that Nicholas is the strangler. What I want to ask you is, does that necessarily mean—as you put it the other day—that he has the *soul* of a murderer?"

"I have been thinking deeply about this," said Galen. "It is not necessarily so. Some people who have been murderers in one incarnation have been near saints in their next. My fears for the soul of whichever of us was guilty were based on the *repetition* of the murdering instinct in a later existence. It is possible, if Nicholas is indeed the guilty one, that this instinct is somehow filtering through in the way that certain other qualities of Antonio have done, without being a definite part of Nicholas. After all, Nicholas is not homosexual, but something in him inherited from Antonio caused him, unconsciously, to participate in life at the Mayfair Gentlemen's Club. I find it almost as hard to think of

Nicholas being a killer as myself, even though I have known him just a few days."

"Good," continued Brough in hushed tones. "I hope for the sake of his immortal soul that your assessment is correct. If it turns out that he is the killer, as I believe, then it is my plan to urge him to remain in Europe. I could hardly drag him back to London to face trial and execution for crimes he has not been aware of committing."

"Why do you believe so strongly in Nicholas' guilt?" asked Galen, earnestly seeking convincing evidence of his own innocence.

Brough champed awhile in silence, and then raised his eyes to the photographs on the wall to the right of the window.

"We have narrowed the field of suspects to two," he said. "You and Nicholas."

Again he stopped, stripped the last of the meat from the chicken bone and ate it.

"I realized something today that should have hit me weeks ago. Certainly I should have latched onto it last week when I started looking into the exploits of the Deptford Strangler in detail."

"Sshhh!" said Galen, putting a finger to his lips.

"What?"

"Your voice is getting louder."

"Let me explain," said Brough, whispering again. "One of the strangest puzzles about the Deptford Strangler's *modus operandi* has been the odd assortment of places in which he has chosen to kill his victims.

"Except with Carew, who was an exception in several ways, the killer has always struck down his victims miles from where they lived or worked or at any time frequented. From what can be gathered, he seems to have lured them to these out-of-the-way spots—on what pretext God knows—and there done them in."

"Done them *in?*" said Galen, bewildered.

"Killed them," said Brough. "Sorry. Your English is so good I forget you might not be up on all the slang. Anyway, when I first visited Rope Walk, Deptford, I knew I had been there before, but for the life of me I could not remember when. Only today did I realize. Thirty years ago in Rope Walk a stevedore found a headless corpse that turned out to be the wife of Black Jim Toynbee, whom I was fortunate enough to run to ground and bring to the gallows. My old brain must be getting addled, I don't know, but it was not until this afternoon that I realized Henry Antrobus was found at the selfsame spot as poor Martha Toynbee. And there"— he pointed to a faded print pasted to the wall above the picture rail—"is a photograph of the place in the seventies. That set me thinking, and suddenly it all fitted into place. The Deptford killer was selecting spots already used by certain killers of the past! The shrubbery in Hyde Park where Manders was found—Lovell on the towpath behind Farringdon Road—Maurice Dakins in Camden Passage—Jessica Twomey on the dustbins behind Piccadilly. *Those places have all been used before*."

He looked across at the door of the spare bedroom and, leaning closer to Galen, said, "What's more, photographs of those exact sites have been hanging in a group on my wall here for years."

"But—" began Galen.

Brough cut him off. "Look!" he said, pointing to the wall. "There they are, the five of them in a row. In the case of three of them the exact murder site was never made public. The killer must therefore be someone familiar with my pictures. We have narrowed our suspects down to two, you and Nicholas. Of the two of you, *only Nicholas*, with whom I have been talking murder these twenty years, could know of these murder sites and the pictures of them I have here."

He stopped again, his old eyes filling with tears at the realization of what he was saying. "This combined with the fact that he actually knew Jessica Twomey convinces me that Nicholas is the guilty one."

Galen tried to speak, but found he could say nothing. He looked at his hands. He had never once felt that these had been the fingers that had throttled six innocent people. But until now he had not been sure. Again he opened his mouth, but said nothing. His relief was inexpressible.

"I still want us to go to Rogano," said Brough. "Apart from it being the best way of getting Nicholas out of England, I want to discover *why* Antonio did what he did, and confirm, if we can, that although Nicholas may be the reincarnation of a murderer, and through an accident in the unfathomable physics of the universe is now unconsciously re-enacting those murders, yet even so his soul is not damned for all time."

His companion nodded, and placed his own hands upon Brough's to comfort the man who in minutes had been transformed from an assiduous detective to a grieving old uncle.

"We are going to have to be actors," said Brough with a lightness that was far from genuine, and he dried his eyes with the corner of the tablecloth. "Nicholas must have no idea of what we know or our experiments and inquiries in Rogano will be ruined."

His chin sank to his chest and he shook his head in sorrow. "Herr van Galen," he said, trembling. For a moment he seemed unable to go on, biting his lip and blinking rapidly as he strove to fight back the tears. "Herr van Galen, I *love* that boy."

30

Last-minute arrangements were made hurriedly. At a few minutes past eight, Brough opened the window and called out to a pair of urchins who for the past hour had been occupying themselves under a lamppost opposite building a malformed snowman with holly twigs for arms and lumps of coal for eyes. That work complete, they were now pelting each other with snowballs. The battle ceased the instant Brough summoned them, and they ran across the street and stood on the pavement looking up at him eager-eyed. They knew of old that an errand for Brough was always worth a farthing or two.

"A penny each and a hot muffin in front of the fire if you'll run round to Piccadilly and order a growler for half past," he said. The boys whisked off as fast as their poorly shod feet could carry them.

Five minutes later they were back and tucking in to a whole plateful of buttered muffins that Nicholas had been toasting on a fork over the open flames. The carriage arrived promptly and their minimal baggage, one fair-sized portmanteau and an item of hand luggage apiece, was stowed aboard. Galen came in from the kitchen with a pile of steaming mince pies, two of which were presented to the boys and the rest wrapped in greaseproof paper for consumption by the three travelers on the way to the station.

Brough scanned his bookshelves in search of a likely traveling companion and selected a small volume of Shakespeare's sonnets. Then he rang Daubeney's night number and told him he would not be available for a week or so as he would be "out of town" on the investigation. By ten to nine they had packed off their little friends with a cheery "Merry Christmas" and set off through the icy darkness of London for Victoria Station and the boat train. The growler, in contrast to the hansom in which the traveler was exposed to the weather, was fully enclosed and upholstered in buttoned leather, with matching carpets. Its solid-rubber tires made it run silently and the rhythmic jingle of the horses' bells formed an appropriately seasonal accompaniment to the three travelers' journey to Victoria. They arrived well in time to catch the 10:40 from Platform One.

31

The Channel was in one of its irascible moods when the little steam packet nosed out of Dover on its choppy voyage to Le Havre.

"This doesn't begin to compare with the nightmare crossing I had on my way out to Florence," said Nicholas to his two companions as they leaned on the stern rail of the ship and watched the harbor lights of Dover and the dimmer glow of the town beyond recede slowly into the impenetrable blackness of night at sea. Soon only the undulating chalk cliffs were visible as a pale ribbon fastening the sea to the sky. Then they too disappeared from sight.

The clouds were low and unbroken. There was no moon and the stars were hidden by an oppressive canopy of cumulus. A few unfortunate souls unable to afford berths, and doing their best to shelter from the slicing westerly wind, were huddling beneath tarpaulins and rugs on the port deck, some securing themselves with pieces of rope or leather belts to the slatted benches which ran the length of the ship's superstructure. The spray that ceaselessly flicked over the side as the boat pitched and rolled through the heaving waves would alone have been enough to ensure their utter discomfort for the duration of the voyage. But the overladen vessel was so full inside that the poorer passengers, many of them French peddlers going home after a stint selling their wares in England, could not even seek shelter when the storm clouds at last carried out their threat and began to pelt the decks with stinging hail. Brough, Nicholas and Galen were more fortunate and retired to their cabin.

While Brough and Galen drifted easily off to sleep despite the noise of the storm and the heaving of the ship, Nicholas found sleep impossible. His mouth felt dry and there was a hollowness in his stomach. But neither storm nor heaving ship were affecting him. Fear was his tormentor. All the evidence, he knew, pointed inexorably to his own guilt. So far he had managed to conceal his own complete hopelessness from the others—even, to an extent, from himself—and with a period out of London he had imagined that the horror would slip away, if only for a day or so. But freed from the crushing burden of the impending murder on the twenty-eighth, which he now felt sure would not take place, and with the all-absorbing investigation temporarily suspended for the duration of the journey, his mind had become prey to other anxieties that until now had not reached the surface. Galen, too, thought Nicholas was the killer. Both of them, whichever one was guilty, were equally committed to discovering the truth. But Galen had said that as they got closer to the truth the baleful influence of the killer's former incarnation could well grow stronger, possibly taking over his mind almost completely. It was even conceivable, he had said, that before the truth they were all desperately striving for could be revealed, the guilty one— Nicholas or himself, though the accent had been on Nicholas— could attempt to kill Brough and the innocent of the two younger men. The thought that on top of everything else he might kill his uncle was insupportable. He tossed fretfully in his bunk.

Eventually the initial anger of the storm abated and the boat was left steaming across a Channel more calm than Nicholas had ever seen it. He crept out of the cabin and mounted the metal ladder to the deck.

He watched the ship carving its passage through the living sea, and the white blood of the sea foaming outward from the wound and congealing behind them in a broad and moonlit highway that vanished over the dark and inscrutable horizon. From the prow, the foam spread outward and back on either side, gradually diminishing from a fierce cascade forward to white-flecked swirls and eddies aft. The sea beyond the foam on the starboard side was as dark as the sky and indistinguishable from it, so that it seemed the ship rode along on an island of foam in the infinite wasteland of space. And then, he fancied (the furious outward motion of the water playing tricks with his vision), the foam was not surging *away* from the vessel, but up, out of the endless void of night, frothing up the side of whatever mysterious summit this strange ark was perched upon, in a vast reverse cataract *toward* the ship.

He stood there, transfixed; haunted by the mystery of life which the mocking, unknowable sea seemed somehow, tangibly, to symbolize.

The Sea.

The Sea, it seemed to Nicholas as he kept his solitary watch under the lee of a rusty lifeboat davit, was the distillation of all the mysteries of the universe. The only way to unlock its secrets was to become a part of it . . . to sink in blissful oblivion through the calm waters beneath the angry surface . . . to embrace the *heart* of the mystery . . . to defeat the misery of life and the fear of death in one glorious act of self-sacrifice to the unfathomable god of the sea. He felt his feet moving forward of their own accord. Step by tortuous step, across the soaking deck, out of the shelter of the lifeboat to the low rail that divided the finite from the infinite, the dark ignorance of life from the bright omniscience of death. He placed one foot on the lowest bar of the safety rail. One, two, three rungs and then release from the petty ills of life. Grasping the top rail with his hands, he placed his other foot on the bar. He looked again at what a moment ago had been three red-painted rails. One, two, three, four, five, six . . . the ivory rungs continued upward from the gently swaying deck a mile below his feet. He raised his head and saw the ladder, straight as a shaft of sunlight, climbing up, past the planets and the stars, to a paradise he had hardly dared hope existed. An irresistible music filled his ears. Soft, whispering cadences that beckoned, "Come, come." He closed his eyes and allowed the joyous hypnotic melody to caress every molecule of his mind and body, and bear him upward, gently upward, to infinity. But all at once his hope of everlasting peace was destroyed. A great raucous peal of thunder cracked open the womb of comfort and warmth in which he snuggled, sending the two halves, like the broken shell of an egg, spinning into the void. He clung to the ladder for dear life as it pitched and swayed under the assault of hellish forces. He saw hideous forms and twisted faces fly at him out of the dark as the ladder was tossed like a straw in the wind. The gleaming rungs above disintegrated in the chaos of the apocalypse. But he clung with superhuman strength to the splintered section of the great ladder still left to him. An appalling scream of hate triumphant tore open his eardrums in a shower of needles of white-hot sound, and a grinning demon fell upon him, sinking its limbs into his shoulders and sending pain searing all over his body. The creature, all its great weight bearing downward, wrenched and tore at Nicholas' paralyzed figure to pry it from the safety of the ladder. He strained his head to look at the evil thing that grunted and groaned with the strain of its task. A sibilant rattle in its throat began to form itself into words. Ni-ch-o-las. There was no doubt about it. It had spoken his name.

"Nicholas," it said again, gasping for breath, "let go!" With a final effort, it forced him from his perch and he fell with a jarring crash onto his back.

Brough had also fallen over with the violence of pulling his nephew from the deck rail. He released his grip on Nicholas' shoulders.

"I was going to kill myself," said Nicholas after a long silence. There was a watery lightness in the east but the sun would not climb over the horizon for at least an hour.

"I know," said the detective gently.

"I had a sort of brainstorm."

"I should have foreseen something like this," he said, putting a comforting arm around his nephew's shoulder. "The strain you have been under has been enough to crush any man's will to live."

"I want to live," said Nicholas absently. They sat there huddled together in the early morning drizzle without speaking a word until it was fully light. When they were in sight of France a fishing smack passed perilously close to the steamer and a loud blast was sounded on the hooter. Nicholas silently noted the sound and realized the source of the "thunderclap" that had begun the disintegration of his deadly hallucination. When he looked again at the sea its illusion was shattered, its spell broken. It was, he realized, no more than a vast acreage of gray water. No secrets, no mystery. A purveyor of ghastly death.

32

The rigmarole of disembarkation and redirection of luggage behind them, they boarded their train for the staggered journey to Munich, Innsbruck and the Brenner Pass. At Bolzano they would transfer to an antediluvian express that made a weekly run through the Dolomites, winding around mountains and through valleys, and finally hugging the banks of the Pergino River as far as the Lago di Garda, stopping at Rogano on its way. The track had been laid on the side of the river opposite the town, but it crossed by an iron bridge to disgorge and take on passengers. Once out of the town it crossed back by a cruder wooden bridge and struck south.

They arrived at the sleepy snow-covered railway station of Rogano late on Christmas Eve. Apart from a bleary-eyed ticket collector in a green wooden box by the exit, the place was deserted, and only one other traveler, also, by the cut of his clothes, English, got out of the last carriage a hundred yards along the platform. With an asthmatic wheeze and a pathetic puff of steam, the train creaked into motion and trundled off out of the station. The rattle of its wheels on the track slowly gathered momentum as it swung, now invisible, around the great sweep of the Pergino, across the bridge, and along the Cavenna Valley. And then all was silence.

No porter appeared to help them with the luggage, so Brough took two of the hand cases and the third was placed on top of the portmanteau, which Nicholas and Galen carried between them. The taciturn ticket collector, hiccoughing from his own private yuletide celebration with a pear-shaped bottle of some coarse liquor, merely took their tickets, belched rather than said, "Signori," and allowed them to pass through into the street.

The almost complete encircling of the city by the river had prevented any great expansion, either industrial or residential, since the fifteenth century. A small factory had been built on the far side of the river in the 1860s and there had been an attempt higher up to sink a mine shaft, but the soil on that side was so soft that further development plans had been abandoned. The only real growth in four hundred and fifty years had been in a trumpet-shaped conurbation fanning out from the quarter-mile section of the town's circumference that was bordered with land rather than water, and this straggled uneasily up the hillside toward the lower slopes of the mountains Arretto and Bellanone. Apart from this, the only modernization that had taken place was where older buildings had been demolished, and this seemed restricted to the outer areas. The center of the city around the site of the old cathedral, now forbidden to traffic, was much as it had been when the Rogano Strangler had stalked his victims. Although the magnificent dominating presence of the cathedral was gone, one of its twin spires, the less bejeweled of Cardinal Montenigro's fingers, had survived both fire and earthquake.

All roads leading from the station sloped upward through the latest architectural additions to the town, mainly small workshops and tenement buildings, past eighteenth-century slums, and wound, cobbled, up to the Rogano of the Middle Ages. The di Corsa Palace and the Piazza del Santa Maria were almost intact, except where the 1819 earth tremor had shaken some of the oldest buildings to their foundations. But even these had been faithfully rebuilt at the behest of a town council already shrewdly aware of the revenue to be had from rich Englishmen on the Grand Tour.

Their first task was to locate a suitable hostelry in the immediate vicinity of the station as none of them felt much like wandering the streets for the next two hours lugging weighty baggage. Brough greeted a gnarled old man bundled in fur who, shoulders hunched and head down, was boring purposefully along like a mole toward a nearby tavern.

"*Signor, un albergo per favore?*" The Italian for *sir, hotel* and *please* was about all he had managed to memorize on the last, tiring lap of the journey. He imagined his *Phrase Book for English Travellers in Italy* blushing to its very spine, but the old man seemed to understand him.

He stopped, and with misty eyes peered at the three strangers through the falling snow. Under his fur hat his whiskery face looked like a dry and wrinkled olive.

"*Si, si!*" He grinned toothlessly, and beckoned them to follow. Burying himself back inside his furs, he made no further acknowledgment of their presence but led them a quarter of a mile through narrow streets bordered by tall, shuttered warehouses and Lilliputian workshops to a well-lit piazza that in contrast to the grimness of the night looked even more spacious and well designed than it was. A hundred-foot-square mosaic pavement in the center was dominated by a fine marble effigy of Christ, a cluster of adoring children at his feet and a dove, somehow by the artifice of the sculptor made to appear separate from the main statue, about to alight on His raised hand. Festive torches lining the square illuminated the buildings on all sides. Every house displayed elaborate Christmas decorations and religious banners.

There seemed to be no part of the city where the soaring valley walls, culminating in the looming snow-laden peaks of the interrupted Dolomiti, were not visible. And from here in the center of the Piazza del Fiore, the enormous bulk of the abbey, still functional and with lights blazing from a pattern of windows, was clearly defined against the moonlit background of the mountains.

Their silent escort led them across the square to a narrow pensione with a carved door, a statuette of the Blessed Virgin reposing in a niche in the yellow plaster wall at first-floor level. The hostelry had four stories of brown-shuttered windows beneath a steeply sloping roof of orange tiles. He turned the handle, swung the door back to reveal a dull but homely vestibule and gestured them to precede him in. An open fire surrounded by an assortment of ill-matched but comfortable armchairs occupied the right-hand side of the room. A long counter ran the length of the

left-hand wall, and behind that was a doorless arch. A hand bell, a
visitors' book and a regiment of bottles were ranged along the
top of the counter. Their companion lifted the bell and swung it
gently to and fro, proclaiming their presence with a deep and
muted clang. In seconds the landlord, a burly Tuscan, materi-
alized in the archway. A few words from the fur man sufficed to
explain the needs of the three travelers, and hearing the word
Inglesi, the landlord raised an eyebrow and revealed with a smile
that he was familiar with his guests' language. Many of his visitors,
he told them, were from "Great British."

Within minutes they had thanked their guide, treated him, de-
spite his energetic protestations, to a warming drink and ascended
a narrow creaking staircase at the heels of the landlord to a room
on the first floor that contained four beds.

"It is few visitors we have in this season," he told them. "You
may occupy this my largest chamber with no charge for the extra
bed."

Lighting the room's two globe-shaped oil lamps, he put a match
to the stack of coal and logs in the grate, which with the help of
some energetic work with the bellows soon crackled into a com-
forting blaze, and he left them with the promise of returning
shortly with a hearty supper. Without a word to each other, the
travelers dumped their trunks into a corner and slumped upon
their beds.

"What's our first move?" asked Nicholas later as they polished
off the last of the *pastasciutta*, cooked in butter with mushrooms
and liver, and washed down with mugs of mulled red wine from
the Trento district to the southwest.

"I doubt if we're going to get into the abbey without some
prior arrangement," said Brough, "and tomorrow being Christmas
Day, the abbess and her sisters of mercy are going to be fully
taken up with their religious tasks. We can either take a climb up
the Santine Hill and locate the cave where all these evil happen-
ings are supposed to have taken place, or seek out the house of the
Aquilina brothers, assuming it still stands. That, surely, would be
the place to start your experimental return journeys into the
minds of Antonio and Giuseppe?"

Galen nodded. "I think we should do that first. After our jour-
ney I think none of us can feel much like hill climbing. And I

think the sooner we get back to the Rogano of the 1450s the sooner we'll learn the truth—once and for all."

The others agreed.

"In which case," continued Galen, "Nicholas should not go to sleep tonight."

"Not sleep? You must be joking!" said Nicholas, horrified.

"No, I'm quite serious. I've been giving the problem of your own regression a lot of thought. As you are not trained in the method I use, you can only rely on your subconscious mind doing the work for you. The dreams you have had already show your subconscious is focused on your Rogano incarnation. What we need to do is make those dreams sharper, better defined. It has been shown that the prime function of sleep is to allow the mind to refresh itself and resolve its conflicts by dreaming. Exactly how dreams achieve this we don't know, but it is a fact. Deprive a man of sleep, and when he does finally become unconscious he will dream earlier, longer, more vividly and more deeply than if he had gone to bed normally."

"Oh well," said Nicholas with a grimace, "*Che sarà sarà.*"

33

When the sun came up Rogano looked splendid in its dazzling winter finery. Draped in its ermine gown, the town and surrounding landscape basked under a sky of pale cloudless blue. Nicholas, however, looked wretched. His near suicide on board ship was yet another indigestible chunk added to the mountain of gristle upon which his mind, choking already on the inedible, was forced to feed. He had slept neither at sea nor during the twenty-hour train journey across Europe. The last eight hours, during which Brough and Galen had slumbered soundly, had completely exhausted him.

He had spent a couple of hours downstairs in yawning conversation with the landlord, who could not understand why a man so obviously tired did not go to bed. Nor did he feel it his place to question his guest, so Nicholas' behavior was attributed, like many another traveler's quirks, to the strange ways of foreigners. After mine host had strode off to bed, Nicholas went out for a walk. The cold blast that met him when he opened the door certainly helped, for a time, in keeping sleep at bay. But his need of rest was so urgent that within twenty minutes his eyelids began to droop despite the swirling snow. He began to occupy his mind by reciting aloud every poem and singing every song he had ever learned. Keep my mind awake, he told himself, and the body will look after itself. At one point, serenading a heedless street with a mournful and tuneless version of "*Questa o quella*," he inflamed the anger of some slumbering opera lovers, who threw back their shutters and heaped him with abuse. After that he subdued his voice and steered clear of Verdi. At about four in the morning he experienced a new surge of energy such as he had identified a day ago as his second wind. The second wind had blown itself out after less than an hour, but this new burst kept him going, with the help of "Little Miss Muffet" and "Mary, Mary Quite Contrary" (his main repertoire exhausted, he was now scraping the barrel of early childhood) until six. Weariness overcoming him again, he turned his steps back toward the Piazza del Fiore.

About a hundred yards from the door of the pensione, he encountered a man in dark tweeds and an Inverness cape.

"*Buon giorno*," said Nicholas to the man's back as he stood motionless on the pavement, looking straight ahead of him. He turned around sharply, a startled look giving way to an uneasy smile as Nicholas came into focus.

"Oh, hello," said the man.

"You're English," said Nicholas.

"Yes—my name is Hutchinson," he said, extending his hand, "Gilbert Hutchinson." He seemed at a loss for anything further to say.

"Happy Christmas, Mr. Hutchinson," said Nicholas.

"What?—Oh yes, the same to you I'm sure."

"Enjoying your walk?"

"Yes." He paused. "I'm just taking a look at the town."

"Won't see much in the dark."

"I'm not here very long. Just passing through. Making the most of every minute, you know the sort of thing."

"Yes," said Nicholas. "Are you from London?"

He nodded.

"Where are you staying?" asked Hutchinson.

"At that little place there."

"Ah well, I must be pushing on," said the man. "Good-bye, Mr. Calvin."

How does he know my name? thought Nicholas as Hutchinson vanished into a narrow passage leading out of the square.

34

Both Nicholas and Galen knew the house the moment they saw it. Even Brough experienced a momentary *frisson* as they rounded the corner of a crumbling thirteenth-century baptistery and found themselves only yards from the curiously proportioned façade of the Palazzotto Aquilina. The detective was astonished how exactly his imagination had reproduced reality. His vision of the house when reading or hearing about it in London might have been a photograph—a *colored* one at that—of the real thing. The windowless rear wall of the house had been built dead against the ancient wall of the city, and to its right was the exquisite but redundant East Gate, erected by Chief Architect Gatta about a year before the murders. The house was bounded on the left by a line of more conventional houses of a similar age, one of which was surrounded by scaffolding and ladders and appeared to be undergoing major renovations to the roof.

There it stood. Tall, narrow and weirdly proportioned, it struck Brough as the sort of place that might have inspired Poe or Hans Christian Andersen to strange flights of fancy. Although no fiction, he thought, could improve upon the true mystery of the house.

The two younger men stopped in their tracks and stared. Suddenly the nightmare of their former incarnations was no longer limited to dreams and academic research. Here, before them, as solid now as it had been four hundred and fifty years earlier, was their first tangible contact with Antonio and Giuseppe. The brothers Aquilina reached out across the centuries and caressed their spines with icy fingers. There it stood. Hardly changed since that Sunday morning in 1455 when, as Giuseppe and Antonio, they had last beheld its brooding grace—the morning they had gone off, suspecting nothing, to mass, and had been hauled away to interrogation and condemnation by the black-hooded inquisitors.

Its over-all proportions were reflected with geometric precision in the doors and windows, which in their extreme height and narrowness were more like glazed or wooded embrasures. The door was no more than two feet wide and was at least eight feet high, curving to a point at the top. It was crowned with a plaque bearing the arms of the Aquilina family. Despite several architectural deviations that would have irritated a purist, the basic style of the building was Italian Gothic. Its roof, which looked original, was low and pyramidal, with semicylindrical tiles grown brown with age. The three ground-floor windows, their apexes level with that of the door, were placed to its left. All were shuttered. At first-floor level a deep balcony, with a whirling Catherine-wheel design on its stone balustrade, ran the width of the house. Behind the balcony was a portico with three arches, identical in shape and size, with the ground-floor windows directly beneath, supported on plain pillars. Symmetry had plainly been a passion with the architect for, exact to the inch, he had repeated the two outer arches of the first-floor balcony on the floor above, each one here having its own miniature balcony. The brick wall between the two top arches was decorated with a scroll pattern in blue plaster.

They had discovered from their landlord that the house was now used as a museum. Although it was closed for Christmas, there was a caretaker living on the premises.

"Say Lombardi sent you," the landlord had called after them. "Old Tommaso will let you in."

Old Tommaso proved to be a shriveled black-eyed man in his early sixties. Apart from a sad relic of youth that clung like a dirty rag to the back of his head, he was completely bald. The narrow but perfectly rounded cupola of his freckled scalp had been brought to a high luster with generous applications of olive oil. He had a thin mustache that lay so precariously close to his top

lip that it seemed in constant danger of toppling over the edge
into his mouth. As if that disagreeable possibility had crossed his
own mind, he kept his lips fast shut. His mouth was like a short
ruled line. He was wearing a cheap, ill-fitting suit.

Brough had ascertained in advance that he spoke English and
so had left his phrase book back at the pensione to revel alone in
its own impeccable grammar.

"Good mor-ning, Sign-or Tom-maso," said Brough, mouthing
each word as if the caretaker were deaf and could communicate
only by lip-reading. "A hap-py Christ-mas to you. My friends and
I are from Eng-land and we would be hon-ored if we could look
ov-er the house. Lom-bard-i sent us."

He had been ready to bolster their case by telling the old fellow
an amended version of the truth—that one of their ancestors had
once lived there—but he did not get the chance.

"Ach, Lombardi!" said Tommaso in tones that left no doubt
that his esteem of the innkeeper was not so high as the latter
seemed to imagine. Without moving, he raised his upper lip a
fraction of an inch and aimed an eloquent lump of spittle at the
ground between his feet. Then, still without taking his eyes off the
strangers, he lifted one hobnailed boot and ground the projectile
into the gravel.

"If to-day is not con-ven-i-ent . . ." began Brough, but Tom-
maso cut him off.

"My mother was a Scot," he said in such confident English
that the detective abandoned his deaf-mute enunciation. He
chuckled lightly in the hope of bringing a thaw to Tommaso's fro-
zen expression and to cover his own embarrassment. Tommaso
remained immobile. He scrutinized them for a full quarter minute
with a dull look in his dark, hooded eyes that told of ingrained
misanthropy.

"We would be happy to pay for the privilege," said Brough,
searching in vain for Tommaso's better nature.

The Italian's only response was to raise his right hand slowly to
his mouth and draw on a previously unnoticed dog end that had
been burning itself down between his chalky knuckles. As he in-
haled, the ragged end of the homemade cigarette glowed brightly.

"I am not speaking of small amounts, signor . . ." began
Brough earnestly, but he was cut off.

"Why do you persist so strongly?" asked Tommaso flatly.

"Because we are in Rogano for only a short time," said Brough, "and it is important to us to see the palazzotto."

"But I have not refused your request. I simply said, 'Ach, Lombardi,' and told you my mother was a Scot. Then you began to offer me inducements."

"But you remained silent," said Brough, his acute awareness of the need for diplomacy struggling with his rising impatience.

"Does not silence betoken assent in British law? Why should you interpret *my* silence as refusal?"

For once in his life Brough felt at a loss for words. He felt that entrance to the house was a vital step in elucidating the mystery, but anything he said, it seemed, was likely to alienate this disagreeable old donkey. He took a gamble.

"Because I don't know what silence betokens in Italian law," he snapped.

It worked. A glint of satisfaction lit Tommaso's countenance: he had succeeded in irritating Brough.

"But do you forget so soon that I am half a Scot. Aren't Scots subject to British law?"

"Thoroughbred Scots, yes," said Brough icily. Tommaso liked that.

"The rightful King of England is a Scot," he said, "not that terrible German you call His Majesty."

Once again, there seemed nothing fruitful to say in reply.

"You have no answer, eh?" said Tommaso, haughty and self-satisfied. "That is good. I will show you the museum." He turned and walked up the steps.

They filed in behind him and found themselves in a square hall with a wooden staircase, polished to almost as high a sheen as Tommaso's head, curving upward on the right. There was an exquisitely carved door set with painted enamel figures on their left, and a passage leading off ahead beneath the angle of the stairs. Tommaso took them into the room on the left. Though now a museum, the building had been in use as a house as recently as the 1880s, and the curator had retained most of the original furniture as the basis of his collection. This room, however, was furnished with monstrous Victorian pieces and clearly formed the living room of Tommaso's quarters.

A large maternal woman was bustling about in the room, needlessly tidying for the benefit of the unexpected visitors she had heard her husband usher in. As they entered she turned, slightly flustered, and bobbed a self-conscious curtsy.

"Emilia, we have visitors," said Tommaso in Italian.

They introduced themselves and Brough added that they were spending Christmas and New Year in Rogano, but from her blank expression it was obvious the signora spoke no English. Tommaso supplied her with a loose translation of what the detective had said, informing her that the three travelers were of "that unhappy race which poisoned one Stuart, beheaded a second, banished a third and deposed a fourth, only to deliver themselves into the hands of cursed Dutchmen and Germans."

His wife was plainly well used to his preoccupation with the fate of the House of Stuart, for she nodded tolerantly, curtsied again and continued about her business. Tommaso had assumed none of his visitors spoke Italian, but Galen now spoke for the first time, in fluent Italian, and informed him, "Signor Tommaso, I must tell you that while my friends are English, I am one of that 'cursed' race of Germans you seem to hold responsible for the end of Scotland's claim to imperial power."

But Tommaso was neither moved nor impressed with the knowledge. His face, expressionless as ever, looked like a drooping mask from some ancient Greek tragedy. He simply shrugged and raised a lazy eyebrow, an act which could be interpreted many ways but which Galen took to be saying, "That's life, signor. We all have our problems. That's yours." Galen perceived that his wife was flushed with embarrassment, and not wishing to add to her discomfort he allowed the subject to drop. Unlike Brough, he had not realized that the way to Tommaso's heart was by allowing him to ruffle your feathers and by retaliating with well-aimed pecks at his own ego. A mild sado-masochist, Brough had decided. But Galen was already too much under the spell of the house to pay close attention to the quirks of an aging Scottish-Italian. Nicholas, too, seemed enraptured with every brick, every stick of original furniture. Both men felt they *knew* every crevice of the house.

Nicholas, who by now was suffering minor hallucinations from being deprived of sleep for thirty-seven hours, began to sway

slightly on his feet. Tommaso was by now in an ungainly crouch-
ing position and was raking in a low cabinet, so did not notice.
But Brough was immediately aware of his nephew's condition and
only too alert to the fact that if the experiment could not begin
soon, Nicholas would collapse in front of Tommaso and his wife.
The ensuing fuss, if not from Tommaso then certainly from
Emilia, would ruin their plans. He was now convinced the house
was vital to the success of the proposed regression to the earlier in-
carnations of the two men. He had understood from Lombardi that
Tommaso was an agreeable old man, and the truth had him tem-
porarily nonplussed. How could they persuade this cantankerous
old beast to leave them alone for at least an hour in a house full
of valuable antiques? They couldn't, but they had to try. Tom-
maso still rummaged in the cupboard. Brough had just begun to
play with the idea of pretending Nicholas' tiredness was a sudden
bout of illness, and perhaps even get him tucked up in bed in the
house (quite a thought if by some chance he was presented with
Antonio's bedchamber), when their host rose and turned toward
them holding a glass decanter of green liquid. He moved to a side
table and poured a single glass of the drink, which without ado he
began to imbibe, after each sip running an ulcerated tongue across
his top lip to salvage the droplets that hung from his wispy mus-
tache. In not offering like refreshment to his visitors the queer old
caretaker was not being consciously rude, Brough decided. The de-
tective guessed that he entertained so rarely, if ever, that he had
never mastered even such basic social graces as proffering a seat,
leave alone a drink. He was not being unfriendly, it simply did not
cross his mind.

"So," he said, swallowing the last of the liquor and sucking his
entire upper lip into his mouth to give it a thorough wash, "I'll
show you the museum."

Without a word to his wife, he shuffled back to the hall with
his hands in his pockets.

"Today I can give you only a short view," said Tommaso. "My
wife and I, we are going to visit her brother and his family, who
live in the house of Emilia's mother. We must leave soon."

"We were hoping to spend some time here," said Brough,
thinking quickly, "as there are certain objects in the museum we
should like to sketch . . ."

As the comment provoked nothing more than Tommaso's infuriating silence, Brough dipped deeper into his sack of mendacity and added, "We are preparing a British Museum report on the private museums of northern Italy."

"The British Museum is like Ali Baba's cavern," said Tommaso. "It is full of stolen treasure. Much of it is stolen from us poor people here and should rightfully be in the museums you speak of. If the British Museum were in its proper place in Edinburgh—the natural capital of your islands—I should not so much mind. No, signor, even if I had the inclination to give up my free time and stay with you while you make your drawings, I should receive not one lira in recompense."

"As I said earlier," replied Brough, striving to remain amicable, "we should be happy to pay for the privilege. And of course, you must go and celebrate Christmas with your family as planned. We could remain here alone. Simply take with you our travel documents, which we have with us. This will ensure that we do not disappear over the horizon with your precious exhibits in three great sacks like a trio of Santa Clauses."

He paused for some flicker of response. "You could even disable our sleigh and impound our reindeer."

Old Tommaso chose not to react to the humor.

"No, signor," he said with finality, and lapsed again into silence.

Each room they entered struck a forgotten chord in the memories of forgotten men deep within the minds of Nicholas and Galen. Even Brough felt brushed by the outer edge of the spell that the house cast over his companions. While Tommaso moved from chamber to chamber grudgingly furnishing them with the briefest details of the contents, Brough became more and more fascinated by the almost hypnotic influence the very fabric of the building seemed to exert over Galen and his nephew. It grew with each step they took, and temporarily at least, Nicholas' exhaustion seemed to vanish.

On the third floor, having shown them the ornate bedrooms, now devoted to sculptures and portraits of the late Renaissance, Tommaso turned to go down. As he did so, Nicholas asked, "What is up those steps, Signor Tommaso?" he was pointing to an old spiral staircase along the landing.

"Junk," said Tommaso. "Nothing but junk."

"Is it an attic?"

"An attic," he confirmed, continuing down the stairs.

"That is *my* room," whispered Nicholas, dawdling at the foot of the spiral staircase. "I used to escape there."

"How do you know?" asked Brough.

"I know," he said.

Brough looked at Galen. Without a word passing between them, they realized that the attic was the place for the first experiment in bringing the fifteenth and twentieth centuries together.

"Signor Tommaso," Brough called out, having indicated that Nicholas and Galen should follow their host downstairs, "Signor Tommaso, I have left my hat in the end room. I shall retrieve it and join you in less time than it takes to rid a country of a Stuart."

That's the way to treat Signor Tommaso, he thought with a grin.

"Silence is assent!" he called down on receiving the customary lack of response, and he walked happily back to the end room, a small chamber given over to icons and a host of beautifully wrought crucifixes. There was a single small stained-glass window in the room that overlooked a narrow alleyway between the palazzotto and the house next to it. The window, depicting the head of Christ in subtle tints of blue and orange, occupied his attention for eight seconds. Then he picked up his hat and wandered leisurely down to his friends. Nicholas and Galen were already in the street. As he passed Tommaso, who lounged by the front door, Brough pointed to an engraved portrait of the Old Pretender in a shrinelike niche on the wall.

"You incorrigible old fraud," said Brough to the portrait, and burying his hands in his greatcoat pockets he walked out of the house without a look at the old caretaker, confident that he had gotten the last word.

"Are you returning to your hostel?" said Tommaso without expression as Brough joined his companions outside. "Tell the landlord that Tommaso sent you. Old Lombardi will let you in." And the door swung gently to behind them.

Brough smiled wryly and looked exceedingly pleased with himself.

"What now?" asked Galen despondently.

"We take a stroll around the block," he said cheerfully.

"Thank you very much!" said Nicholas in a burst of impatience, "I am just about sick of this bloody charade. I have not slept for two days. I have been tramping around all night to keep awake and now you propose *a stroll around the block!* Well that's it. You two can do what you like. I'm going back to the hostel to get some sleep."

"Follow me," said Brough, regardless. And he marched off through the snow.

For a long moment Nicholas was tempted to throw up his hands, scream, "You obstinate old bugger!" and storm away in the opposite direction. But something held him back, and with Galen at his side he trekked after his uncle without a word.

Brough led them along the street past the East Gate and turned right up a steep flight of stone steps between two buildings. The spirit of the hunt had possessed him and for a time at least his aching mind was numbed. He felt like taking the steps two at a time, but remembering his age and the hard-packed ice underfoot, he rejected the idea. Besides, he told himself, now was the time to conserve energy for use later on. They traced a wide circle around a cluster of buildings, finding themselves at length at the rear door of the octagonal baptistery that stood opposite the palazzotto.

"Talk about going round in circles," grumbled Nicholas under his breath. "What the hell's going on, Uncle?"

Brough employed Tommaso's favorite tactic and pretended not to hear. Swinging open the door, he motioned his friends through into the yellow gloom. Without faltering, he led the way past dusty pews, around ancient marble-faced pillars to a stone font in the form of an enormous clam shell borne upon the shoulders of John the Baptist. Brough skirted it without mishap in the pitch darkness and led them to the far corner of the building, where there was another door.

"Have you been here before?" whispered Nicholas.

"Why?" said Brough in low tones. "And why are we whispering?"

"I don't know, but have you?"

"What?"

"Been here before?"

"No."

"How can you find your way around so well in the dark?"

"I send out signals like a bat," laughed Brough, and pushed open the door. No light percolated into the side gallery in which they now stood. Brough took out a box of matches and struck a light. As it flared they got a transient vision of decay, with crumbling idols and rotten paneling lining a long corridor with a lofty wooden ceiling and a black and white-tiled floor. Like three live chessmen on a deserted board, they moved swiftly along, passing under an arch at the end and on to the foot of a winding stone stair.

"This place would have been under ten feet of water when the Pergino broke its banks in 1692," murmured Nicholas. "It must have been left derelict since then."

"Very likely," said Brough, supporting himself on the wall each side and leading the way up the curving steps. Soon the darkness began to recede as they approached a broken window where light filtered in. Upward they climbed. Fifty steps, eighty, one hundred. By now it was fully light, with a window at each turn of the stair. One hundred and ten . . . twenty . . . thirty . . . thirty-five. One hundred and thirty-seven steps. Another door, hanging open on sagging hinges. They passed through onto a narrow balcony that lay under a foot of snow.

"The tower of the baptistery," said Brough with a histrionic sweep of his arm.

"Superb," said Nicholas. "I can think of nothing I'd rather see than the tower of the goddamned baptistery."

"From here we get a perfect view of the front door of the palazzotto. We can not only see when the delightful Signor Tommaso and his long-suffering wife leave the house. We can also track them to their destination without the slightest likelihood of being spotted ourselves. Look what a wonderful view of the city we have from here."

"And when we've done that?"

"We break into the palazzotto," he said matter-of-factly.

"How exactly do you propose we do that?"

"By removing one of those ladders from the house where the roof is being repaired, taking it along the alleyway between the palazzotto and the big house next door and climbing up to the window which I unlocked when I returned to the end chamber for my hat."

"The result could be disastrous, perhaps even fatal, if Tommaso returns and disturbs us during our regression," said Galen.

"I realize that," said Brough.

"And there is no guarantee that we could return to consciousness before he came back."

"No."

"And discounting the risks attached to the regression, if we are caught we'll finish up starving to death in an Italian prison."

"Yes," said Brough with a grin, "exciting isn't it?"

35

Old Tommaso emerged from the palazzotto with his wife three steps behind at precisely eleven o'clock. Cloaked in a long tartan overcoat that all but covered his regulation-issue army boots, he ambled up the road, untouched and untouchable.

"In the midst of a vast crowd that man would be alone," said Nicholas grimly. "I have never seen anyone so utterly isolated from his fellow men."

"It has been his own choice," remarked Galen.

"I wonder," said Brough, screwing up his eyes and concentrating on the retreating figures. "It would be illuminating to know *his* side of the story."

They watched Tommaso and Emilia's microscopic forms move through the almost deserted streets, along the Via Gatta and left into Il Prato, the town's main thoroughfare. From there they branched off through a maze of side streets and alleyways and for several minutes were lost to sight. They reappeared four streets to the north and at last entered an apartment block near a spindly clock tower.

"So much for 'the house of Emilia's mother,'" said Brough, switching his gaze from the ramshackle tenement to a street map of Rogano, which he had borrowed from the landlord. Locating the baptistery on the map, he traced the route taken by Tommaso and Emilia and concluded they were in the Via Angelo Manzini.

"By the shortest route that's a good half mile from here," he said, "even though it's only a third of that as the crow flies."

They waited a further ten minutes until they were reasonably confident that Tommaso and Emilia were enmeshed in all the fuss and noise of Christmas in the bosom of the family.

"Let us gamble that Emilia's relatives are a typical Italian family," said Brough. "Possessive, emotional and apt to play dangerous games with each other's vulnerable areas. If Tommaso and Emilia have got themselves into that jungle, never more raw than at Christmas, they'll not escape for several hours at least."

"If my guess is accurate they will not want to escape," said Galen.

The three men climbed back down the tower and moved purposefully toward the palazzotto.

Looking for all the world as if they had every right to the ladder which lay on its side against the partly repaired mansion, they walked back along the middle of the road to the house. Brough carried the front of the ladder, Nicholas the middle and Galen the rear. The detective whistled an unidentifiable Italian-sounding tune.

"Make yourself as obvious as possible when you're up to no good," he had told them. "Villains skulk. If you walk in the open, whistle merrily and bid passers-by 'Buon Giorno,' you must be on the right side of the law. That's the universal notion. And rather than revise their thinking people will let you get away with murder if you do it with a smile."

In the event, no one did pass by, and Brough was relieved that his debatable view was not put to the test.

The major problem proved to be the ladder's weight and length. It was by no means a simple task, even with three of them working on it, to lift it from a horizontal to a vertical position. The narrowness of the passageway and the slippery ground made things immeasurably worse. But when at last they heaved it into position under the window, the closeness of the wall opposite proved a positive boon: without its presence as a bulwark the ladder would have slipped away from under them as they climbed up.

Galen moved to the end of the passage and took a final look for signs of Tommaso returning. There was no one in sight. With Brough leading the way, they clambered up the wooden rungs to the stained-glass window high in the wall. The detective slipped his hand inside and released the catch, opening the window outward. In less than a minute they were all inside the little room of icons and crosses.

Brough had learned many things in India, as he regularly professed. Part of his studies had rewarded him with a working knowledge of an esoteric philosophy of the physical and spiritual nature of man. It was his belief, which he had taken to the length of proof on more than one occasion, that the best way to keep an exhausted man awake was to push either his mind or body *beyond* the point of exhaustion. In unusual circumstances it was possible to act on mind and body together. Once pushed past what would normally be considered the limit of human endurance, the body switched itself into an energy source few Western people knew existed. When this too was exhausted, he had been taught by a one hundred and nineteen-year-old yogi, it was possible to go still further. By subjecting the body to an incredible strain one could reach an energy source that was virtually inexhaustible. In switching into this so-called cosmic energy, one's whole perception of life and the universe was turned upside down. Truths which before were hidden and unattainable were now commonplace: the first step to understanding existence had been taken. Brough had never seen evidence of this latter stage, and he knew many people had died attempting to reach the final energy threshold. As an acolyte, he would never dare attempt such a feat. But the first stage was simple mechanics and it was this that the detective had been diligently practicing upon his nephew—hence the killing climb to the top of the tower, the mental stimulation of the break-in and the wearying problem of the ladder. The ploy had succeeded, and for as long as his new energy had been needed it had burgeoned. Once inside the house, however, able at last to relax physically if not mentally, Nicholas found his additional energy reserves beginning to dissipate. Suddenly he was transformed from a man with the stamina of an athlete to a miserable husk on the brink of collapse. His eyelids, which had begun to look swollen, were edged with mauve.

"Let's get up there," said Galen, grabbing Nicholas by the arm to prevent him keeling over. Brough took up a like position on his nephew's right and they heaved him onto the landing and up the spiral staircase. It ended in a plain wooden door, one panel of which seemed to have been replaced at some time long ago, for although it looked as old as the rest of the door it was plainly of another type of wood. The dampness of winter had swollen the door and it took a hefty push from Galen to get it open. They entered the attic, the dust of years thick under their boots. The room, devoid of windows, was in complete darkness apart from the short wedge of daylight that crept across the floor from the door. Brough hastened to an oil lamp hanging from a bracket near the door and lit it with a match. They were in a room about twenty feet square. From each wall, no more than six feet high, the ceiling sloped upward to the apex of the roof. As Old Tommaso had told them, it contained a great deal of rubbish, but this was chiefly confined to the farther end, the area near the door having been roughly cleared for the storage of some of the fine furniture displaced when the palazzotto became a museum. This now lay under gray dust sheets. Despite the decline in its fortunes, the room had obviously been an imposing one in its heyday. The low walls were paneled in carved sandalwood and adorned with some striking portraits.

"Merciful heaven," said Nicholas, stumbling forward and retching with the nausea of exhaustion, "a couch." He reached the couch, a rickety old thing upholstered in purple satin which stood on the bare floorboards in the middle of the room. Gently he lowered himself onto it, and almost at once he was asleep.

"We have no time to lose," said Galen quickly. "I must enter a trance immediately and try to link up with Nicholas. Theoretically it is possible, but I have my doubts in practice. If I succeed, it is conceivable that with our combined wills we shall be in a position to direct ourselves and select an exact moment of our past lives."

He looked frightened. There was an awful truth awaiting them in the fifteenth century. Whatever it was, he was not eager to confront it. And once the truth was faced, it was by no means certain that they would be able to return consciously to the present.

"Keep a watch on the door and ensure that your friend Tommaso does not literally catch us napping," said Galen. "Any violent interruption could have dire effects."

Brough moved to the door while Galen stretched himself out on the floor close to the couch. He placed his arms at his sides, the palms of his hands facing upward, and began deep, controlled breathing, filling the lowest parts of his lungs. He allowed his eyes slowly to close as every muscle in his body relaxed. Brough watched with fascination as Galen traveled down through the levels of consciousness toward the mind of Giuseppe. A sound on the landing at the foot of the spiral staircase caused Brough suddenly to freeze. He strained his ears to catch any repetition of the noise, but none came. The possibilities reeled through his mind: Was Tommaso back? Was there someone else in the house all along? Had a neighbor seen the ladder and summoned the police? No further noises rose from the landing. The sounds of his own body chugging through its daily routine hammered in his head. If there was anyone down there they must surely be able to hear him. After two more minutes of silence he placed his hand on the doorknob and turned it silently. He drew the door toward him with ponderous slowness, so that the unavoidable creak of its old hinges was so muted it would never be heard from below. Not breathing for fear he would give himself away, he crept down the spiral staircase. Looking, listening, smelling. Nothing. As he reached the bottom step he saw it standing in the doorway of the end room. A dark, ugly creature with bulbous eyes and a wagging tail.

"A ruddy bulldog," he muttered, giving the animal a reluctant pat on the head to keep it happy. At least it was friendly enough, he reflected gratefully, probably just heard noises and came to investigate. Some guard dog, giving burglars a welcome like that.

When he re-entered the attic room Galen had stopped breathing. His body was rigid and for a second it crossed Brough's mind that he had died. Then he remembered. Galen's method was to bring about a self-induced cataleptic fit. Catalepsy, he recalled, slowed down the pulse and respiration of its victims to such an extent that they looked dead even to those trained in medicine. Visions of a woman whose body he had been instrumental in having exhumed swam before his eyes. She had been buried three months before the exhumation and there was suspicion that she had been poisoned. The suspicion proved unfounded for on the opening of the coffin it was evident she had not been dead when buried. A victim of catalepsy, she had been cast into the ground during a prolonged fit and had wakened in her coffin some time after the grave had been filled in. The memory of the deep scratch marks on the inside of the coffin lid and the splinters of wood driven deep into the skin beneath her fingernails still filled him with horror eleven years later.

For the briefest moment Galen's body seemed to go out of focus. It shimmered like the air above a cornfield on a hot September day before harvest. As the German entered more profoundly into his controlled trance state his soul had become momentarily free of the body and had begun to rise upward, giving Brough his unnerving double vision. But Galen, in control despite his deathly appearance, prevented the usual separation of the two parts of his being and proceeded on his voyage of discovery.

36

His exhaustion had been so complete that at first he felt mildly surprised that he was awakening so soon. His eyelids flickered open and without moving his head he looked slowly around the room. It was different, there was no argument about that. But it was the same room. The same ceiling sloping from the central point of the roof to the four paneled walls. Apart from the couch on which he lay the only other item of furniture was an elaborately carved oak chair ten feet away on the opposite side of the circular rug. An elegant brass tripod in the center of the rug held a shallow dish of burning incense. Its bittersweet fumes rose in a thin perpendicular column that shimmered and twisted like a strange, slow whirlwind where it met an air current about two feet from the ceiling. The room was newer, somehow, the wood paneling lighter in color than when he had entered a few minutes earlier with Galen and Brough. That was a point. Where *were* Galen and Brough? It was a nagging point, but not a very important one. His mind began to drift to other things, subjects closer to his heart and more vital. More vital not just to him, Antonio, but to the whole of mankind.

His work.

Once back in the mainstream of thought, his entire being became suddenly alive. He sat up and discarded the remnants of his physical exhaustion as easily as he might at another time have thrown off his cloak and boots.

Spread before him like a written summary of his achievements, like some dread testimony to his life to date, was his work—hundreds of sheets of parchment, all covered with notes and diagrams, strewn across the rug.

Like an unfinished epitaph, he thought. Well, when it is finished they might write my epitaph. My purpose will be fulfilled.

He leaned forward and extracted a page from the heap of his past, and smiled ruefully at his own lack of system. If I took time off to catalogue my work, he thought, I'd not need to rely on my memory. As the years pass it needs to be ever more capacious. But then, he mused with a smile, my disorganization will probably be my salvation. None of those accursed familiars of the Inquisition could make sense of my notes. But it is so much a part of me that I know the exact sequence of the pages, although none of them is numbered, and I know the precise meaning of each symbol.

He knelt down with his entire universe spread before him on the floor. Diagrams of the planets and the stars tracing their pathways through the black ocean of the firmament were surrounded by densely written notes. Each page was decorated with signs clearly astrological in origin, but somehow unlike the familiar twelve zodiac symbols.

Magic, thought Nicholas in horror. Not magic, countered the much stronger presence of Antonio. Not magic but the means whereby mankind reaches the truth. He leaned forward and placed the palms of his hands reverently upon the papers that he had decided were his reason for living. In doing so some of the pages were moved, and part of the pattern on the carpet was revealed: more abstruse signs. A magician! thought Nicholas in desolation. Before Antonio could deny the charge brought by the unknown observer floating inexplicably, yet somehow naturally, in the deeps of his own brain, there was a sound of feet on the landing below. Then, before Antonio could even rise from his suppliant position on the floor, the feet were clattering up the spiral staircase.

The Inquisition! he thought, seized by a sudden dread. They have come at last.

Filled with unreasoning panic, he attempted to rise, with the thought of doing the impossible and hiding all evidence of his work in the fleeting moments before the door burst open and he was carried off to the torture chamber beneath the cathedral crypt. But in getting up so quickly he trod on the hem of his gown, stumbled and landed with a crash on top of the damning pile. He looked helplessly across at the door, which was now straining under the savage blows being rained upon it from the other side.

Holy Mother of God, he trembled, they are using an ax. Seconds later the upper panel of the door splintered and the head of the ax came right through. Antonio was paralyzed with fear. He could do nothing as a hand forced its way through the rent in the wood and groped for the bolt. Then the door was thrown back and there, framed in the doorway, the cowering Antonio was confronted by . . . blackness! It descended like a cloak of invisibility over the intruder as Nicholas, possessed with terror, forced himself out of the mind of Antonio and upward, straining ever upward, toward the real world. Toward 1902 and Brough and Galen and . . . something was restraining him, pulling him back. . . . Oh God, he begged a moment before sliding back into the pit that was Antonio's consciousness, Oh God, let me not go back . . . but the prayer went unheeded.

The problem with the attic, mused Brough, surveying the shabby room and its two unconscious occupants, was that it had no windows. There was nowhere he could get a view of the street, nowhere at all to keep watch. There was only one thing for it, he would have to go down to the third floor and take up his position by the tall windows of one of the bedchambers. It was twenty-five minutes since Galen had entered his trance and it could be another hour before the two men awoke. Staying here

was worse than useless. With hardly a sound he opened the door
and made his way down the spiral staircase to the landing.

He had been at his new post no longer than seven or eight min-
utes when his worst fears were realized. A police vehicle drawn by
two stallions came flying down the road from the direction of Il
Prato. At first he thought it must be out of control it came so fast,
but the thundering hoofs never faltered. The uniformed *carabi-
niere* at the reins drove the horses onward to the limit of their en-
durance, and at the last moment brought them to a standstill
outside the front door of the *palazzetto* with all the adroitness of a
circus performer. While the police officer jumped from his perch
on top of the carriage, the skinny figure of Old Tommaso scram-
bled from the inside and led the way at a run up the steps to the
door.

"Christ," whispered Brough.

Nicholas repeated his prayer to an indifferent deity as his own
consciousness tumbled, helpless, back into the mind of his for-
mer self. But, for the time being at least, he was delivered from
the valley of death. As his eyes focused again on the Rogano of
the 1450s he realized he had returned to another moment in An-
tonio's life. He was not, as he had feared, face to face with a mob
of Inquisition thugs about to arrest him for practicing witch-
craft. He was not even in the attic room of the palazzotto. He
stood in his tight-fitting puce skull cup, tailored to cover his hair
and ears, and a voluminous crimson gown whose hem brushed the
polished floor. At first he could not tell where he was, or even
whether he had regressed to a time before or after the episode in
the attic. Then suddenly he knew: he was in the chamber on the
third floor which Giuseppe used as a study. As children they had
used it as their schoolroom. Giuseppe was there too, seated in a
high-backed chair near the window. A pallid sunlight filtered
through the bubbly glass of the window behind him, and his odd
eyes burned with a ferocity that made Antonio ill at ease.

Nicholas had barely taken in the room and gleaned a superficial
idea of the troubled emotions of Antonio, when the scene began
to fade. Once again he found himself rising slowly upward and
the room lost its clarity—sights, sounds and feelings alike becom-
ing vague and gray. Then he was back and all his senses regained

their former sharpness. Now, again, the picture was lost. The back
and forth swing into and out of Antonio's mind seemed to be tak-
ing on a rhythmic pattern, as if two fluctuating but equal forces
were fighting for possession of him. When at last, after staring at
each other silently for a long time, Antonio and Giuseppe began
to talk, Nicholas was able to register only parts of the dialogue as
he swung from an eerie limbo to the ancient room and back
again.

"Where is the cave? Where is the cave? . . ." said Giuseppe.

"I can't tell you . . ." said Antonio.

"Why? . . ."

". . . it is a secret what happens at the cave . . ."

". . . what happens there . . ."

"I won't tell you . . ."

Silence. Then Giuseppe again:

"The Inquisition would soon get at the truth . . ."

"Are you going to tell . . . the Grand Inquisitor?"

"Never!" said Giuseppe. "You are my brother."

". . . But this *is* a case of murder . . ." said Antonio quietly,
with solemn deliberation.

"A brother cannot betray a brother," said Giuseppe.

"What will you do? . . ."

Nicholas was hearing less and less of the conversation as with
each swing into limbo it took him longer, despite desperate striv-
ing, to return to the correct moment of his former life. His own
thoughts whirled in confusion as he realized he had at last re-
ceived definite confirmation that Antonio had been the brother
who made nocturnal excursions to the cave on the Santine Hill.
Therefore Antonio was the leader of the Gormini. Antonio was
the Rogano Strangler. And he, Nicholas, was the Deptford
Stranger.

He heard just one further snatch of the dialogue between the
brothers before leaving it behind forever. Again, Giuseppe was
addressing Antonio.

"You are . . . a mass murderer, a strangler."

Antonio stood, eyes downcast, saying nothing.

Brough began to sweat. He could hear Tommaso's key sliding
into the great padlock on the front door. There was no time for

him to rouse his companions and attempt an escape down the ladder. There was not even enough time to get back up the spiral staircase. In less than a second the caretaker would be inside the house with the police officer at his heels. How on earth was he to explain their breaking into the house, and the fact that one of his friends was fast asleep and the other apparently dead? He had to think of an answer—quickly.

"I have been contemplating the nature of God," said Antonio, sitting down on a pile of cushions in the corner of the library and placing his hands in his lap. Giuseppe lay nearby, his head pillowed on a massive handwritten Bible.

"For me," said Antonio, "the Christian concept of an all-loving creator is unsatisfactory in the extreme."

"You have other ideas?" inquired Giuseppe with genuine interest.

"Yes. I have come to the conclusion that God is neither good nor evil. God is a neutral force of enormous power, a virtually limitless store of spiritual energy somewhere—perhaps everywhere —in the universe. We humans can draw upon that power for good or for evil. The power itself is disinterested."

"A provoking argument," observed Giuseppe, "and one that will surely brand you heretic if you ever breathe a word of it outside these walls."

"Perhaps. But since our great dissension last year I have regarded the Inquisition with little fear."

"I have grown up a great deal since then, Antonio," said Giuseppe. "I have learned that the universe is not as neat and perfect and secure as our spiritual rulers would have us believe."

"As neat, yes. Neater by far than anyone has hitherto imagined. But secure?" He shook his head gravely. "No, never secure."

Antonio reflected a moment before resuming.

"When you charged up those stairs with an ax I was sure my time on earth was at an end. As I lay helpless on the floor with all my work spread out beneath me I lived in my imagination through every detail of torture, trial and execution. When the door finally gave way and you lumbered in bellowing, 'Magician! Black magician!' I could have cried with relief. In those moments I had known the worst horrors man could perpetrate upon man.

And my greatest misery had not been the thought that my life
was at an end, but that it was ending before the consummation of
my mission. After that the Inquisition held no terror for me."

"I truly believed you were a magician," said Giuseppe. "We
had drifted so far apart I found I did not know you at all."

"I know." He placed a comforting hand upon his brother's
shoulder. "According to the laws of the Church I am a magician.
But now my work is done. One day seekers after truth will no
longer be hunted to the ends of the earth by ignorant men intent
only on preserving their own power in the world. One day it will
no longer be a crime to think."

He closed his eyes and tried to visualize man's blind, groping
form stumbling not into greater depths of ignorance but toward
a distant enlightenment.

"I can see a time," he said, "perhaps a generation from now,
perhaps longer, when my discoveries will be debated freely in
every university and household in Italy."

"But by then you will be dead. For you all the struggles will
have been in vain."

"Giuseppe, I have not striven as I have for personal aggran-
dizement. I have zealously pursued Truth not for my sake but its
own. I have proven that the earth is not the center of the uni-
verse. The sun and stars do not revolve around us. What some
men have long suspected is true—the earth is not like a plate sup-
ported by gargantuan elephants or some other fanciful concep-
tion. It is a sphere spinning on its own axis. I have gone beyond
that. I have shown that the earth is simply one of several planets
revolving around the sun, and that the sun is nothing more special
than an ordinary, medium-sized star. There could be thousands of
other planets in the universe which support intelligent life. Many,
perhaps, support life aeons more advanced than we are. At times
that is not difficult to envisage."

"And I was convinced you were up there in the attic room,
locked away for hours each day and often long into the night,
summoning the Evil One and weaving diabolic spells. I had
brooded about it for months. Then that day some overwhelming
fear gripped me. I had to confront you with your sins and demand
you turn your back on sorcery. I was outraged that you should pu-
trefy the house of our fathers, angry that you were jeopardizing

your immortal soul by dabbling in the supernatural, and panic-stricken that you were laying both of us open to investigation by the Inquisition."

"Ha!" laughed Antonio. "How our actions can be misjudged, even by those who profess to love us. Now *you* have been behaving curiously of late. Where do you go when you sneak out of the house at night? I've asked myself that question a hundred times. It is the measure of our characters that in bewildering circumstances you suspect me of being a magician—while I, on the other hand, lean toward the view that your late-night assignations are less likely to be with the devil than with a woman."

"It is not a woman," said Giuseppe, suddenly on his guard. He sat up and looked deeply into his brother's eyes. For a moment he seemed about to speak, to share a confidence of great weight. Then the rapport between them unaccountably dissolved and he climbed to his feet, flushed and confused. "It is *not* a woman!" he cried, and hurried out of the room.

It was the first time Nicholas had gained any real insight into Antonio's thinking. His previous perception of his former self had been limited chiefly to sights and sounds. He had been wrong in thinking Antonio was a magician. Now, as he lingered for the last few seconds in the mind of the elder brother Aquilina, he realized there had been a mistake, too, in his interpretation of the earlier dialogue about the cave. Antonio's secret was nothing more sinister than his study of the universe. It was *Giuseppe* who had made the nighttime visits to the Santine Hill.

A rush of wind he could hear but not feel took him up and bore him outward and away to the bizarre limbo between Antonio's fragmented consciousness and the upper levels of his brain where Nicholas reigned supreme. In an instant he was out of the nothingness and tumbling headlong toward the present.

If escape was impossible, Brough decided, then at least he could prevent disaster befalling Galen and his nephew. Perhaps whoever had alerted Tommaso had seen only the ladder, and not the three men who used it. If that were so, he might yet convince his captors that he had been alone in his housebreaking enterprise. If he were then carted off to the nick, Tommaso would doubtless come too, blown up with satisfaction at scoring the final point.

That would rule out the unthinkable dangers that threatened his friends if their experiment were interrupted. He began his slow, anxious descent of the first flight of stairs as Tommaso threw open the front door and blundered in with the *carabiniere* behind him.

"You look in the kitchen, I'll search the bedroom," he heard Tommaso tell the policeman as he reached the second-floor landing.

If I'd been alone, he thought, making a face, I'd have been out of here and down the ladder before these buffoons had finished checking the ground floor. They haven't even posted anyone at the foot of the ladder.

The caretaker's apartment was a hive of furious activity as Brough rounded the final curve of the stairs and made his way down to the hall.

"Where are they? Where are they?" Tommaso was saying with uncharacteristic agitation.

Then the policeman spoke for the first time. "Oh my sister. My poor sister," he wailed.

Brough frowned and pulled himself up with a jerk outside Tommaso's door.

"Emilia will be all right," said Tommaso. "You know she has had these turns before. But we must find her *tablets*."

"They are not in the kitchen," said the policeman.

"And they are not in the bedroom," said Tommaso, beside himself with worry. "Oh Luigi, what am I going to do?"

So our friend Tommaso has a heart after all, thought Brough.

There were frantic scrabbling sounds as Tommaso began turning over the living room in search of the precious tablets.

"She told me they were in the bedroom or the kitchen," he moaned.

There was something funny about all this, thought Brough. He couldn't think what it was.

"Ah! Tommaso!" cried Luigi in triumph, "I have them!"

Brough beat a silent but hasty retreat up the stairs.

"Emilia, Emilia, why do you not take care of your tablets?" sang that unfortunate woman's husband as he tore out of their apartment and through the front door with his brother-in-law at his heels.

A real emergency, thought Brough as he stood by the first-floor window and watched Tommaso clamber back into the carriage without even locking the front door behind him. In a second Luigi had turned the vehicle around and they were disappearing as madly as they had come.

Hoping Emilia would emerge from her "turn" none the worse for the experience, Brough bounded back up the stairs.

Luck, like lightning, rarely strikes twice in the same place, he thought. We must get out of here fast.

He waited in the doorway at the top of the spiral staircase, straining his nostrils at every scent in the air and his ears at every sound, for a further twelve minutes. Then Galen began to show signs of emerging from his trance. His breathing was again perceptible. In another minute he was inhaling and exhaling air at the same slow, deep rate as when the experiment had started.

"Herr van Galen," said Brough, crossing to him when he awoke, "we must get out of here quickly. Tommaso came back for his wife's tablets and he forgot to lock the door. As soon as he realizes the omission he will be back. And he has a policeman for a brother-in-law. This time I doubt if they'll fail to notice the footprints leading into the alleyway. Can we wake Nicholas?"

Galen looked strained. He briefly examined Nicholas.

"Yes, he is all right," he said. "He is now simply sleeping. He must have returned to a normal level of consciousness before I did."

They managed to rouse Nicholas with some difficulty.

"He is, after all, still very tired," said Galen.

Once he was on his feet they made their way down the spiral staircase to the landing.

"We might as well take the front door," said Brough.

"No!" said Galen tensely. "We're much more likely to be caught that way."

Brough shrugged. There was no time for arguments.

They walked swiftly along to the icon room and pushed open the window. Galen went first, then Nicholas, then Brough.

The cold air was only beginning to bring some clarity to Nicholas' thoughts when Brough joined him on the ground.

"Uncle," he said with sudden excitement, "it worked! I got back into the mind of Antonio!"

"And?" asked Brough, as thrilled as his nephew.

"And he was innocent!"

"Who?"

"Antonio. He was innocent. I don't know how, but all the evidence is wrong. I got inside that man's mind. He knew *nothing* about the Rogano killings."

"Maybe you got inside his mind at a time *before* the killings took place?"

"No. He was talking about the cave . . ."

"With whom?"

"Giuseppe, his brother. He was asking him, 'Where do you go at night?' Uncle, do you realize what this means? I *know* I am not the Deptford Strangler!"

"If Antonio was innocent," said Brough, "then the killer must have been . . ."

"Giuseppe," said Nicholas.

"And the Deptford Strangler . . ."

". . . is Galen."

"Where *is* Herr van Galen?"

In the exhilaration of the discovery they had been oblivious of the German's absence. They ran to the end of the alleyway and surveyed the street in both directions.

But Galen was nowhere in sight.

37

"Who was the dark lady?" asked Brough pensively as they tramped back through the snow.

"Which dark lady?" said Nicholas.

"Shakespeare's. The one in the sonnets?"

"Oh her," he said unenthusiastically. "I don't know. At this moment I can't say I really care."

They walked on in silence for a few minutes, Nicholas peering along each alleyway and street they passed in the hope of catching sight of Galen.

"I expect he'll be back at the pensione," he murmured more to himself than his uncle.

"What about Mr. W.H.?" asked Brough.

"Mr. Who?"

"W.H."

"Who is Mr. W.H.?"

"No one knows. He's the man Shakespeare dedicated his sonnets to."

He produced his little volume of the sonnets from his pocket.

"Here we are. 'To the onlie begetter of these ensuing sonnets, Mr. W.H.' But who was he?"

"Are you really concerned at this time with an academic problem like that?"

"Not really, just a diversion. Interesting though, isn't it—the language I mean. *The only begetter*. Shakespeare must have thought of his writings as his children. I suppose a lot of writers think that way about their creations."

"I suppose so," said Nicholas, hardly listening.

"Especially in the 1500s when Shakespeare lived. They seemed to find ways of personifying almost every idea and inanimate object in those days."

Nicholas marveled again at his uncle's ability to cut himself off completely from the trials of the present, refreshing his mind with forays into the obscurest avenues of thought. The old detective chattered on unhindered, receiving an appropriate-sounding "Yes" or "Hmmm" where his pauses seemed to call for some response.

Galen was not at the pensione. The landlord had been at home all morning and he had seen no one enter the house.

"Strange fellow," muttered Brough. "Doesn't he realize we want to find out about his experiences this morning?"

"Isn't it clear to you what those experiences were?" asked Nicholas. There was a lightness in his voice that had not been present for weeks.

"Surely you can see," he continued. "Galen received definite proof too. He knows now that Giuseppe was the Rogano Strangler. How *can* he face us after believing all along in my guilt? Galen has to come to terms with the fact that he is a murderer."

"I'm not convinced of that," said Brough, slamming shut his *Sonnets* and stuffing it back into his pocket, "but right now what I want more than anything is to make a pig of myself. Turkey and mince pies might be too much to expect in a remote north Italian town even on Christmas Day. But one of those little restaurants along the way should be able to provide something nourishing. Food or sleep for you?"

"Food," said Nicholas, "then sleep."

They walked along to a *trattoria* that snuggled in a corner of the piazza between a barber's shop and a tailor. Only one or two tables were occupied and the two men found themselves a private corner where they could talk undisturbed. Despite his hunger, Brough barely noticed as waiters arrived at the table and disappeared again, depositing steaming dishes and removing used plates. Indeed, he was hardly aware even of ordering the food or eating it, so engrossed was he in Nicholas' description of his journeys into the mind of Antonio.

Over coffee he suggested that he take a precise note of the two sections of dialogue Nicholas had heard.

"Do you remember it clearly?"

"Every word. I shall never forget it."

While Nicholas unfalteringly dictated, Brough took notes in his own peculiar form of shorthand.

"That's the bit that rankles," he said after recording the partly heard conversation between the two brothers, in which Giuseppe had seemed to be interrogating Antonio about the cave. "It completely contradicts their later talk on the subject."

He ran his eye over what he had written.

"Giuseppe finishes up telling Antonio, 'You are . . . a mass murderer, a strangler.' Explain that."

"I can't," said Nicholas almost flippantly. "I don't care what was *said*. I know what Antonio *thought*. He was not a murderer. He was not involved with the goings-on at the cave. He knew nothing—I repeat, nothing at all—about the Gormini. I swear to you on the life of my mother that he was innocent."

"We'll leave that for the moment," said Brough. "Let's examine some of the other evidence that still seems to tell against you. And let's resolve it if we can."

He got out his pipe and began to fill it.

"There is still the question of your dreams. On the night of each murder in London you dreamed you were in the act of strangling someone. How does that square with Galen being the killer?"

"I've come to the conclusion that some telepathic link existed between Antonio and Giuseppe. They were very close, especially as children. If some such link were forged it is possible that *Antonio* had dreams of killing people while *Giuseppe* was committing the murders. If that were so, the dreams simply form another facet of Antonio's mind that I have inherited along with the other traits."

"No. It still doesn't fit."

"But why? You of all people can't deny the existence of thought transference. My father has often said he thinks I have some sort of ability in that line. Look at that time when I was about eight. I *knew* my mother had collapsed in the street and been taken to hospital—when she had the miscarriage—even though I was asleep in bed two miles away at the time. I did not know my mother had gone out. I wasn't even aware that she was pregnant until that moment."

Brough nodded attentively.

"Then there was that other occasion when, on my way to visit you in Jermyn Street, I had a vivid picture of you standing under one of the great trilithons at Stonehenge. When I got to your place you weren't there. You'd been called out at short notice by the Wiltshire Police to help them out of a mess they'd got into over a murder at Devizes. We later worked it out that at the moment I'd had my mental picture of you, that you were in fact at Stonehenge."

"I'd got a couple of hours to spare so I did a bit of sightseeing."

"You see! And what about when—"

"I'm not denying the existence of telepathy," interrupted Brough. "What I'm saying is, if Herr van Galen were the murderer, why did you have your dreams on the very nights the killings took place? You had never met Herr van Galen. How *could* there be a telepathic link between you and him?"

"I don't know. What I do know is that Antonio was innocent, and I am innocent."

"The other point is one that I have so far not mentioned to you, although I did confide in Herr van Galen while we were in London. The Deptford Strangler chose to kill his victims in the exact locality of previous London murders. The vital importance of this is that with at least three of them, no member of the general public could have known the grisly association the sites have. But each of those murder sites is depicted in photographs in a group on the wall of my living room. Now Herr van Galen had not been to Jermyn Street until after the last murder had taken place."

A trace of surprise registered on Nicholas' face, giving place almost immediately to a look of intense concentration as his mind digested the problem.

"Of course!" he said after a few moments, "Galen's soul! His *soul* must have entered your rooms before the murders even began."

Brough pursed his lips and dissected the theory. Slowly and with precision.

"What other explanation is there?" cut in Nicholas, impatient to be vindicated in his uncle's eyes. "In fact, bearing in mind his uncanny ability to send out his soul, and his desperate need to observe me at that stage, it is inconceivable that he would *not* have had his soul enter your rooms invisibly."

"Perhaps," nodded Brough, "perhaps."

Galen had still not returned when they got back to the pensione at a few minutes past three.

"What unnerves me most of all," said Nicholas, "is Galen's warning that the guilty one of us might try to kill the other two when we got close to discovering the truth. We must take every precaution to protect ourselves in case the murderous spirit of Giuseppe has begun to exert a stronger influence over him."

They climbed the stairs to their room. It was locked. Brough fumbled in his pocket for the key.

"Galen was the last one out of here this morning," said Nicholas. "He must have it."

"I'll borrow the landlord's duplicate," said Brough, going downstairs once more. He came back with Lombardi close behind. Lombardi took out a bunch of keys, knotted together on a length of string, and let them into the room. Detaching their key from the bunch, he said, "I shall hang it on the hook in the vestibule. Just take it if you need it."

Nicholas threw himself down on the bed, intent on finishing his interrupted sleep. Brough, meanwhile, sat down by the fire to put his thoughts in order. His gaze drifted listlessly about the room, eventually coming to rest upon the richly bound writing book, embossed with the letters R.v.G., in which Galen had made notes on his research into the Rogano case. The detective picked it up and settled down at page one to see in detail what Galen had discovered before meeting Nicholas and himself.

In the course of their long discussions the German had imparted almost every grain of information contained in the book. However, it made compulsive reading and Brough read on and on, recapping on life in Italy in the fifteenth century; the personal details of the victims of the Rogano Strangler; the methods of the Inquisition; the background and characters of the brothers Aquilina. He read on until the fire burned low in the grate and the sun disappeared behind Mount Bellanone. At length, with barely enough light left to read by, he came upon Galen's notes on his earlier regressions to the mind of Giuseppe. It seemed that each of the seven experiments recorded had been vague and unsatisfactory. Sensations had been broken and unclear. He had been able to exert only feeble control on the timing of his regression. Each occasion had drained him physically and mentally and he had to wait days, sometimes weeks, between sessions. From Galen's description, the regressions compared unfavorably with the two out of three episodes Nicholas had detailed with such clarity.

Obviously, thought Brough, being in the palazzotto—in the very room where Antonio had worked—had contributed beyond measure to Nicholas' success.

If Herr van Galen returns, he pondered, we shall know if he had like success in the mesmeric ambience of the house.

Only one of Galen's earlier experiments seized Brough's interest. It was recorded thus:

> *Dialogue between Giuseppe and Antonio. Place: Giuseppe's study. Giuseppe seated near window, Antonio standing. Only parts of the conversation were discernible, viz.:*
>
> GIUSEPPE: . . . *That's all you ever say.*

ANTONIO: . . . *you how anxious I am about you.*

GIUSEPPE: . . . *You have no need to be.*

ANTONIO: *I know you say it is . . . but can you not trust even your own brother?*

GIUSEPPE: *If I told you . . . it would do you no good.*

ANTONIO: . . . *you the horrible possibilities that have suggested themselves.*

GIUSEPPE: . . . *at the truth. Ask them to find out for you.*

ANTONIO: . . . *me you seriously think I'd go to . . .*

GIUSEPPE: *Never . . . my brother.*

ANTONIO: *Yes I am. . . . A brother who loved you less might think differently.*

GIUSEPPE: *A brother . . . a brother.*

ANTONIO: . . . *if one of your friends betrays you?*

GIUSEPPE: *All my friends are dead.*

ANTONIO: *Do you want pity?*

GIUSEPPE: . . . *my brother, Antonio. Do you really think I am . . .*

Beneath the dialogue, Galen had written:

Upon waking I remembered distinctly every syllable of the dialogue that I had heard. From the cold words on the page it might be deemed debatable where in such a jumble new sentences begin. I have split them into sentences as I heard them spoken. The nuance of each word, the stress, accent and tone is with me still. I feel positive this conversation would have provided important insights into the characters of both brothers. As it stands it is worthless. Strive as I might I could not make out any more than I have recorded. I could hear the entire dialogue, but much of it descended beneath the level of intelligibility and became a meaningless jumble of sound. It might be possible to return again to this moment and fill in the gaps. I shall strive for this.

Brough reached across to his greatcoat, flung carelessly over the bed, and extracted his own notebook. Thumbing through the pages of notes he had made at the restaurant, he found the beginning of Nicholas' report on the conversation between the brothers. He placed both books side by side on his lap and looked from one to the other. His resultant exclamation—a loud "Ha!"—awoke Nicholas with a start.

"What is it?" he demanded, jumping up before his eyes had even come into focus.

"It's a cue for eureka in a minor key," said Brough without looking up. Nicholas scrambled across to him and peered over his shoulder.

"I can't see," said Nicholas. Quickly he reached for a spill on the mantelpiece, stuck it in the embers of the fire and lit an oil lamp with its glowing end.

"In my right hand," said Brough like a poor stage magician, "your version of a conversation between Antonio and Giuseppe. And in my left, Herr van Galen's version of the same episode. He heard one bit of it. You heard the rest. Where you had gaps he had words. Where you had words he had gaps. Some of it appears in both versions, but not much. Put 'em together and what have we got?"

He tore a sheet from his notebook, and resting on the end of the bed with both reports in front of him, he began to write.

GIUSEPPE: *Where is the cave? Where is the cave? That's all you ever say.*

ANTONIO: *I can't tell you how anxious I am about you.*

GIUSEPPE: *Why? You have no need to be.*

ANTONIO: *I know you say it is a secret what happens at the cave, but can you not trust even your own brother?*

GIUSEPPE: *If I told you what happens there it would do you no good.*

ANTONIO: *I won't tell you the horrible possibilities that have suggested themselves.*

GIUSEPPE: *The Inquisition would soon get at the truth. Ask them to find out for you.*

ANTONIO: *Are you going to tell me you seriously think I'd go to the Grand Inquisitor?*

GIUSEPPE: *Never! You are my brother.*

ANTONIO: *Yes, I am. But this is a case of murder. A brother who loved you less might think differently.*

GIUSEPPE: *A brother cannot betray a brother.*

ANTONIO: *What will you do if one of your friends betrays you?*

GIUSEPPE: *All my friends are dead.*

ANTONIO: *Do you want pity?*

GIUSEPPE: *You are my brother, Antonio. Do you really think I am a mass murderer, a strangler?*

"That reverses the whole meaning of the confrontation," breathed Nicholas, striving to contain his elation and avoid the recurring pitfall of overstating his case. "It was *Antonio* who was the interrogator and Giuseppe who was being quizzed. Now do you believe that Antonio was innocent?"

"Yes," said Brough absently, yet even now he seemed puzzled, ill at ease, "I do."

An ominous click of metal against metal suddenly arrested Brough's attention. The shadow of a frown passed across his face. He rose without a sound, and motioning Nicholas to remain silent, he padded to the door. He pressed his ear to the wood and listened intently for sounds on the other side. He breathed smoothly and deeply through his nostrils but no clue, nasal or aural, was perceptible. Stealthily he grasped the door handle and turned it. They were locked in.

"Someone is playing a nasty game, Nicholas," he said, low and cheerless.

"Who in the name of God would want us holed up in this benighted place?"

"Who indeed? It wouldn't do the landlord a lot of good."

"No. And who in Rogano apart from the landlord is even aware of our existence?"

Brough gave a grunt of dissatisfaction and moved away from the door.

"Whoever it was he moved fast," he said. "He'd gone by the time I reached the door."

As he spoke someone in the street below threw a handful of gravel at the closed window of their room. It rattled stridently against the pane. Brough pushed open the casement and looked down. At first he could see nothing except the uneven outline of the buildings on the opposite side of the square and the dusky silhouette of the Christ statue in the center. Then the dark watchful presence of Arretto and Bellanone, keeping their vigil over the heedless town, gradually materialized as his eyes adjusted themselves to the night.

All at once he sensed, rather than heard or saw, a movement on the pavement immediately beneath the window. He searched the street as far as he could see but the pavement was hidden by the wide snow-covered gable of the pensione. There was a brief rasp-

ing sound as someone lit a match. He saw its yellow halo flare and
fade, and smelled the unmistakable odor of burned phosphorus.
Then darkness and stillness reigned again for a long moment.

Gloom and calm were dispelled together by a sudden roaring
blaze that leapt into being where the stranger was lurking. At last
a figure emerged into view. A man. He was swinging a yard of
cord in wide circles around his head. A fleeting picture of a South
American gaucho armed with a bola flashed through Brough's
mind. But any similarity between the man below and a pampas
cowboy ended with his swift, swinging action. For the rope ended
not with a cluster of stone weights but in a great ball of roaring
fire. On the third circle, the man, his face obscured by a scarf, let
go of the missile and it soared upward in a broad arc toward
Brough. Time seemed almost to hang motionless. In the fraction
of a second the fireball took to complete its short trajectory, the
detective was able by some trick of the senses to perceive every de-
tail of the scene in which he had become the central figure. He
saw the piazza spread out before him, deserted on this Christmas
night by all but the fearful Prometheus and his deadly gift of fire.
He saw the enigmatic gaze of the stone Christ looking deep into
his own eyes and seeming to challenge him with the central riddle
of Christianity: Who was I, What am I? He saw the uplifted
hand and the fluttering dove. He saw the three white points of
Orion's belt low in the sky behind Arretto's curving shoulder; so
mathematically precise in their relative positions that they defied
the observing Brough, trapped awhile in an endless moment, to
think the universe was an accident. He saw the lighted windows
and the dark rooftops of Rogano. He saw the faceless man who
would kill him, frozen in the act of lobbing his deadly missile into
the air.

And then, hanging motionless on its upward path, the fireball
began to move again and the stranger was swallowed up by the
shadows that had spawned him.

As the blazing bringer of death reached its zenith before plum-
meting down into the room, Brough saw a face picked out in the
darkness by its ever-changing light. A face only partly obscured by
a black scarf. A face wild-eyed, pale and staring. A face frozen in a
strange, unfathomable mien surrounded by night of such impene-

trable blackness that it seemed to float in air. The face of Rudolf van Galen.

The odd eyes were unmistakable. Galen's gaze met Brough's and in the instant of recognition, he ran off into the darkness. The flaming projectile continued its descent. Brough threw himself flat across the window sill just in time to avoid being hit full in the face. It caught his shoulder a glancing blow and singed his hair and ear. The flames licked at the muslin curtains as the fireball passed through the window, and immediately they were ablaze. The missile itself was now recognizable as a mass of oily rags soaked in some highly flammable liquid, probably naphtha, and weighted—it seemed with a hefty stone. Bound to it with wire was a glass bottle, securely stoppered, containing the same liquid.

It crashed onto the floor, the bottle shattering on impact. The liquid spattered in all directions, carrying fire to every part of the room. Nicholas and Brough howled with pain as the fiery rain smacked against their bare skin. They shrank back, trying to protect their faces with their arms. The missile rolled beneath Nicholas' bed, setting fire to the bedspread as it went. Fires were now breaking out all over the room.

Nicholas hurled himself across to the bed and tried to lift it. It was too heavy. Brough, suffering with a long vertical burn on his cheek where the naphtha had landed and rolled down, and another on the back of his hand, hurried to his aid. They raised the bed and overturned it. The fireball blazed furiously. The underside of the bedclothes was already ablaze.

"The mattress!" said Brough.

He tore the covers from his bed and dragged off the mattress. Together they threw it down over the mass of burning rags. Nicholas jumped on top of it to help smother the fire.

The curtains had nearly gone. Flames now licked at the pelmet. The other fires were spreading outward and joining up. A corner table draped in lace was an inferno.

Brough was beating away at the bedclothes.

"This bit's out!" cried Nicholas through the smoke. They looked under the mattress. The missile had burned out. It was now a mass of smoldering rags with a blackened boulder at its center.

Nicholas seized Galen's umbrella and tried to rip down the burning pelmet.

Brough, bellowing for the landlord, was trying to contain a blaze by the door.

"We're losing!" shouted Nicholas. "We need water!"

"There is no water!" cried Brough.

Nicholas looked desperately about the room. "The chamber pot!" he cried, bounding across to Brough's bed and pulling out the big china pot.

He took it to the window. He gripped the mullion of the window with one hand and leaned out with the pot in the other. He scraped it along the sloping gable, filling it to the brim with snow.

He carried the snow to the fiercest of the fires and emptied it onto the flames in a lump. An angry hiss. A fierce ejaculation of steam. But the fire roared on.

"Grab the vase!" shouted Nicholas.

Brough was throwing bedclothes and other easily combustible items out of the window. Then he snatched up the vase.

They worked in unison, hardly pausing for breath. Soaking the carpets, they isolated the fires and stopped them spreading. Then they heaped snow into the flames in such quantities that a turning point in the battle became inevitable.

Toward the end the snow near at hand was depleted and they had to strain farther and farther along the gable on each side of the window. When they had done, the fires were all out and the room was a shambles of charred wood, smoldering piles of cloth, ashes, heaps of melting snow and great puddles of water.

"It looks like the end of the world," said Nicholas, surveying the chaos.

"A great reckoning in a small room," said Brough.

"Thank God there's been so much snow. Without it we'd have been burned to cinders."

"If the gable had been free of snow we could have climbed out of the window and shinned to safety. But maybe it's just as well. While we were doing that, Signor Lombardi's house would have burned to the ground. Besides, that stuff's all right for the intrepid heroes of *Boys Own*, but it doesn't suit my aging bones."

There was a sudden rapping on the door.

"Signor Brough," said Lombardi's voice from the other side, "did I hear you calling?"

Brough looked at his nephew. Nicholas looked back. It was too much. Despite the burns on their faces and hands, which had turned to evil-looking blisters, their faces creased up with laughter.

"Signor Brough?"

"Yes, I am here, Signor Lombardi," he said, suddenly sober.

"Did you want me?"

"Yes," the detective called back. "I have some grave news for you."

"Pardon my language," said Nicholas as his uncle picked his way across to the door, "but did you see anything of the bastard who did it?"

Brough stopped.

"I saw Galen," he said without turning around.

Nicholas nodded. He registered no surprise.

"I notice you've dropped the 'Herr,'" he said.

"Yes. I wonder why."

38

Brough found it hard to imagine a man more reconciled to his destiny than Lombardi. After the first shock of seeing his best room laid waste, during which his eyes swam in tears, he was pacified with remarkable ease.

"When my dear Rosa was alive this was our bedroom," he said, nodding sadly and turning back into the passage. "It is for Rosa that I weep, not the room."

Not wishing to raise a time-consuming hue and cry, they told him the inferno had been caused by a log rolling out of the fire onto the rug. They would secretly dispose of the fireball's blackened heart later. The greatest obstacle should have been the key, which their attacker had left in the outside of the lock, but in his anxiety Lombardi did not see the strangeness of having to unlock the door and let them out.

He was thankful the catastrophe had happened while his guests were indoors, for the alternative of the fire gaining hold of an unoccupied room and spreading to the whole house terrified him. It was hardly dishonest to refrain from telling him that without their presence the fire would never have happened.

"It is good for me it happened in winter," he said with a shrug of resignation. "I should have lost much if my main chamber had been out of use in summer."

"We shall do everything to help you clear up the mess," volunteered Nicholas.

"There are a lot of rugs, cushions, articles of bedding and the like completely unharmed by the flames," said Brough. "They might be a bit wet out there in the snow but that's all."

"I have deferred renewing my furniture and decor these past ten years," said Lombardi. "It is so easy to put off those tasks which are not essential. Especially here, where Rosa's presence is still so strong for me. But now I must spend winter renewing the whole room. It will be the envy of the piazza by the spring. It will also be good for my health to do some work in the cold months instead of drinking Barbaresco and playing cards with my neighbors."

"He's too good to be true," said Nicholas later.

"Do I detect a budding cynic?" said Brough. "I disagree that Lombardi's philosophy is too good to be true. In this essentially pessimistic world he is rather, I think, too good to be believed. I am sure he is true."

After bathing and changing, they went out for dinner with Lombardi's assurance that another room would be ready for them when they returned. By now a crowd of Roganese on their way to mass had gathered beneath the scene of the drama.

"Pity they weren't around when we needed them," said Nicholas.

"Few things will induce the average Italian out of doors on Christmas Day before the tolling of the vespers bell," said Brough as they walked to the little *trattoria*. "And if Lombardi heard nothing from downstairs in the same house, which I find amazing, I doubt if anyone else heard or saw anything."

As they stepped into the light of a streetlamp, Brough heard a hollow footfall and a rustle of clothing in an alleyway to their left.

He tensed himself for action or flight, whichever proved most likely to end in survival, and silently cursed his lifelong disdain of firearms.

Another stealthy movement was heard by both of them, but outside the lamplight all was darkness.

"Another attempted murder?" whispered Nicholas. "Or will this one succeed?"

"Ssshh!" replied Brough, moving out of the light. "Just keep by me, say nothing and be ready for anything."

A dark figure was emerging from the alleyway. The two men stood in the shadow of a doorway and watched. Still in silhouette, the figure hovered by the entry and looked to right and left. He saw their outline ten yards away and began moving slowly toward them. As he passed under the lamp their suspicions were confirmed.

"Galen!" whispered Nicholas to his uncle.

The German walked toward them, his face downcast. He nodded self-consciously in greeting and his gaze did not quite connect with theirs.

"He got away," he said sheepishly. "I nearly had him but then he gave me the slip down by one of the wharves. I've been searching for the past two hours. Thank heaven you are both safe."

"And who is this man of mystery?" said Nicholas icily.

"I have no more idea now than when I came upon him hurling that fireball up into the room," said Galen.

"You deny that it was you who threw it then?" said Brough.

"*I?*" he said, goggle-eyed. "How can you think that *I . . .*" The sentence trailed away to nothing.

"Just who are we talking to at this moment," pursued Nicholas, "Rudolf van Galen or Giuseppe Aquilina?"

"I see," said Galen. "So you also know the truth about the murders."

"We know that Giuseppe was the murderer," said Nicholas. "We know therefore that you are a murderer. And we remember vividly your warning that the guilty one of us could well try to kill the others."

"It is true that Giuseppe was the guilty brother," said Galen wretchedly. "That I must therefore be the Deptford Strangler is inescapable. But I did not try to kill you tonight."

"Who else would want to do so?" asked Nicholas.

"I don't know."

"Where is the key to our room which you had this morning?" Galen searched his pockets.

"I must have lost it during the chase," he said.

Nicholas snorted with contempt.

"I am not going to try to convince you. You must believe what you will. I think I have never been in greater need of true friendship than I am at the moment, but if you cannot give that friendship I must try to cope alone."

They began to walk slowly on to the *trattoria*.

"Why are you looking so shifty?" asked Nicholas.

"Oh Nicholas," said Galen with an earnest passion he had not revealed to them before, "can't you tell the difference between a man so deeply troubled he can hardly face his friends, and one who has something to hide?"

There was no answer.

"Let me say just one thing," continued Galen. "When we did not know the truth about the brothers we were friends. We knew that one of us was a killer but there was a bond of"—he searched for the right words—"a bond of shared adversity between us. That bond still exists. That I am a killer I must accept. But I beg you to accept of me what you accepted about yourself in your dark weeks of uncertainty—that these actions have been outside my control. Even if it had been I who tried to kill you, it would not have been any evil in myself that was the cause, but the malevolent influence of my earlier incarnation."

"When we thought I was the killer I was in despair," said Nicholas. "I was on the brink of suicide. If it had not been for my uncle I should be dead now." He fixed Galen with a leaden stare. "*That's* how much I suffered."

"I know," said Galen, "and believe me I suffered too as I stood by helplessly and watched you in your torment. But would it help you now if I killed myself? Is it revenge you want?"

"No," said Nicholas weakly, waking up to the lethal game he had been playing. "No, what you say is true. I don't believe that on a conscious level you are a killer."

He looked away, past Galen to some point on the other side of the square, hesitating before delivering the sting.

"For all that, we have to protect ourselves," he said. "If your past existence is beginning to gain greater control of your mind, we are courting danger at every moment. The risk is increased a thousandfold by your ability to send out your soul. If you chose, you could kill us as you slept."

"Keep me under close observation," said Galen. "Watch my every move. But do not, I beg you, abandon me. Part of the mystery might well be solved, but there are still far more questions than answers."

They had stopped in the pool of green light shining from the lattice windows of the *trattoria*. Nicholas looked at Brough, who had remained silent throughout the exchange, for guidance, for some pearl of wisdom that would decide the next step for him.

"Let's eat," said Brough.

39

The detective was preoccupied with his own thoughts throughout the meal. His taciturn mood served to inhibit Nicholas and Galen more even than their sour confrontation in the street. Both factors undermined their sporadic attempts at conversation, and an atmosphere of unease closed around them. Not until the table had been cleared did Brough stir from his meditation.

"You made a discovery during your regression this morning," he said, addressing Galen.

"Yes. That's why I walked off and left you. I had to be alone to sort out my thoughts. My mind was reeling at the sudden twist events had taken. Until this morning all three of us thought Antonio had been the murderer. Suddenly and irreversibly I had to find the means of accepting that *I* was the killer. I have been wandering about the city all day. I went down by the river earlier and sat on the hull of a rotted old barge. I remained there for about two hours, not moving, not thinking of moving, hardly aware of the cold. Then I walked up the lower slopes of the mountains toward where the cave must be, but it was becoming so dark I turned back. I was coming along the side of the piazza on my way to the hostelry when I saw that weird figure swinging his ball of fire around his head. As soon as he let go he vanished into a passageway along the street. I stepped into the road to get a view of what he'd been aiming at, and to my horror I saw you standing at the open window with the missile soaring toward you. I rushed off after him. But as I told you, I lost him."

"It's a pity you don't have anyone to corroborate your account of your movements," said Nicholas, not unkindly. "You must admit that as far as we know, you could just as easily have been buying naphtha and constructing a fire bomb. Perhaps your walk up into the hills was earlier than you say, and that's where you picked up the boulder for weighting the weapon."

"How did you discover the truth about Giuseppe?" asked Brough.

"I failed to link up with Nicholas," said Galen. "I told you I was doubtful about the idea working in practice. Nevertheless, once unconscious I found my mind sinking slowly but unfalteringly toward the level where the fragmented memories of Giuseppe are strewn.

"I was aware, as I floated, of wild images of intervening existences—confused, distorted pictures like viewing a magic-lantern show through a glass bottle and having no time to stop and watch it unfold. I was weeping at a graveside by a shelled church. The tumult of guns, wounded men and screaming horses was all about me. There was a boy with his legs blown off, still alive and lying limply in a little grassy hollow, his head propped up on the edge of his shattered drum. I saw my dark, calloused hands as I wallowed in mud and stones, working feverishly with a team of men to shore up a bursting dam somewhere in the Low Countries. I was riding upon the shoulders of a happy, laughing man along a woodland track. The rustle of life was all around us. Squirrels, dragonflies, tattered rooks. We came out into an open meadow, my father laughing still, and at the end of the track we could see a little timber cottage. Then I was back inside the mind of Giuseppe. The vision was more clear than any I have previously experienced. There can be no doubt that the palazzotto played a vital part in the clarity of the regression.

"I was in my study at the palazzotto. Antonio was not at home.

It was December seventeenth, 1454. I know that because as the vision began I was seated at my high desk in an alcove, writing my journal. The date—*Die Jovis, 17 die Decembris 1454*—was clearly visible at the top of the page. I completed the writing, laid down my pen and rested my face in my hands. The dominant emotion was anger, but I was aware too of a deep-seated fear, and an almost fanatical determination to achieve some goal. I placed my hands on the desk in front of me and slowly raised my eyes. In a tiny plaster niche on the wall above the writing desk there was a mark in the dust in the shape of a cross. There had once been a silver crucifix hanging there. I looked at the mark and remembered the great burst of anger with which I had torn down the crucifix and cast it into the fire.

"I rose and went to the window. It was as dark as the underworld in the unlighted streets. I looked up beyond the limits of the town into the hills. Suddenly the first words of one of the psalms was in my mind, cruelly changed. *I lift up mine eyes unto the mountains, whence cometh my death.* In great bitterness I turned back to the journal and scrawled a final sentence."

"What did it say?" asked Brough.

"I don't know. I can remember every word clearly but it was in no language I have ever seen."

"What were the words?"

"*Li oippod ocoig id leuq olovaid id oibesue eved eresse otalevir* —totally meaningless."

He recited the words again, letter by letter, and Brough recorded them in his notebook.

"What happened next?" he said when he had finished.

"I rushed out of the room. I stopped outside and listened for any sounds of Antonio having returned. All was silence. I crept along to the end room—that little one where we made our entry into the house this morning. Its walls were bare. No icons, nothing. The room contained only two enormous wooden chests of silver plate.

"I closed the shutters and dragged one chest aside, revealing a panel in the floorboards about a foot long and eight or nine inches wide. I lifted it out and reached into the space underneath. My hand grasped something that felt like a pillow and I brought it out. It was a faded linen bag."

"What was in it?" asked Nicholas.

"It contained a black tight-fitting suit such as those clothing the bodies of Maria Bellini and the sister of mercy; such as the Grand Inquisitor later told the town was the uniform of the Gormini; such as the guilty of the two brothers was seen wearing by the prying townsman who followed him to the foot of the Santine Hill."

"What did you do?"

"I put it on," said Galen, "and I went out. I had a sense of terrible foreboding. But I had to go. No power on earth could alter that. I crept out of the door and into the street, hugging the shadows of the city wall as I made my way to the gleaming East Gate. I had a vague suspicion as I went that I was being observed, but the imperative nature of my task pressed me onward. I strode on across the rocky countryside outside the town, consciously fighting to overcome my fears. I began to climb the hill. The curse of the Santine Hill unsettled me, but it was by no means my main worry. A far greater anxiety filled me. Strangely, though, the sharpness of the regression had started to diminish the moment I left the house. It was now no longer sufficiently clear for me to tell what that great fear was."

He stopped and thought for several moments.

"When I was about halfway up the hill, the moon came out from behind the clouds that had hidden it all evening. For a second the landscape was bathed in its frosty light. I am certain this was the night when the townsman who reported the brothers to the Inquisition dogged Giuseppe's steps."

"What happened then?" asked Brough.

"There was a long blankness. Then I was aware of other people around me—eight of them. I recognized Lorenzo, the old astrologer Festa, and Maria Bellini. I'm sure they were all eventual victims of the strangler. It was clearly another time from the night of my walk up the hill, because by then all but one of the victims were dead. But whenever it was, we were in the cave."

"And next?" said Brough.

"Nothing. I returned against my will to consciousness. Perhaps one part of my mind had attuned itself to your anxiety about the impending return of Tommaso."

Again he fell silent. "So you see," he said at last, spreading his hands in despair, "it was Giuseppe who stole to the cave wearing the black uniform of the Gormini. There can be no doubt that he was the leader of the heretics."

Nicholas recounted to Galen his own experiences in the experiment and summarized the full conversation between the two brothers, confirming beyond all doubt that Antonio had been guiltless.

"Have you ever been to the East End of London?" asked Brough, looking up from his notebook when Nicholas had finished.

"I think not," said Galen.

"Well worth a visit," said Brough. "No place like it in the world. Its thieves are among the most likable, honest criminals it has ever been my good fortune to know."

He was drawing spiky patterns in his book.

"Cockneys are immensely proud of their culture," he continued, "and one of their greatest sources of pride is their rhyming slang. East Enders invented it, there's no doubt about that. . . ."

"What is it?" said Galen.

"Oh, it's an obscure way of speaking English. Anyone not initiated to its secrets wouldn't know what the hell it meant."

"How does it work?"

"Let me give you an example. The rhyming slang for 'suit' is 'whistle and flute,' but most cockneys have abbreviated that to 'whistle.'"

Galen looked at him in mild disbelief.

"So," continued Brough, "one cockney might say to another, 'I went up the apples wearing my new whistle and found my trouble and strife and my bath-bun having their Tommy Tucker.'"

"That would mean something?" asked Galen. Nicholas grinned.

"It would mean, 'I went upstairs wearing my new suit and found my wife and my son having their supper.'"

Galen's blank expression became blanker.

"Apples and pears—stairs; whistle and flute—suit; trouble and strife—wife; bath-bun—son; Tommy Tucker—supper," explained Brough.

"Ah," said Galen, nodding.

"But you've rather deflected me from my point," said Brough. "I was going on to say that while rhyming slang is unquestionably an invention of the cockneys, a phenomenon called backslang, to which they also lay claim, is not theirs at all. It is one of the oldest and most rudimentary forms of coded speech. Exactly how old it is no one really knows, but Giuseppe Aquilina was evidently adept at it."

"The sentence in the journal?" asked Galen.

"Exactly. It's a variation of good old 'cockney' backslang. In this case, the letters of each word are simply reversed. I doubt if it would have fooled anyone even when it was a new idea. When spoken perhaps, but not when written."

He indicated his notebook.

"I don't know much Italian, but the sixth word jumped right out at me—*olovaid*. Reverse it and it's *diavolo*. And that, I know, means devil."

"Devil," repeated Galen as visions of Giuseppe performing satanic rites with his evil Gormini confederates rose before him.

"Yes," said Brough, "the whole of it reads, *Il doppio gioco di quel diavolo di eusebio deve essere rivelato*. I'll wager that word *eusebio* should have a capital E."

"The Italian equivalent of Eusebius!" said Galen.

"Of course!" said Nicholas. "The Aryan heretic whose ideas were the basis of the Gormini's doctrines."

"What's the full translation?" asked Brough.

"I'm puzzled by this," said Galen, looking at the sentence in the notebook. "The simplest translation is, *The duplicity of that devil Eusebius must be exposed*. What does it mean? Giuseppe is supposed to have been a latter-day disciple of Eusebius. Why is he calling him a devil?"

"I think I have a good idea," said Brough thoughtfully. Then, suddenly animated, he patted Galen on the arm and said lightly, "Don't upset yourself. I've often told Nicholas there is very little in detection that's straightforward."

"You're looking pleased with yourself," said Nicholas.

"Am I?" said Brough, smiling.

He beckoned a hovering waiter, paid their bill and led the way into the street.

40

Lombardi, who with the help of a band of neighbors had restored a semblance of order to the gutted room, showed his three guests into a smaller chamber on the second floor.

They were all exhausted by the day's harrowing events, and Nicholas and Galen decided to retire immediately. But Brough, despite physical weariness, was mentally wide awake and hungry for more knowledge of the case. He decided to sit up and read through Nicholas' box of research notes.

His nephew's arrangement of his notes was erratic and untidy, unlike the methodical work of Galen. Instead of a single fat book of systematic notes, there were bundles of papers carelessly clipped or tied together. It took Brough more than half an hour to sift the vital material from the rubbish. For another hour he read on by the light of a candle and a cautiously stacked log fire, chiefly re-examining points he had already fully discussed with Nicholas. Then he came upon a typed transcript of the account of Duke Lorenzo's life, written by the Grand Inquisitor who had sentenced the two brothers to death. Why had he written the life? According to Nicholas' research he was not even a native of Rogano. There were city states all over northern Italy and Rogano had been among the least important. Was it purely anti-Gormini propaganda? If so, what was the point? After the execution of the brothers there was no further activity by the Gormini. Anywhere. If they had been destroyed, why take the trouble to villify them in print?

In print.

Why, further, did the Grand Inquisitor omit all reference to Lorenzo's strange withdrawal from society, his refusal to have his son baptized? If Lorenzo had been "got at" by the heretics, why did the Grand Inquisitor not say so? It would have been more ammunition to fire at the heretics. *The heretics who no longer existed.*

Brough turned to the notes written by Galen, who had delved more thoroughly into the life of the Grand Inquisitor. About a third of the way through the book he found a list of personal data:

Vincenzo Palestrina: Born 1393, Rome. Took Holy Orders 1418. Appointed Bishop of Coranta in Sicily 1426 by Pope Martin V. In 1431, as an emissary of the Vatican, he was instrumental in bringing about the execution of Joan of Arc. His appointment at Coranta was a sinecure and from about 1432 onward he was fully occupied as a driving force of the Inquisition, searching out heretics and destroying them by whatever method he could devise. He established a complex and amazingly efficient spy network all over continental Europe, which he called, euphemistically, the Holy Order of St. Jerome. By means of this sophisticated organization, he was able to root out opposition to the Church almost as soon as it erupted. He was perfectly ruthless, as his destruction of both brothers Aquilina testifies. Nevertheless he was a brilliant planner and an expert judge of public opinion, which even a powerful figure such as he could not afford to ignore. With a mixture of cruelty, deadly cunning and a regard for popular taste, he kept not only the peasants but also the wealthy classes almost completely under the control of the Church. A schemer of the first water, but one who believed totally in the ultimate good of his actions.

A formidable opponent, thought Brough. He put down the book and allowed his mind to wander over the multitude of unanswered questions about the Rogano murders which, in their anxiety to find out about the two brothers, Nicholas and Galen had rather neglected.

How had the strangler gained access to Lorenzo's palace on the night he was killed? How was it that his fifth victim, the girl Maria Bellini, had disappeared from her bed when there had been no noise, and no signs either of a struggle or of any doors or windows having been forced? Even more baffling, how had the abduction of Sister Ruffo been achieved from the impregnable abbey? The words of Nicholas on that first night at the Beggar's echoed in his mind: "No one heard or saw anything and all the doors of the place were bolted on the inside. No one could explain how the kidnaper or kidnapers had scaled the wall of the abbey, for the drawbridge, which was its sole link with the world beneath, had been raised hours before, and would have been heard had it been lowered. The mother abbess was emphatic that nothing had happened to raise anyone's suspicions."

And what, finally, was the "infernal machine" the Inquisition guards had discovered in the cave?

Brough smiled grimly. Nostradamus knew the answer, but his quatrains were almost as cryptic as the riddle itself.

Before that bloody train had damn near killed him *he* had known the answer too. Or at least he'd known three quarters of it. The hypothesis he had constructed on the night before Peterson tried to kill him had fitted every point so exactly it had to be the right one. It answered every single question he had just raised. But the shock of that fall in front of the train had been far more serious than he had imagined. That, combined with his meeting with Meg Brandon and his discovery about the photographs of the murder sites, had led him badly astray. The trouble was, from the beginning he had been emotionally involved. And emotion played havoc with your reasoning powers. After that it was Nicholas' near suicide, a cold and exhausting journey across Europe, Tommaso, the experiment, Galen's disappearance, the fire . . . small wonder he'd been confused. But now, with the new discoveries about Antonio and Giuseppe, he was beginning to think clearly again. There was still a long way to go, but he knew he was on the right road.

He clambered into bed and fell asleep.

41

At about two o'clock in the morning Nicholas stirred briefly and turned over.

As he did so, he was surprised to glimpse Galen, fully dressed, standing by the door with his back toward him. Pretending to be asleep, Nicholas waited tremulously for any sounds that would tell him what mischief the German was planning. None came. After a full minute he could tolerate the tension no more, and he decided on action even if it put him in danger. Yawning realistically, he stretched and opened his eyes. Galen had gone.

He looked across to his right at the slumbering form of his uncle, uncertain whether to wake him. He sat up in bed to contemplate the problem, and as he did so he sensed a presence to his left. In defiance of the warnings being fired at him by his subconscious, he turned his face slowly toward Galen's bed. The German was under the covers sleeping soundly, his hat and coat on a hook near the door.

Nicholas whispered his name, but there was no response. Galen did not seem to be breathing.

Possessed suddenly by an absurd idea, Nicholas climbed cautiously out of bed and tiptoed to the window.

There was no moon but the streetlamps were alight and most of the piazza, at ground level at least, was clearly visible. He scanned the square from one extremity to the other. Almost at once he saw a man walking under an archway on the south side, tall and bowler-hatted.

It was unmistakably the figure of Galen.

42

Before breakfast Brough found a post office and put through a call to the abbey. The telephone was answered by a gruff female who was unable, or perhaps refused, to understand English. In his best phrase-book Italian the detective asked for the mother abbess. After a wait of several minutes he was connected to the office of the reverend mother. She sounded much younger than he had anticipated, and mercifully she spoke English.

Brough explained that he and two friends were re-examining the frightful case of the Rogano murders of 1454 and after exhaustive research they had concluded that vital evidence lay in the abbey.

"My dear man," said the reverend mother without a trace of an accent, "I am fascinated by murder. Do come and see me and have a look around whenever you like."

He suggested the following morning at ten o'clock and she agreed immediately.

"Pardon my asking, Reverend Mother, but have you ever lived in Britain? You speak such perfect English."

"My mother was a Scot," she replied.

I don't believe it, he thought. Then aloud, he said, "So too is another of the people we have met in Rogano—Signor Tommaso at the museum."

"The same mother," she said. "Tommaso is my brother."

Coincidence after coincidence, he reflected as he hung up the receiver a few minutes later. The problem was, which coincidences were relevant and which were just . . . coincidental?

On their way to search for the cave later in the morning, Brough, Nicholas and Galen passed the site of the old cathedral. It was surrounded by high, spiked railings. To their surprise on this bleak Boxing Day morning they found the big wrought-iron gates were open. At the edge of the ruins, two men, their outlines uncertain in the mist, were engaged in earnest discussion. They ventured inside the gate.

All signs of the hospital that had been built on the site had vanished. The foundations of the cathedral had been painstakingly cleared and the crypt exposed. A low wall had been built around the perimeter of the site to prevent visitors toppling to the floor of the crypt fifteen feet below. They had reached the wall and were gazing at the crumbling sepulchers and the huge pillars that had once supported the vaulted ceiling of the crypt before the taller of the two men noticed their presence.

"We are closed today!" he called to them in Italian. Brough spoke a few words to Galen, who approached the two officials.

"We are representatives of the British Museum in London," he said, reviving the story that Brough had told Tommaso. "We are not long in Rogano and would value the chance of viewing the crypt."

His explanation brought a change to the stony faces of the officials. The taller man even smiled and shook the hand of each of them in turn.

"My name is Francesco Matteotti," he said. "I am the superintendent of the Rogano museums and overseer of our historical sites. This is my assistant, Gianni Mangora."

The shorter man nodded.

"Gianni is a wonderful linguist," continued Signor Matteotti. "He deals with all my correspondence with museums abroad."

"Our main task is the preparation of a report on the private museums of northern Italy," said Galen, "but naturally we have an interest in all historical sites."

"Of course," said the superintendent. "And of course you must see ours. You are lucky to find us here today. We had a report this morning that someone was seen walking around in the grounds of the cathedral during the night. How that could be we don't know —there is no sign of anyone having climbed over the gates or the railings. But now that matters little. It is fortunate we were called here for we have discovered an area of subsidence. A gang of workmen are on their way here now to shore it up."

"Where is the entrance to the dungeons?" asked Galen.

"Dungeons?" asked the superintendent. "There are none."

"There most certainly are," said Galen, "directly beneath the crypt."

"But that's impossible. We would know about them. The entrance would have been unearthed when the site was excavated."

"Ask Signor Matteotti if we might call back tomorrow afternoon," Brough said to Galen. "If we don't set out for the cave soon it will be too late."

The superintendent said that he would be pleased to see them at the site at half-past two the following day.

Galen, who had accompanied Giuseppe part of the way to the cave in his most recent regression, led them out of the town by the same route. He stopped at the point where the clarity of his vision had faded beyond the level of recognition. But by now the Santine Hill was in sight. They walked toward it in silence.

A quarter of a mile outside the ancient walls of Rogano, at the foot of the hill, they came upon the bed of a dried-up mountain stream. Diligent peasants of a world long departed had turned the useless gulley into an easily negotiated pathway by paving it with large flat stones. The pathway wound upward between steep banks and around humpy knolls. Where its course became too steep to climb in comfort, at a place that had once been a waterfall, the forgotten laborers had hewn a rough stairway.

"This makes life a bit easier than if we had to climb the bare hillside," said Brough as they straggled up the slope.

"Why did they go to such trouble?" asked Galen, who at Nicholas' request walked ahead of the others.

"Probably for the benefit of shepherds," said Nicholas. "There aren't many now, but at one time these foothills were teeming with sheep and goats."

Although spared having to clamber up the hill on all fours, they still had to cope with snow and ice, which in places badly hindered their progress.

Two hours after leaving the city behind, they reached a point where the river path intersected a track that encircled the hill. They stood on the track and surveyed the valley spreading out beneath them. Arretto and Bellanone towered passive and eternal behind them. The Santine Hill, dotted with isolated clumps of woodland, looked like an odd-shaped human head ravaged by alopecia. The Pergino wandered along the valley bottom to a glistening Rogano. High on the opposite side of the valley stood the Abbey of Alba d'Amprizzio, its turrets and round towers gleaming white against a livid sky. A solitary camion pottered along the road between Rogano and the abbey, and on a path between two vineyards a donkey struggled upward under the weight of a woman, her spade thrown over her shoulder like a musket.

"This is the path I trod in my dream," said Nicholas, "the dream I had after knocking myself unconscious outside Potts's house. I know it wasn't a proper regression—more a blend of all the events at Rogano interwoven with my own personal nightmare of the Man with Odd Eyes. But the landscape was exactly the same as this. I'm certain this is the path taken by the woodman who found the body of the final victim. Hold on."

He motioned Brough and Galen to remain at the crossing of the two tracks and began to walk along the horizontal path, superimposing the memory of the dream landscape upon the real one. He stopped and looked about him, a faraway expression in his eyes.

"This is the *lower* path, which the woodman used to traverse each day," he called to his companions, "but that night he walked into a patch of mist and climbed higher up the hill. Follow me."

About thirty yards above the track the river path ran off in the wrong direction, so Brough and Galen abandoned it at the intersection and trudged after Nicholas. Eighty feet farther up the hill they came upon another flat section about fifteen feet wide, which ran around the hill parallel to the track below. It was overgrown with nettles and wild blueberry thickets.

"This is the site of the upper path, I'm sure of it," said Nicholas, looking down and picturing the old woodman climbing up out of the mist.

"It is becoming familiar again," said Galen. "For a while back there it meant nothing to me, but now I have an overwhelming feeling that I have been here before."

"In one of your regressions do you mean?" said Nicholas.

"No. Nor in a dream or any sort of experience in my present life. The hill casts the same sort of hypnotic spell that the palazzotto did."

"Which way do you think?" asked Nicholas.

"Along here to our right," said Galen, striving to concentrate his entire mind on an elusive memory four hundred years old, "and then up again somewhere near that stricken tree."

"Yes, that's what I thought," said Nicholas.

The ancient path was so densely overgrown that it was easier to skirt it and hike along the sloping ground above. At the dead cypress tree they stopped again.

"'Climbing the hill in the hope of rising above the mist, he went into a clump of trees which he had never before explored,'" said Brough, recalling Nicholas' description of the woodman's route.

"That must be the clump of trees," said Nicholas, pointing to a ragged spinney clinging to a part of the hill which until now had been hidden from view. They walked into the trees.

"'He had not taken many steps into the gloomy wood when he stumbled across a dark object on what turned out to be an overgrown track, long disused, that ran around the hill parallel to the path he normally used,'" said Brough.

"This is it then," said Nicholas. "The spot where the final victim was discovered."

"It doesn't seem at all familiar to me," said Galen.

"Nor me."

"From what you said, Nicholas, the cave was near the crest of the hill directly above this spot," said Brough.

He pushed onward into the trees and continued the upward climb, the others following.

"There *is* an odd sort of feeling about this place," he said, pausing for breath about halfway to the top.

"Yes," said Nicholas, "there is a tangible sense of evil all about us, even in daylight."

"I wouldn't put it that strongly," said Galen, "but there is certainly something. Perhaps it is this quality, somehow exuded by the earth hereabouts, that earned the hill the reputation of being haunted."

"Or perhaps it really is haunted," said Nicholas. "I wouldn't want to spend the night here."

The hill spread out in a broad plateau at the top. On the other side, it sloped gently down for about a hundred feet before rising steeply toward the two great mountains.

It took them more than an hour to find the cave. When at last they came upon it they could hardly believe they had already crossed and recrossed the spot a dozen times without observing it.

The mouth of the cave was a short climb down on the far side of the hill. Partially hidden by the undergrowth, it was located in a stretch of hillside that fell almost sheerly, like a cliff face inset on the sloping hill, capped by a boulder-strewn shelf thirty feet beneath the plateau.

It was smaller than Nicholas had imagined, but exactly as Galen had pictured it: a gaping hole, roughly circular and eight feet in diameter. It narrowed gently and about six feet from the entrance a boulder as high as a man barred farther passage.

" 'And the cave will be sealed up that no man may look upon the place of the antichrists,' " said Nicholas.

"Seal it they did," said Brough, "very effectively."

"I doubt if anyone who has ventured up here in the past four hundred years has realized there's anything beyond the boulder," said Galen.

"At least we've found it," said Brough, "but we're going to need a couple of horses to shift that. Can we hire them, do you think?"

"I'm sure Lombardi will know someone," said Nicholas.

"Yes. A local tradesman might be happy to make a few lira on the side if business is a bit slack after Christmas."

Before leaving they searched the floor at the entrance to the cave, but found nothing.

"If we can organize the horses for tomorrow we can perhaps rearrange our visit to the abbey for Sunday or Monday," said Brough.

"Monday's a better bet," said Nicholas. "I doubt if they'll want to know on the Sabbath."

"Sunday," said Galen. "December twenty-eighth."

"The date of the seventh Rogano murder," said Brough.

"Mercurio Ferruccio," said Nicholas. "Aged forty-two, bachelor. An apothecary. Found strangled near the East Gate of the town."

"At least whatever poor wretch fate had singled out to die at the hands of the Deptford Strangler is now safe," said Galen, staring at his own hands with a mixture of disbelief and disgust. "And the reincarnations of Ferruccio and Sister Ruffo, whoever they are, will never suspect how closely the shadow of death passed over them."

It was already twilight as they left the cave and climbed toward the plateau. The easiest route to the top was a circuitous one, and with nightfall imminent they considered taking the shortest way—straight up the cliff face to the shelf and then a fairly gentle climb to the plateau.

"There are plenty of footholds," said Brough. "Let's be daring and take the quick way."

They were halfway up to the rock shelf when it happened.

Their objective from the moment they had set foot on the cliff face had been a large round boulder on the edge of the shelf, which would provide a handhold when they reached the top. Suddenly it began to move. They all saw it at the same moment, and they all knew it could be no accident. The boulder must have been lying there for hundreds if not thousands of years. There was no sign of any sort of earth tremor which could explain its steady forward movement: someone was deliberately heaving it toward the edge. Though they appreciated in a moment the deadly gravity of their position, there was little they could do except try to climb out of the path of the rock, which was now teetering on the very brink of its downward plunge. Their would-be murderer was still hidden by the bulk of the rock, though Nicholas fancied he could hear him grunting under the strain of his task. In another second the assassin, with a final effort, heaved his burden over the edge of the plateau. The three companions, clinging like petrified sea birds to the cliff face, watched paralyzed as a quarter of a ton of granite plunged toward them. The killer was now visible. He stood looking down on them with dull, soulless eyes.

"Hutchinson!" exclaimed Nicholas in astonishment.

The face of Gilbert Hutchinson disappeared from view as the rock crashed downward. A yard or so above their heads it struck a knotty root and bounced slightly away from the cliff face. The collision saved them from being smashed like snails—and Nicholas and Galen, who had scrambled in opposite directions, escaped without a bruise.

Brough pressed himself into the face of the cliff, but the edge of the rock struck his head and sent him toppling backward down the slope. He hit the ground at the mouth of the cave with a hollow thud. Nicholas and Galen looked down. The old detective lay motionless on his back, his right arm bent unnaturally under him. They looked up to the shelf. The villain had gone.

In seconds they were at Brough's side. His head was bleeding profusely.

"Is he all right?" asked Galen.

Nicholas frantically tore open his uncle's clothing and listened for his heartbeat.

"I think he's dead," he said.

43

Nicholas took off his overcoat and covered his uncle.

"I'll stay here," he said to Galen. "You go down to Rogano and fetch help." The German hurried off.

Nicholas considered shifting his uncle into the cave. He had at last detected a sign of life. The heart, stilled between beats for about half a minute by the shock of the fall, was again beating, and he was breathing shallowly. He would certainly be more protected in the cave, and exposure to the elements was one of the worst hazards in a situation like this. But if he had broken any bones, and it seemed likely, moving him could do untold damage —might even be fatal. He decided to leave him where he was, keep him as well covered as possible and to light a fire nearby.

He gathered dry twigs and leaves that had found their way into the entrance of the cave. The only paper they had was Brough's notebook. He tore out the blank pages and crumpled them separately. Clearing a place in the snow, he made a neat pyramid of the kindling and searched Brough's pockets for his matches.

Only when he had finished and the fire was alight did he realize how cold he was, and how arctic the night was becoming. He marched up and down inside the entrance to the cave and saw the first flakes of a new snowfall drift down into the flickering light of the fire.

Yesterday fighting fire with snow, today fighting snow with fire.

He began to dwell upon the memory of the man who had tried to kill them, and upon horrible imaginings of the malevolent specter of the Santine Hill.

Why should a traveler called Gilbert Hutchinson make two attempts on their lives? And having twice failed, how likely was he to try again?

All things considered, he concluded that he stood in greater danger of being sought out by the traveler than by the phantom.

He prayed that Galen would arrive with help before Hutchinson reappeared.

44

Even the police captain to whom Galen reported the attempted murder was reluctant to venture up the Santine Hill in the dark.

"Look," rasped Galen in Italian, "there is a man seriously injured up in those hills and if he is not brought down soon he will die. Are you going to allow that to happen because you are afraid of ghosts?"

His vehemence seemed to work. Within ten minutes a band of four *carabinieri* carrying lanterns, blankets and a stretcher—the captain himself at their head—were climbing into two police coaches like the one driven by Tommaso's brother-in-law.

Their first stop was the infirmary, where the captain, a man called Fabriano, enlisted a doctor. Almost before the doctor had taken his seat in the second carriage the convoy was surging forward on the snow-covered road to the East Gate. They drove on across country until Galen pointed out the spot where they must abandon the vehicles and continue on foot. Each of the five policemen carried a lantern to light the way. Even though Galen was by now familiar with the route, it took them more than two hours to reach the cave.

"Not before time," said Nicholas in a hoarse whisper. "I'm damn near frozen to death."

While three of the *carabinieri* scoured the hillside for signs of the would-be murderer, the others lifted Brough onto the stretcher. Nicholas took back his coat while his uncle was festooned in blankets.

After an onerous journey down the hillside lasting nearly three hours, the stretcher was stowed aboard a horse-drawn ambulance which, on the instructions of the doctor, had followed the tracks of the police vehicles.

By half an hour before midnight Brough, still unconscious but breathing steadily, was tucked up in bed in the infirmary.

"There is nothing you can do tonight," the doctor said, looking at the miserable figures of Nicholas and Galen. "Call here tomorrow morning."

Without a word they tramped back to the pensione.

45

"Who is this murderous Hutchinson customer? How in hell does he think he will benefit by our deaths?" asked Nicholas as he lay fully clothed on his bed. Galen secured the bolts on the door.

"Aren't you going to undress?"

"I don't have the energy."

There was a long pause as Galen removed his day clothes, folded them in a neat pile on a chair by his bed and donned a nightshirt.

"I can't begin to guess at his motive," he said, responding at length to Nicholas' question. "But it was certainly he who tried to kill you and your uncle with the fire bomb. I saw his face clearly both then and when he heaved the boulder over on top of us."

"Oh, it was him all right. I was no more than a yard from the cuss when he was hanging around outside the pensione on Christmas morning."

Both men lay in their beds ruminating for more than five minutes.

"Your soul . . . it . . . it happened again last night," said Nicholas. Although he trusted Galen in his normal state, he hesitated to confront him now lest Giuseppe had taken over his being. There was no way of knowing when the transition might take place. He certainly expected a crisis on the twenty-eighth.

Galen looked startled.

"You know?" he said.

"I saw it."

"I was trying to trace Hutchinson," said Galen. "My body was tired and I had to sleep, but it struck me as foolhardy to let up on the quest. While my body refreshed itself in sleep, my soul was able to scour Rogano."

"Any luck?" said Nicholas dubiously.

"Er . . . no. There was no sign of him."

Another prolonged silence.

"The figure behind the cathedral railings," said Nicholas, "was it you?"

"Yes. It was I. At least there I achieved something."

Nicholas threw him a questioning glance, but he had already turned on his side and closed his eyes.

46

"Signor Brough has the saints on his side," said the paunchy senior physician when Nicholas and Galen returned to the infirmary early the next morning. "We at first feared that his skull was fractured but it turns out that he is no more than severely concussed."

"Is he conscious?"

"No. He stirred during the night but not for very long."

"What about his other injuries?"

"It is difficult to assess his exact condition until he is fully awake, but we are reasonably sure no bones are broken. He will be uncomfortable, though. He will be uncomfortable for a long time."

"May we see him?"

"I think it would be better if you came back after lunch. He could be conscious by then."

Captain Fabriano had seen no reason to trouble Nicholas and Galen after their ordeal the night before, but in order to clarify the danger in which they found themselves, he had asked them to call in at his office early in the morning. So when they walked out of the depressing brown-painted passages of the infirmary into the alabaster whiteness of the Via Calabria, it was toward the police office that they turned their steps.

"My men have been out all night searching hotels, pensioni and hostelries for your mysterious Signor Hutchinson," said the captain, who had the face of a Dobermann pinscher, "but Rogano is a large town. There is no sign of him."

He spoke in Italian and Galen translated for Nicholas, who

could cope with the written language but was lost when it came to conversation.

"Yesterday evening was his second attempt to kill us," said Nicholas. "On Christmas afternoon he hurled a fire bomb through our window."

"You saw him?"

"I did," said Galen. "Signor Calvin and Signor Brough were inside the room at Lombardi's house. I was coming along the street. I looked up just as this madman let go of his missile. I gave chase but he eluded me. There is no doubt that the fire bomber and the man at the top of the cliff were one and the same."

"Did you receive any threats or warnings before the attacks began?"

"None."

"I see," said the captain, low and grave. He fell silent and contemplated his predicament.

"When troubles come," he said at last, "they come not single spies but in battalions."

Galen, perplexed, translated the comment.

"*Hamlet*," explained Nicholas. "I wish I could quote Dante like that."

"You have other troubles?" Galen asked the captain.

"Crime is generally not a problem in Rogano," the captain said. "The last robbery we had was four years ago. The last murder was in 1827, and that was a domestic affair. But now, in the space of two days, we have two big cases on our hands."

"What's the other one?" asked Galen.

"As well as searching for the man who is trying to kill you, we are trying to solve a mystery concerning the town's largest private museum."

"Oh?"

"Yes. The caretaker of the museum, a Signor Tommaso, discovered a ladder propped against an upper window of the museum late on Christmas Day. It is clear that someone was planning to break into the building, but they must have been disturbed by a passer-by at the last moment. But they will try again. Mark my words, signori, they will try again. And when they do, we shall be ready for them."

Galen could barely suppress a smile.

Fabriano questioned them on Hutchinson's appearance and asked which direction he had taken from the Piazza del Fiore on the morning Nicholas had met him. He promised to keep in close contact with them and asked them not to leave Rogano without first reporting to him.

On their way back to the hostelry they stopped off at the post office to telephone the abbey. The mother abbess was most concerned about Brough, and assured them that she was in no way inconvenienced.

"Do let me know how Mr. Brough goes on," she said, "and as soon as you want to make new arrangements to visit us you only have to telephone again."

Lombardi thought he knew just the man to help them in their quest for two strong horses, and Galen went off with him to see about hiring the beasts, while Nicholas remained at the pensione and composed a letter.

When he had finished he read it through:

Rogano, December 27th

My Beautiful Meg,

This is the very first moment I have had to write to you since we arrived here. Unfortunately you won't receive this in time for your birthday on the 30th, but news such as this is most definitely better late than never.

Meg, I am innocent. We have proven it beyond doubt. Sadly, that has to mean that Galen is the Deptford Strangler, and the realization of that fact has quite stunned him. But at least by remaining abroad he can ensure that no further murders occur. Another would have been due tomorrow, and the final victim would have been found two days later. London can rest secure at last. What we don't know is whether it will ever be safe for Galen to return to London. Apart from him, and this too seems inexplicable, all the Rogano people reincarnated today have lived in England. If he steers clear of England, the malevolent influence of Giuseppe can do little to affect him. It may be that when the dates of the murders are passed he will be safe to return, but that is a gamble I wouldn't care to take.

I know what he has done is appalling, horrible. But he, Galen, is not responsible. It would be immoral for us to turn him over to the authorities. Hanging him would be criminal. He is basically, I am sure, a good man. That he is the reincarnation of a man who was a mass murderer and a heretic is hardly any fault of his present self.

There is still a legion of questions that must be answered before Uncle and I return home, but the one which troubles me most of all arises from Jessica's dreams. Do you remember she told you that as Maria Bellini she had dreamed of being involved with Duke Lorenzo and seven of his friends in some dark secret to do with the cave? Nostradamus also spoke about the group in his forty-fourth quatrain. In Galen's most recent regression he too was in the cave with eight people.

How, I keep asking myself, could one man alone compel eight other people to take part in devilish ceremonies? How could he force them to go to the cave in the first place? What power could he have had over them? There was a lot of talk about Giuseppe's "confederates," but where were they? Once the brothers were executed, nothing further was heard of the Gormini.

One can answer only so many questions with speculation. Until we conduct further research there are some riddles which guesswork can never solve. What, for instance, was the dark secret of the group? Was it, as I suggested when we were in London, the identity of the leader of the heretics? Did they know of Giuseppe's secret life with the Gormini? Was that why they were rounded up and murdered? I find it hard to believe. It doesn't ring true. If that were the case, why was Lorenzo murdered in his bed and not at the cave? And how was it, unless all the heretics lived in Rogano, that they risked their lives entering the town to kill six of the remaining seven victims, when they could easily have disposed of them in the cave? Only Sister Ruffo was found murdered outside Rogano.

No, my suggestion as to the nature of the secret does not really hold water. But as yet none of us has come up with a better idea.

Tomorrow we go to the cave. God knows if that will bring us any nearer a solution.

I love you, Meg, more than I would have thought possible. I shall write again soon. With luck I shall be home before too long.

Nicholas

He refrained from mentioning Brough's incapacity. That would mean telling Meg about the attempts on their lives, and he had no wish to alarm her. Positive news was what counted at this stage.

Galen returned shortly before lunchtime, having concluded a deal with Lombardi's crony. The horses would be delivered the following morning at nine o'clock.

They joined Lombardi for a light snack downstairs and left the pensione in good time to meet Superintendent Matteotti at the ruins of the cathedral at half-past two.

"We've found the dungeons!" he bellowed triumphantly when he caught sight of them entering the big gates. "Holy Maria, how did you know they were here?"

"We have an original plan of the cathedral in London," said Galen, surpassing Brough in his confident delivery of untruths.

"I would love to see it," said Signor Matteotti, leading them down a wooden ladder into the crypt and across to a spot in the southwestern corner of the site.

"The subsidence revealed it all," he said. He pointed down through an enormous rent in the stone floor. Beneath the crack a flight of narrow worn steps curved away into a darkness underneath the floor of the crypt. There were sounds of movement beneath.

"I have my workmen down there still," he said. "Come, follow me."

Grasping a lantern that hung on a post by the top of the newly discovered steps, Signor Matteotti scuttled down into the hole. The steps curved around on themselves at the bottom and, disappearing into the darkness, continued down for another ten feet. The whole of the dungeon cellar was built of ancient brick and extended over almost as large an area as the crypt. There were five dungeons, each with its iron-faced door, its manacles and its stench of damnation. There was, too, a torture chamber, an arsenal of torture implements rusting away on wall hooks and on a low bench. The whole place was dank and insect-ridden, fungus proliferating where nearly a century of rainwater had run down through the cracks from the exposed crypt above.

"Was there only a stone concealing this entire network?" asked Nicholas.

"Yes," said Matteotti, "the subsidence moved the stone, somehow cracking it in two, and here we are. It must have been placed over the entrance after the fire of 1781."

"Why?"

"In 1781 the Inquisition was still wielding a lot of power in Europe," said Galen. "But its strength was declining and it was relying more on the good will of the people. It would have been most unfortunate if it had become public knowledge that the Inquisition had its own dungeons and torture chambers beneath cathedral crypts."

"This was where Giuseppe and Antonio must have been tortured nearly to death," whispered Nicholas when Superintendent Matteotti walked on a few paces to shout an order at some workmen.

"Yes," breathed Galen, "I can feel the oppressive atmosphere that enclosed us when we were strapped to the racks—good God, the racks are still here!"

He was pointing into the shadows beyond the bench of torturer's implements.

"We must come back here tonight," continued Galen. "There can be no knowing what valuable memories of our past lives will come to us in this of all places."

Nicholas nodded. "How does a disembodied soul, physical or not, cause the floor of a building to subside?" he asked.

Galen did not reply.

"Signor Matteotti," he called. "Signor Matteotti, might we speak with you a moment?"

Matteotti returned from his conference with his underlings.

"I am sorry," he said, "it is very easy to become engrossed with such a major discovery. . . ."

"Signor Matteotti, my colleague and I should like to return here tonight to make some notes on the dungeons, and also some drawings. We would have preferred to stay here now, but alas our time is all spoken for. Besides, as it is totally dark down here without lanterns it matters little whether we are here in the day or at night."

The superintendent, flushing with pride at the thought that his name might go down in a British Museum report—even perhaps in some learned journal in an account of the finding of the dungeons—agreed to lend them the key to the site if they called on him at his home in Il Prato that evening.

"I must of course ask you to deliver the key back to me in time to open the gates in the morning," he added, imaginary headlines like "The Matteotti Discovery" shimmering in front of his eyes.

.

47

Brough had been awake for about an hour when Nicholas and Galen returned to his little cell-like room at the infirmary. In that time he had helped the doctor confirm finally that he had broken no bones and he had eaten a pot of sickly milk pudding.

"I'm badly bruised and my limbs ache as if I'd gone the distance with Jem Belcher," said Brough. "But these good people say I should be out of here by Tuesday."

The younger men gave him a quick summary of the arrangements they had concluded concerning the abbey, the examination of the cathedral ruins and the exploration of the cave.

"We've lived night and day for weeks with the prospect of entering that cave. Now it's at hand it's rather intimidating," said Nicholas.

"As I shall not be there to test my own reasoning, I shall have to be more forthcoming than I have been to date," said Brough weakly.

He looked up at them for a moment before continuing.

"I have a theory," he said, "which relies heavily on there being the remains of a printing press in the cave."

"That's impossible," said Galen. "There were no printing presses outside Germany when the cave was sealed up."

"What about the Grand Inquisitor's life of Lorenzo?"

"No copy of that has yet been traced. References to it could be the result of a clerical error. I do not believe it ever existed."

"I have seen a copy!" said Nicholas.

"Let me say this," said Brough. "If I am right I have the framework of an explanation for the Rogano murders. The details will still need to be filled in, but half the battle will be won. I do not wish to raise false hopes, so until we have more information I think it best if I say nothing further and continue to mull over the problems in my own muddling way."

"Come on, Uncle. Any ideas you've come up with in this convoluted case can't be more than guesswork. There have been no clues."

"The case has been riddled with clues from the first," said Brough. "Not only that, we've had the advantage of Nostradamus' words on the subject. Pass me my notebook, will you?"

Nicholas picked up the notebook from the bedside cabinet and handed it to his uncle. Taking a fountain pen from his pyjama pocket, Brough wrote thirty-five words, tore out the page and folded it.

Handing the paper to Galen, he said, "If you find a printing press or the remains of one in the cave, read this. If not, destroy it without reading it."

As Galen, intrigued, secreted the paper in his breast pocket, Brough looked again at his notebook and turned rapidly through the pages.

He spread the vital quatrains of Nostradamus' Century Seven before them once again:

43 *A puzzle. And a struggle over crimes long dead. The strangling hands of Rogano kill again and London walks in fear. C. knows not himself and the terror of the night haunts him.*

44 *Beware the son of Peter. Lorenzo and his confederates meet him and they die. Their design is ill advised. One of the children of Peter is true and one is false.*

45 *The son of Peter reappears and kills again. He must be destroyed or great misery will follow. The great untruth of Eusebius must be preserved. It will die a natural death.*

46 *The pious lady knows but cannot tell. The citadel holds their secret. Behind the altar the true son of Peter is concealed. HE MUST BE DESTROYED OR GREAT MISERY WILL FOLLOW.*

"What do you notice?" asked Brough when he had given his companions ample time to redigest the quatrains.

"How do you mean?" said Nicholas.

"There is a crucial point we have so far not discussed."

"What is it?" asked Galen.

Brough picked up the notebook and read.

"Quatrain forty-five," he said. "The son of Peter reappears and kills again. He must be destroyed or great misery will follow. . . ."

"We *have* already discussed that," said Galen in a sudden passion. "Do you think I don't know that he who predicted so much with perfect accuracy also foresaw *my* destruction?"

"You are still missing the crucial point I mentioned," said Brough. "Would you like to read my quatrain forty-six?"

Galen read, "The pious lady knows but cannot tell. The citadel holds their secret. Behind the altar the true son of Peter is concealed." He broke off. "The last line is in capital letters. HE MUST BE DESTROYED OR GREAT MISERY WILL FOLLOW."

"Well?" said Brough.

"Well what?"

"When we first read that quatrain we were so absorbed interpreting 'the pious lady' as the mother abbess and 'the citadel' as the abbey that we missed entirely the importance of one four-letter word."

"Which word?"

"'*True.*'"

Galen looked at him blankly.

"Behind the altar the *true* son of Peter is concealed," said Brough. "*He* must be destroyed or great misery will follow. There can be no other meaning. The juxtaposition of the two sentences means undeniably that it is the *true* son of Peter who must be destroyed."

"That's right," exclaimed Nicholas and Galen together.

"But why?" said Nicholas soberly after a few seconds. "Why should the true son of Peter be destroyed?"

"Read quatrain forty-five carefully and you'll see that it is the true son of Peter, not the false, who is the killer," said Brough.

"What are you saying?" said Galen.

"Come back tomorrow and tell me if I'm right about the printing press," said Brough.

At Nicholas and Galen's request, Captain Fabriano placed a guard on Brough's door to ensure his safety should the murderous Hutchinson decide to attend to his unfinished work. But beyond granting the younger men permission to sleep in the cell at the police office, he could offer them no positive protection. Reluctantly they declined his invitation, explaining truthfully that they had a great deal to do, and returned to the pensione.

"If we insist on going out tonight," said Nicholas, looking down into the dark piazza, "we might get as far as the ruins but I doubt if we'll return—ever."

He turned back into the room.

"Hutchinson is down there," he told Galen. "He just stepped back into the shadows."

"Then we must stay here," said the German. "God knows, two of us should be able to deal with one, but I'd hate to think what weapons he has. Whatever you do, don't open the window."

"Pity Lombardi doesn't have a telephone," said Nicholas, watching a lonely lamplighter making his round of the main streets. "One call to the captain and our worries would be finished. He could fill the square with men before friend Hutchinson knew what was happening."

"Why should a complete stranger want us dead?" said Galen.

"The victims of the Deptford Strangler might have asked you the same question."

Galen opened his mouth to speak, but decided otherwise.

"I'm sorry," said Nicholas hastily, "that was unforgivable. I wasn't meaning to be unkind. It just struck me as the same sort of mindless destruction."

"Whatever the reason, it seems certain that this man does want us dead," said Galen. "We must pay Lombardi's horseman handsomely to stick with us tomorrow. I don't fancy a second encounter with Mr. Hutchinson on the Santine Hill."

A gormless-looking fellow called Grimaldi arrived at the pensione leading two powerful stallions at precisely nine o'clock the next morning.

The first animal, distinguishable from its companion only by a honey-tinted discoloration of its chestnut hair above one shoulder, had three lanterns and a long coil of sturdy rope fastened neatly to its back. The other carried the harness and bridles necessary for the task ahead.

The climb to the cave took almost four hours, the drifting snow causing many a slip on the part of the horses, neither of which had any experience of hill climbing.

It had begun to rain by the time they reached the plateau. After the hazardous journey down the other side, along the sloping narrow path around the cliff face, they sheltered awhile in the entrance of the cave. Nicholas built a fire and brewed some tea while Galen and Grimaldi brushed the hailstones and the rain from the horses' coats. Then Grimaldi produced some small loaves and pâté from a threadbare rucksack and shared it with his companions.

Afterward he inspected the stone that had been used to seal the heart of the cave, and harnessed the horses together. Unhitching the twenty-foot length of rope, he secured one end to each horse, leaving a long loop dragging on the ground behind them. Working together, the three men raised the loop into the narrow cleft between the top of the rock and the hidden part of the cave, forcing it securely down behind the rock as far as it would go.

Grimaldi eased the horses forward until the loop of rope was taut. At first nothing happened. The great beasts strained forward, the double halter that joined them riding up and back to the limit of its massive straps.

The rock stood defiant, seeming to turn the horses momentarily into a primitive stone relief.

"They work together so beautifully," said Nicholas, unconsciously stiffening the fibers of his own body in sympathy with the straining sinews of the relentless horses, "but they are losing."

"They are brothers, signor. For eleven months they shared the same womb. They were suckled at the same nipple. They are as one. My Alfredo and Alfonso, they will not lose."

He turned to his stallions. Only the oils glistening on their hides, the look of startled determination in their bulging brown eyes and the jets of steaming breath pumping rhythmically from each nostril told of the almost unquenchable life force in those frozen bodies.

"They are indefatigable," said Galen.

Grimaldi held no whip. No harshness invaded his voice as he addressed his workmates in fluid Italian: "Pull Alfonso. Pull Alfredo. Strive as one soul. Be fired with righteous strength and the wall will tumble down."

The level, gentle tones settled like balm upon the turbulent waters of the equine minds. As one they responded to the coaxing of their trusted master. Imperceptibly at first, then in a graceful craning motion, the four velvet ears pointed forward.

"On my comrades!" urged Grimaldi. "You are the brothers Joshua and this is your Jericho!"

Still the leaden portal to a world of menace and mist ponderously withstood the great force they exerted.

Then, as the bugle call of defeat sounded across the desolate battlefield of Galen's mind, and as the words "The rope must break!" formed themselves in Nicholas' head, the gap between the rock and the black hole behind undramatically widened.

The bodies of the stallions slid smoothly forward while their iron-shod hoofs remained rooted to the barren earth. As if one brain governed both creatures, each raised its right foreleg in an exactly synchronized motion and planted it firmly in the ground two feet ahead. The stalemate was over.

Within three minutes the boulder had been dragged far enough forward for a thin man to squeeze in behind. Nicholas' automatic response was to step eagerly toward the opening, but his progress was arrested by a gesture from Grimaldi.

"One moment, signor," he said, as gentle and confident as when he had spoken to his steeds.

He darted forward to the rock. At a single word of command, Alfonso and Alfredo allowed the rope to slacken. Keeping the loop behind the rock, he raised it to a point near the top, securing it behind a knob-shaped eruption on its surface. Holding it in position, he ordered the horses to move gently forward again. When the rope was once more taut he let go and dodged clear.

"Pull, my friends, pull!" he urged, and the stallions obeyed.

With all their weight centered upon the topmost part of the rock, it began to teeter forward on its broad base. For seconds it balanced motionless at an impossible angle before crashing onto its face amid billows of dust and shale. The rope flicked out from behind it like the string of an immense catapult.

Nicholas and Galen looked into the cave. Beyond the point where the boulder had stood, its roof sloped upward to a height of just over seven feet. As yet they could not see how far into the rock the cave extended, but for a length of at least ten feet it was as wide as it was high.

Having rewarded Alfredo and Alfonso with a nose bag full of oats, Grimaldi approached Nicholas and Galen with two of the lanterns. As they lit them he said, "It will soon be dusk, signori. Dusk is no time to linger on the Santine Hill."

"We shan't be on it, we shall be *in* it," said Galen without a smile. Grimaldi shrugged and attended to his own lantern.

"Make sure you are here when we come back," said Nicholas pointedly.

Holding their lanterns before them, Nicholas and Galen left Grimaldi to his horses and walked cautiously past the vanquished boulder into the heart of the cave. A black dustlike fungus grew on the dribbling walls. Beyond the initial limits of visibility, Galen stopped and held his lantern aloft. By its light they could see the cave continue at its present dimensions for another twenty feet or so, when it narrowed to a passageway little more than four feet in diameter.

Only then did Nicholas remember the date. December 28th. The day the next killing would have happened if they had stayed in London. So far he had noticed nothing strange or menacing in Galen's demeanor. But it would come. Sooner or later, he was certain, it would come.

Bending nearly double, they entered the passage and followed its slight upward gradient for about twelve feet. Toward the end they observed how dry the rocky floor and walls had become. No particle of the moisture in the wider part of the tunnel penetrated into the desiccated rock of the passage. It seemed that in the four hundred and fifty years since men had last set foot here, not even a primitive lichen or fungus had been able to find the means of supporting life. The passage unexpectedly curved upward and to the left. The low ceiling compelled them to adopt an ungainly crouching posture, and they scrambled uncomfortably along. Galen, who was leading the way, stopped so suddenly that Nicholas collided with him. The passage had come to an end in a sheer drop. Reaching out over the ledge with the hand holding the lantern, Galen illuminated the dark heart of the cave. From where they crouched, the rock fell away beneath for about eight feet. Above and on each side, it spread out into a roughly spherical cavern about twenty feet high.

Without conferring with his companion, Galen handed him his lantern and shinned down the sheer wall onto the floor. The remains of a wooden ladder, evidently smashed up deliberately, had been strewn about under the mouth of the passage. The German reached up and relieved Nicholas of the lanterns, lighting his way as he followed him down into the gallery.

By now their vision was better used to the dancing lantern light and the surrounding gloom, and they began to scan the stony floor for signs of the "devil's paraphernalia," said by the Grand Inquisitor to have been found in the cave.

"*The vile impedimenta of the antichrists is sealed up in the eternal darkness of the accursed hill*," said Nicholas, reciting the words of the oration from the steps of the cathedral. "*The evil magic books of the heretics will lie forever entombed with the unspeakable disfigured idols of Our Lady and with the upturned crucifixes with which they sought to overcome the power of Our Lord.*"

"*And then voices in the crowd spoke up*," said Galen, "*asking what was the machine seen by the soldiers who entered the cave to rout the execrable Gormini?*"

"*To which*," said Nicholas, "*the Grand Inquisitor saith that it was an* infernal *machine.*"

To one side of the gallery were the remains of a large fire.

Nicholas and Galen placed their lanterns on the floor and, dropping to their hands and knees, they minutely examined the blackened remains.

"It looks like paper," said Nicholas.

"The magical books?" said Galen.

"No. There was no word of the books having been burned. They were abandoned here untouched."

"Then where are they?"

They continued their search among the embers. All at once Galen stiffened and whispered Nicholas' name.

"Look!" he said, gingerly holding on the palms of both hands what looked like a ragged scrap of old leather. He brought it into the light of the lanterns.

"What is it?"

"A piece of old parchment, and"—he screwed up his eyes to see if it bore any clues—"my God, Nicholas. It's printed!"

Nicholas said nothing.

"I can't quite read the words," said Galen between clenched teeth. "It's obviously the topmost part of a page. The rest has been burned."

Every muscle in his body seemed to strain forward in the effort to focus his eyes upon the charred and faded pigment. He was hunched motionless over the parchment for nearly half an hour.

"It's in Italian, of course," he said distractedly, still staring at his prize, when he had finished.

"For God's sake, man, what does it say?"

"It says, *To All the People in Christendom—Hark to the Message That Will Deliver You From Bondage.* There are some other words which I can't make out."

"What does it mean?"

"Perhaps the Gormini were committing their heretical precepts to print."

"But how? In 1454 there were no printing presses outside Mainz in Germany, where Gutenberg had his equipment."

"Uncle said he expected there to be the remains of a press here. That parchment certainly supports his belief."

Nicholas rose to his feet and held up his lantern. It threw its uncertain light halfway across the gallery. Almost at once he saw a dark, hunched object near the end wall. At first he thought it was a rock, but . . .

He strode across to the object, Galen at his heels. A filthy leather sheet thrown over the object had given it the rocklike appearance. Nicholas removed the sheet.

It looked to Nicholas like a medieval cheese or cider press. A sturdy table of rough wood, it stood about three feet high. The table was surmounted by a carved wooden screw, one end of which passed vertically through a hole in its flat top. A wooden lever for insertion in a hole in the side of the screw was lying in the stones at their feet.

"It is a printing press," said Galen. "A homemade printing press."

"How does it work?"

Galen seized the lever and inserted it in the screw.

"By turning the lever," he said, "the screw pushes down this plate onto the tabletop. You can see the remains of the frame that would have held the type. The type would have been soaked in ink, the paper would have been placed on top of it and the plate screwed down to press the two together."

"But it's so crude."

"It is not that, Nicholas. Believe me, it is not crude for Italy in the 1450s. It is twenty or thirty years before its time."

Suddenly Galen remembered the note that Brough had handed him the previous day. He reached into his breast pocket and brought it out. For a moment he held it in front of him, looking steadfastly at Nicholas with his burning odd eyes. He unfolded the paper.

"Herr van Galen," he read aloud, "if as I believe the cave contains a printing press, I feel confident in assuring you that you have not been guilty of murder either in the fifteenth century or the twentieth."

"What?" exclaimed Nicholas. "But we *know* Giuseppe was the guilty brother—our regressions prove that. He can't believe after all we have discovered that Antonio was the killer!"

"Just tell me this," said Galen after reading through the note twice more in silence. "The Grand Inquisitor spoke of disfigured idols and inverted crucifixes. Where are they?"

They both held their lanterns aloft and scrutinized every inch of the cave's floor. There was nothing there but the trophies they had already discovered.

The fire.

The parchment.

And the broken printing press.

50

Darkness had enclosed the desolate plateau by the time they scrambled back to the cave entrance. Grimaldi, haunted by the ages-old Roganese fear of the specter of the Santine Hill, had abandoned them and fled to the sanctuary of the town.

"Curse these damned bogymen," said Nicholas. "With three of us and two horses, we might have stood a chance against Hutchinson. But alone, and with surprise on his side, we are practically helpless."

Taking the long, smoother path up to the plateau, they then climbed down the other side toward Rogano, scrutinizing every rock and gulley for signs of movement. In their imaginations a sanguinary Hutchinson haunted every shadow.

"The most horrible crimes could be committed with impunity on this hill after dark," said Galen. "Even the police are terrified of the ghost. I have never known such deeply rooted fear in a population."

They strained eyes and ears for the warning tread, the hunched figure detaching itself from the plunging blackness. But the avaricious darkness clasped its secrets to its breast and told them nothing.

They reached the road shortly before five o'clock. They had taken barely a dozen steps in the direction of Rogano when the stillness was shattered by the clatter of horses' hoofs on the road ahead. They looked up. A carriage was hurtling toward them on the snowy road.

Hutchinson!

The same thought possessed both of them at once. They

smashed their lanterns on the road to extinguish the telltale light, and scrambled from the path of the carriage as it bore down on them, now less than three hundred yards away. Sliding down the low embankment to a drainage ditch bordering the road, they cowered in the shadows and prayed that he had not seen them. As the carriage rattled onward they looked desperately around for a proper hiding place. But only one moss-covered outcrop of rock would have afforded better cover than the ditch, and to make a run for that would be to expose themselves to full view.

They sank as low down into the ditch as they could and pulled their coats up over their heads. But their hope was not to be rewarded. Above the clatter of the wheels they could now hear the voice of the coachman calling to his horses to stop. The vehicle came to a halt almost above them. They heard a door open and shut, and the sound of heavy boots on the road. Staring up from their hiding place, the fugitives could just see the top of the carriage and the coachman seated on his perch, whip in hand, peering into the darkness with stony eyes. Then the dark-hatted figure from inside the coach, hands buried deep in overcoat pockets, walked into view. He knew they were not far away, but as yet he was unsure of their exact position. He walked from one side of the road to the other, straining his vision to catch a glimpse of the men he sought.

Then he saw the lamps. Slowly he walked along to where they had dumped the lanterns and scrambled off into the ditch. He looked from the broken lanterns to the driver and back to the lanterns. They saw his silhouette rearing up not six feet above them and strove to control their heaving hearts and lungs. But he knew they were there. Taking one hand from his pocket, he looked down at their crouching figures.

"Why do you hide from me?" he said softly. "I have been looking for you for more than an hour."

"Captain Fabriano!" called Galen, clambering up the bank to the perplexed policeman. "We thought you were Hutchinson."

"It is about Signor Hutchinson that I must talk to you," said the captain, helping Nicholas up onto the road. "It is from Signor Hutchinson that I come to protect you."

He looked sadly from one to the other.

"Well?" said Nicholas anxiously.

"Signor Hutchinson has committed a murder at last," said the policeman.

Nicholas could barely speak. "My uncle . . . is . . . dead?" he said at last, unable to look at his two companions.

Captain Fabriano stared at him. "Uncle?" he said. "Ah, I understand. Signor Brough is your uncle."

He again sank his hands in his pockets and walked a few steps along the road. The clouds had parted, and the moon, like a sliver of phosphorus, glinted in the starless sky.

Without turning, the policeman continued, "That is part of my problem, signor. It is not Signor Brough who has been murdered. If it were him my troubles would not be so heavy."

"Not Uncle?" said Nicholas quickly. "Then who is it?"

"As I tell you, signor, that is my problem. We don't know who it is. When my man brought me the report this afternoon I immediately thought it must be one of you two gentlemen or Signor Brough. I telephoned my officer at the infirmary and he assured me that no one had visited Signor Brough's room all day. That was not too depressing. As I have told you, I then assumed the victim must be you, Signor van Galen, or you, Signor Calvin."

He sighed and raised his hands, palms upward, in a gesture of grave disappointment. "Not so. When the corpse was carried into the police office it was at once apparent that it was neither of you two gentlemen. The body of the dead man was older and altogether more heavily built than either of you. I then sent for Signor Lombardi, who told me you had left for the hills with his friend Grimaldi early this morning. I must tell you my heart was very heavy indeed."

"You seem to be saying that you wish the dead man was one of us," said Galen.

"Nothing personal, signor. But it would have left me with a much tidier case." He raised one hand to tick off on his fingers the points he had to make.

"I am searching for a man who for some reason wants to kill three others. Then a body turns up. It is not the body of one of the three. Therefore I am left with two alternatives. One, there was someone else in Rogano whom Signor Hutchinson wanted to kill. Or, two, Signor Hutchinson is a homicidal lunatic who is not selective about the identity of his victims. Either way, I not only have to track down Signor Hutchinson before he kills you or someone else, I also have to identify the body of his first victim."

"Murder cases never seem straightforward do they?" said Galen.

"I don't know, signor. No one has been murdered in Rogano for seventy-five years."

"Where was the body found?"

"Not far from the East Gate."

Something clicked in Galen's mind. "It's the twenty-eighth!" he said, looking at Nicholas.

"Yes, signor, it is the twenty-eighth."

"My God," breathed Nicholas. "Mercurio Ferruccio. The seventh Rogano victim. Found near the East Gate."

"Signor?" said Fabriano. "You know the dead man?"

"Aged forty-two," said Nicholas, ignoring the question.

"The police surgeon says the dead man *was* in his early forties," said Fabriano.

"Strangled," said Nicholas, far away.

"The man *was* strangled, signor! How do you know all this?"

"Found on December twenty-eighth, 1454."

"Signor?"

"It's too much for coincidence," said Nicholas, still ignoring the captain and addressing himself to Galen. "The Deptford Strangler has committed his seventh murder. And this time it not only tallies with its fifteenth-century counterpart in the method of killing and in details of the victim's age and sex. This time he used the selfsame spot as the Rogano Strangler."

"What time was the body found?" said Galen to Fabriano.

"At half-past three. He had been dead about an hour."

"We were both in the cave at that time!" said Galen, turning back to Nicholas.

"Which means Uncle is right. You are not the murderer," said Nicholas.

"Nor are you," said Galen, staring.

"Antonio and Giuseppe were . . . *both* innocent?"

"Signori," interrupted Fabriano, "I am telling myself that you know more about this case than I do. This is not right. Be fair."

He leaned so close to Galen that their noses almost touched. "Who," he said, clasping his hands, "is Mercurio Ferruccio? Who are Antonio and Giuseppe? Who is the Deptford Strangler?"

"Captain Fabriano," said Nicholas, "I think we should climb aboard your vehicle and drive back into town. This case is astonishingly more complex than anything you might conjure up in your worst nightmares. There is only one man who has any hope of unraveling this mystery. And he lies in a dingy room at the infirmary."

As they sat in the cramped interior of the jogging carriage, for the most part side-stepping the captain's agitated questions, both men tried hard to grasp the new reality of the situation.

Antonio and Giuseppe had been innocent. It was obvious from the regressions that Antonio had believed in his brother's guilt. But he had been mistaken. Giuseppe had certainly gone to the cave, but he was not the killer. And if the seventh Deptford strangling had been perpetrated by Hutchinson, surely it was he who had killed the other six people in England.

But who, in the name of the devil, was Hutchinson? Whose reincarnation was he?

And where was he now?

51

"Well?" said Brough almost before Nicholas and Galen were through the door.

"As you said," replied Galen, "a printing press."

"Good!" said Brough, and sank back ruminatively onto the pillows.

"How do you feel?" asked Nicholas.

"Stiff," said Brough after a thoughtful pause. "Very stiff." He eyed his companions quizzically and smiled. "Bruised I am," he said, "beaten I am not. I can leave my sterile prison in the morning."

"Uncle," said Nicholas, hardly reacting to Brough's announcement, "about Hutchinson."

"Hutchinson?"

"The man who's been trying to kill us."

"You know who it is then?"

"Yes, I met him near the pensione on Christmas morning, and Galen of course saw him at the time of the fire. We both recognized him as he heaved the boulder down on us."

"On me," corrected Brough. "Why didn't you tell me this yesterday?"

"I don't know," said Nicholas impatiently. "There was so much to talk about in so little time. We were all pretty frayed. Anyhow . . ."

"He's English then?" interrupted Brough.

"Yes, but more important than that, he has now actually killed someone."

"Who?"

"That we don't know. Nor do the police. But we are certain this is murder number seven by the Deptford Strangler. It corresponds in every way with the seventh Rogano murder."

"And that," said Galen, "makes Hutchinson the Deptford Strangler and explains why he wanted us dead."

Brough reached for his pipe. "It fits," he said.

"Your theory?" said Galen.

"Yes. Where is Hutchinson now?"

"He has to be somewhere in Rogano. There is no way out of the valley at this time of year until the express passes through again from Bolzano on Tuesday."

"That makes life *rather* difficult. I wonder if there is a gunsmith in Rogano."

At that moment a doctor walked in without knocking.

"Signor Brow," he said, "I must ask your visitors to leave now."

"Not another injection?" said Brough dejectedly.

"I am afraid so."

"No. This time I refuse. Last night I did not sleep because I *chose* not to sleep. I was thinking. This morning I agreed to accept your sedative, and I have slept most co-operatively all day. Tonight I shall sleep or stay awake as my body pleases—without the interference of drugs. And that is my final word in the matter."

"Yes, signor. Roll up your sleeve please."

Nicholas and Galen discreetly withdrew as the altercation proceeded. As they walked to the exit where Captain Fabriano waited to escort them safely to their lodgings, they could still hear Brough protesting that artificially induced sleep was worse than insomnia.

"Signor Brow," they heard the doctor say, "be quiet."

To their amazement he was.

Back inside the carriage, Fabriano explained that he had to call at the police office to dispatch an urgent message about the murder to regional police headquarters at Venice.

"We shall go there first," he said, "then we shall return to your hostel."

At the police office he showed them into an untidy waiting room and sent a swarthy *carabiniere* to fetch them some coffee. Fabriano returned before his underling and suggested they accompany him to the outhouse at the back where the body of the strangler's latest victim lay awaiting transportation to the pathologist's room at the infirmary. Despite the anxiety it caused him, there was in his manner an underlying pride at being the first Rogano policeman for generations to be in charge of a murder hunt.

They followed him through the dim, ill-furnished rooms of the office and out of a barred door into the high-walled courtyard at the rear. Several low, dark sheds, their flat roofs lying under a foot of snow, were humped together in a corner. Leading the way with a lantern, Fabriano walked to the largest of the sheds. He hung the lantern on a peg by the door and fiddled with a corroded padlock. The door swung back and the captain led them into the darkness.

It was bitterly cold in the shed, which by the clutter of old pots, broken chairs and lumps of twisted iron they judged had never been intended as a mortuary. The corpse, fully clothed in a thick winter overcoat, lay on its back on a wooden bench. Fabriano approached it with his lantern and peered into the open eyes.

"There is a look of terror on this face," he said. "To die by strangling is to die horribly."

Beckoned by the captain, Nicholas and Galen moved forward out of the shadow. At his first sight of the face Nicholas gripped Galen's arm in astonishment.

"Look," he whispered, pointing at the body, and he moved back so that Galen could see clearly. "Look!"

Galen stooped over the body, visibly starting at what he saw.

"What is it, signori?" whispered Fabriano, subdued by the tenseness of the atmosphere. "What alarms you?"

Galen stood upright and, brushing past the captain, walked out of the shed without a word. The others followed him outside. He was standing in the tiny courtyard, looking up at the narrow patch of sky visible between the dark bulk of the neighboring buildings. For the first time since reaching Rogano, Nicholas noticed how clear and clean seemed the air, like vaporized snow.

"Captain Fabriano," said Galen without looking around, "part of your problem is solved."

"Tell me!"

"We know the identity of the man in the shed. But far from helping you, it turns your case upside down."

"What do you mean? Tell me, who is it? Half my troubles are over when I identify the body."

"Not this body," said Nicholas, breaking his silence for the first time since leaving the shed. "It is Hutchinson."

Fabriano's eyes widened.

"The man who would have murdered us has himself been murdered," said Galen.

"And the Deptford Strangler is still on the loose," said Nicholas, looking steadfastly at Galen.

52

Before they left the police office, Nicholas telephoned the abbey and rearranged their appointment with the mother abbess for the following afternoon.

Fabriano, more confused than he had ever been in his routine thirty-year career, accompanied them back to the pensione.

"I think, signori, you could help me if you wished. We shall talk again."

Securely locked in their room, they reviewed the rapidly changing situation.

"Say what you like," said Nicholas, "there is a power in the universe akin to what our forefathers called Fate. Hutchinson was the reincarnation of Ferruccio, the last but one victim of the Rogano Strangler. How, except by the word 'fate,' can we explain this presence in Rogano at all?"

"I agree," said Galen.

"The further the case proceeds, the more obscure it becomes. We began with two suspects. Both have been exonerated. Who else in fifteenth-century Rogano had a motive for killing eight reincarnation of Ferruccio, the last but one victim of the Rogano today who is that unknown murderer's reincarnation?"

"What was Giuseppe doing in the cave?" added Galen.

"And on top of all the other questions piling up in front of us there is Nostradamus. He said the murderer was Peter's son. If that didn't mean the son of Pietro Aquilina, who did it mean?"

53

Brough, a neat dressing on his head, was discharged from the infirmary after lunch the next day.

After paying his bill, he joined Nicholas and Galen in the corridor. Captain Fabriano was with them.

"Good afternoon, Captain," said Brough.

"Captain Fabriano has just delivered the body of Hutchinson to the pathologist," said Nicholas.

"Good. Perhaps I might look at it later?"

"Of course, signor."

"Tell me, Captain, what have you found out about Hutchinson?"

"Too little, I fear. He carried no papers. We have not yet discovered where he was staying. A post-mortem examination is due to be carried out later today. That might tell us something, but I doubt it."

"Well, we must ask you to excuse us," said Brough. "We are

expected at the abbey very shortly. Perhaps late this afternoon I might call back and view the body."

"It will be my pleasure," said Fabriano with a cursory inclination of the head. He was beginning to feel badly neglected.

"It was a great pity, Nicholas, that you told Mr. Hutchinson where we were staying when you met him in the piazza," said Brough as they settled themselves into a waiting four-seater cab.

"The abbey, driver!" Galen called in Italian.

"Yes, it was a pity," agreed Nicholas as the cab jogged into motion.

Brough listened awhile to the regular clip-clop of the horse's hoofs on the slushy cobbles.

"What followed seems clear," the detective said at last. "While we were at the palazzotto conducting our experiments, Hutchinson entered the pensione and ascertained the precise position of our room. Then, when you and I returned, he entered the house, took our key from the hook in the vestibule and locked us in. Then he went outside, drew me to the window by throwing up a handful of stones and the rest we know."

"But why did he want to kill us—*and who killed him?*"

"As you have already deduced, the Deptford Strangler must have killed Hutchinson."

"How did the strangler get to Rogano?"

"He arrived on the same train as we did. Foreign visitors are few and far between in Rogano at this time of year. The report of *four* English travelers arriving by the express on Christmas Eve had spread all over the town within a day. I was told about the fourth man by an orderly at the infirmary."

"I heard about the fourth traveler too, but I assumed it must have been Hutchinson himself."

"Why Hutchinson? He might have arrived weeks ago. But the strangler was in England as recently as the fourteenth, when he killed old Carew."

"I still can't see why Hutchinson, a man whom none of us knows, should want to kill us. When we thought he was the strangler it made sense. But he was the victim. Why kill us?"

"Do you think he could somehow have been in league with the strangler, and at the last moment have fallen foul of him?" suggested Galen.

Brough was filling his pipe, deep in thought, and seemed not to hear his companions' exchange.

"Your trouble all along," he said, looking across at them, "has been that—as a fenman might put it—you've been too 'imbrangled' in the case. The solution hinges on Nostradamus' cryptic comments about 'the son of Peter.' You have insisted on interpreting Peter's son as the son of Pietro Aquilina. I have had another idea, and it has led me far away from your hidebound view of the mystery."

"Tell us," said Nicholas.

"Our respective views of the case parted company at an early stage," he said. "My own theory began to take shape when you first told me of the almost supernatural qualities attributed to this Rogano Strangler. If one accepted the orthodox account of the murders, there was an ever-present sense of dealing with a killer so fiendishly cunning as to be superhuman. It sounded more like the exploits of Frankenstein's monster than a man."

"In what way?"

"We are told he gained access to Lorenzo's palace, killed the duke and escaped without leaving any trace. He had entered the mansion of the Bellini family, abducted the girl Maria without anyone hearing any screams or sounds of a struggle, and leaving no clue as to how he had so silently entered a locked house. None of the windows or doors had been forced."

Nicholas nodded agreement as his uncle listed the points.

"With the final murder we are asked to believe that this uncanny creature not only gained entrance to the abbey after the drawbridge had been raised, but that he also found his way to the West Tower and escaped again carrying Sister Ruffo with him— and again no one heard a sound. It seemed impossible. But there had to be some explanation."

"What did you come up with?"

"The killer must have had help. Lorenzo lived alone except for a pair of Sicilian dwarfs who had arrived in Rogano from Rome only months before. If the killer got in and out of the di Corsa Palace, one of those dwarfs, perhaps both of them working together, had to let him in and lock the doors after he had gone."

"What about the cases of Maria Bellini and Sister Ruffo?"

"Those crimes differed from the murder of Lorenzo in that the

victims disappeared from their beds and were murdered elsewhere.
It has been established that no human murderer could have got
into the Bellini mansion without being detected. Our only alter-
native therefore is that Maria was not abducted at all—that she
crept out of the house of her own free will."

He paused while the idea settled into their minds.

"And Sister Ruffo?" said Nicholas.

"Her case is different again. Abducted or leaving of her own vo-
lition, either way her exit would have been heard. The only way
out of the abbey was across the drawbridge, which had already
been raised. The door of the dormitory from which she disap-
peared was bolted on the inside—therefore someone bolted it after
she had gone. We are left with two main hypotheses. One, that
someone in the abbey was in cohorts with the murderer. Or two,
that Sister Ruffo, wanting to go out in secret, had a helper. As the
only possible explanation for Maria Bellini's disappearance is that
it was her own choice, the odds are strongly weighted in favor of
the same deliberate choice by Sister Ruffo. This argument is sup-
ported by the fact that the mother abbess swore on oath that no
one had heard or seen anything. This had to be a lie. So it is not a
great step to identifying Mother Maria d'Aprillia as Sister Ruffo's
accomplice. The line of thinking is further strengthened by Nos-
tradamus, who wrote that 'the pious lady knows but cannot tell.' "

The cab had now passed out of the town and was following the
road that hugged the banks of the river for about a mile before
winding steeply up the mountainside toward the Forest of Ampri-
zio and the abbey.

"*Why* would they have crept out in the dead of night?" asked
Nicholas.

"I'll come to that in a minute. What we know for sure is that
before or after they had accomplished their errand they met the
strangler."

"What errand could conceivably induce two women to behave
so strangely, especially as both of them would have known a mur-
derer was on the loose in Rogano?"

"The answer to that lies in the dreams of Jessica Twomey. Jes-
sica was convinced that in her incarnation as Maria Bellini, her
lover, Duke Lorenzo, had introduced her to seven friends. They
always met in secret and at night. They had made a fearful discov-

ery, but from her fragmented dreams all she could tell was that it was to do with a cave and a man called Aquilina."

"And the friends were the people who later became the victims of the strangler," said Galen.

"Correct—Pietro Gatta, Giovanni Crispi, Brother Domenico, Ruggiero Festa, Mercurio Ferruccio and Sister Ruffo."

"That's only six," said Nicholas.

"Yes. The seventh was the only other person we know to have been associated with the cave."

"Giuseppe!"

"Exactly."

"Giuseppe was a *friend* of the others?" said Nicholas.

"What other explanation is there? We have established that he was not their killer. But as Herr van Galen's most recent regression showed us, he was one of the mysterious group of nine. If you recall, Herr van Galen recognized Lorenzo, Maria Bellini and the astrologer Festa."

"So the group comprised the eight victims of the strangler plus Giuseppe?"

Brough nodded.

"We're getting further and further away from identifying the killer," said Nicholas.

"No, we're on our way. But we must take it step by step."

"Where do the heretics come in?"

"That was the stumbling block for a long time," he said, struggling in vain with matches and damp tobacco. Then a tiny flame spread across the top of the shag and Brough settled back in a sweet-smelling applewood haze. "There were no heretics," he said at last.

"*What?*" said Nicholas and Galen together.

"There was a great deal made of the evil Gormini and their devilish rites in the hills. There was talk of the 'confederates' of the guilty brother wreaking vengeance on the quaking townsfolk. But we have found that neither brother was guilty—and no sign ever appeared of any confederates. You have both conducted exhaustive research, but have you found a single vestige of a clue to indicate the existence of the Gormini, either before or after this time?"

He looked from one to the other.

"No."

"No."

"Not a single clue!" pursued Brough. "Because the Gormini never for one moment existed. And Nostradamus, who of us all seems to have known what happened, referred only to *Lorenzo's* confederates—that enigmatic band of nine conspirators who within three months of the murder of their leader were all dead."

"But the black uniforms," said Nicholas.

"There," said Brough heatedly, jabbing the air with the stem of his pipe, "is the sole reason why the population of Rogano accepted the existence of the imaginary heretics. The bodies of Maria Bellini and Sister Ruffo were clothed in strange tight-fitting black garments with breeches instead of skirts. In the end room at the Palazzotto Aquilina they found an exactly similar outfit, which we now know Giuseppe wore when he went to the cave at night. And if you call to mind the evidence of the old herdsman, the men he saw with torches high up on the Santine Hill also wore the black outfits."

"Why else would the garments have been worn if not for pseudo-religious purposes?"

"Practical reasons. These nine people were creeping around at night pursuing some clandestine purpose. They did not want to be seen. So they dressed in black from head to foot. Skirts are hardly the best clothing in which to move quickly and nimbly, as Joan of Arc discovered. So the women as well as the men wore breeches."

"He's right, Galen!" said Nicholas suddenly. "The Gormini did *not* exist. What evidence of devil worship did we find in the cave? None. No magical books, no idols, no crucifixes. Nothing."

"Just a printing press," said Galen.

"The Bishop of Rogano was therefore misleading the townsfolk when he spoke of devilish paraphernalia," said Brough. "And remember, it was he, too, who was responsible entirely for the story about the Gormini. And reading your notes on his speech, it is clear that he was not intending even to mention the machine found in the cave. But some of the soldiers had seen it and rumor had spread. Challenged, he dismissed it as an 'infernal' machine, which silenced the curious while telling them nothing."

"How did you know it was a printing press?"

"I didn't know. It seemed logical, but I didn't know. When you proved that point, the rest of my theory fell into place."

"What made you suspect the true nature of the machine?" said Nicholas.

"First a comment by Herr van Galen when you mentioned the printed version of the life of Lorenzo which had been distributed at the time of the brothers' execution. He said that there must have been some mistake—that it must have been much later because, although Gutenberg had a printing press at Mainz in the early 1450s, printing did not spread to Italy until much later in the century."

"Well?"

"Then I remembered what you had told me at the Beggar's about Chief Architect and Engineer Gatta, the strangler's second victim. 'He was a well-traveled man,' you said, 'who had spent several years in a high civic position at Mainz in Germany before returning to Rogano about 1451.'"

"Of course! He must have been well acquainted with Gutenberg," said Nicholas. "An engineer could hardly fail to cultivate a neighbor like that. It would have been Gatta's professional duty to keep track of new inventions in case the corporation could make money out of them."

"Before I started thinking about the printing press I had already decided the people gathering in the cave were not the heretics but the people whose deaths were laid at the heretics' door. It was evident they were working together on some secret and dangerous project. We knew from the existence of the Lorenzo pamphlet that Rogano possessed a printing press. It was hardly coincidence that the chief engineer of that same town had been to Mainz."

He eyed them gravely. "The secret project of the nine was the building of a printing press under Gatta's supervision."

"But why? What was the purpose of the project?"

"I knew from the beginning that the task must be of the most deadly significance," said Brough. "So deadly that men of the power of Lorenzo and Gatta, men of high birth like Giuseppe, had to conceal themselves in a remote cave on an accursed hill where no ordinary citizen would stray. These were no common men. And yet they went in fear. And every one of them died in pursuit of their dread goal."

"Why? What had they found out?"

"They had found out about Peter's son," said Brough. "Remember Nostradamus—*Beware the son of Peter. Lorenzo and his confederates meet him and they die.* If my reasoning is sound, Peter's son is still concealed at the Abbey of Alba d'Amprizio, and is as dangerous today as in 1454."

"What for God's sake are you saying?" said Nicholas.

"Just this—ah, here we are."

The cab had negotiated the final bend on the road and come to a halt to await the descent of the great drawbridge.

54

"Old Ragusa," murmured Galen as he stepped out of the cab after it had trundled across the wooden drawbridge into the stone-flagged courtyard.

"Old who?" said Nicholas, walking around from the other side of the vehicle and standing nearby.

"Ragusa," said the German. "It's the ancient name for Dubrovnik. This place is just like it."

"Never been there," said Nicholas.

"It has the same enormous walls scarred with narrow unrailed stairways going up to the battlements," said Galen, looking about him. "And there is a strangely similar arrangement of buildings and streets huddling behind the fortified walls. This is much smaller of course."

In front of them, directly opposite the main gate, was a tiny white chapel with a domed roof, and on either side of it two parallel roads led into the heart of the abbey. Another road that followed the perimeter wall led off the courtyard to right and left.

The door of a circular gatehouse to one side of the lofty arched entrance stood open. After a few moments a middle-aged nun appeared in the doorway. She was clad in the same deep-blue habit worn by members of her order in the fifteenth century. Beneath it was the familiar shift-like undergarment visible at hem, collar and cuffs.

"Nothing has changed," whispered Nicholas.

The nun was leading three donkeys, linked one to the other by a long frayed rope looped around their necks. Harnessed to a three-spoked horizontal wheel, which in its turn drove a system of chains and pulleys, the donkeys had provided the motive power for lowering the drawbridge.

The nun's face, cupped in the porcelain whiteness of her wimple, looked haggard from care or physical suffering—the visitors could not decide which. But in her being there was a certain grace, a serenity born of triumph over pain. As she tethered her donkeys to an iron ring set in the stone wall of the gatehouse, Nicholas observed that her left arm, sewn into her sleeve, hung uselessly at her side.

Polio, he reflected sadly, recalling all at once the withered body of a baby cousin which he had seen lifted tenderly from her cot into a tiny coffin one distant autumn of early childhood.

Brough was trying to indicate by means of sign language and comically exaggerated speech that they wished the cabby to remain where he was until they returned. As the nun turned away from the donkeys and began with difficulty to cross the snowy courtyard, Galen went to the detective's rescue.

The muscles of her leg are wasted too, thought Nicholas.

With a sullen inclination of his head, the cabby prodded his horse in the buttock with the handle of his whip and eased it forward to drink at a moss-covered fountain.

Eyes downcast, the woman approached them, and placing one hand upon her breast, she said, "I am Sister Giotto." Beckoning them to follow, she led them in silence into the left hand of the two narrow roads past the chapel.

It was not a part of the creed of her order to shun contact with the outside world, but by the very remoteness of the abbey, the sisters had developed over the centuries into an almost completely self-contained community. Nearly five hundred in number, they tended their own sheep and goats on the lower slopes beneath the fortress. They hewed their own firewood from the forest, collected wild fruit and berries and cultivated their own crops on a terraced hillside midway between the forest and Rogano. They coped alone with repairs to roofs and drainpipes, constructed their own furniture from the wood they cut and made their own clothes from wool they sheared and spun on homemade looms.

Each sister had a particular function within the community, and the primacy of the mother abbess was unquestioned. Where many another society would have foundered through internal dissension, the community of Alba d'Amprizio had sailed smoothly onward since the beginning of the thirteenth century, secure and stable on its keel of obedience.

In addition to their individual roles as woodcutters, goatherds, carpenters, weavers, seamstresses and bakers, the sisters had the vital tasks of their calling to perform—their religious devotions, their teaching of the children of the valley, their tending of the old and infirm.

This is the other side of the Christian coin, thought Brough as they followed the diminutive form of the sister past a square granite building used as a corn store and granary. This, he thought, is just a small part of the good which has flowed in a seemingly endless stream from the wounds of the man they called Christ. It puts in perspective the evil which has gushed from the same source. Nearly nineteen hundred years of bigotry, torture, religious wars, and persecution and murder by the Inquisition. It changes the perspective. But does it balance or compensate for the evil? Would it have been better if Christianity had never been born?

He shook his head unhappily and realized he might never know.

Brough's telephone conversation with Mother Sebastiano had banished his preconceived ideas of austere and sagacious old age— her voice was as young as a girl's. Now, meeting her face to face in her magnolia-walled room, one aspect of his first mental picture of her was vindicated: despite the youthful richness of her voice, Mother Sebastiano was very old indeed. She had said she was Tommaso's sister. If that were so, she must be at least fifteen years his senior. Brough doubted if Napoleon had been long in his grave when the reverend mother had come into the world. Physically, she reminded him of Cézanne's *Old Woman with Rosary*, but there was something more robust in her spirit, and the wrin-

kles around her eyes and mouth looked more due to laughter than
to sorrow.

She had been sitting on one of four wooden forms placed
around a low pine table, and when they entered she sprang up
with all the agility of a freshly received novice. A china teapot and
four cups were set out on the table.

"Mr. Brough," she said, coming forward and taking his hand
tenderly in both her own, "I am happy your injuries were not
serious."

Brough smiled, and introduced Nicholas and Galen.

Mother Sebastiano returned to her seat and bade her visitors
join her.

"I'm sure you've not tasted tea since you left England," she said
as they grouped themselves around the table, "even if some amia-
ble innkeeper has served you the insipid beverage which the aver-
age Italian in all innocence calls tea."

"We haven't," agreed Brough with an uncomfortable smile.
After such a boulder-strewn journey he could summon no energy
for trivial conversation. The end was in sight. It was impossible to
call a halt now in order to talk about tea.

"Mother Sebastiano," he began, "as I explained on the tele-
phone, our purpose in Italy is—"

"Murder!" interrupted the mother abbess with relish.

"Murder, yes," said Brough, a mote taken aback by her undis-
guised enthusiasm.

"Are you shocked?" she asked. "Does it seem incongruous for a
sister of mercy to be fascinated by the subject of murder?"

Without waiting for a reply she said, "It is not so far removed
from my calling as you might imagine. One of God's own com-
mandments was that we should not kill. I am deeply interested in
the minds of those who oppose the Lord in this most funda-
mental law."

She paused, analyzing her own motivations. "Yes, it is the *mind*
of the murderer that fascinates me," she said. "And on a more
commonplace level I must confess to a predilection for mystery.
Even nuns relax sometimes, and my own favorite pursuit is detec-
tive fiction. I have read and reread *The Moonstone* in both Eng-
lish and Italian, and have puzzled interminably over the possible
solutions to *Edwin Drood*."

"Ah, there you enter a field very close to my heart," said Brough. "Alas, I cannot now expound my own rather abstruse theory to you. Suffice to say that I find your absorption with murder, on whatever level, totally comprehensible. I have, after all, made a career of it."

"My mother used to sit us down on wet afternoons," said the mother abbess, "and regale us with gruesome tales of Sawney Bean, who with his vast family had terrorized a section of seashore in Galloway near where she had lived. In twenty-five years they carried off and devoured more than a thousand people."

"Did Tommaso share your interest?"

"No. He never listened when we spoke of murder. Mother was a MacAvoy, and the MacAvoys, I fear, fancied they were descended from the Stuarts. Mother was not bothered much about politics, but Tommaso took after his grandfather. While she and I were conspiring together over some unsolved murder mystery, Tommaso would be re-enacting Culloden with his lead soldiers and turning the tables on the Duke of Cumberland. Or he'd be devising a family tree that linked us with the Pretenders. It was his conviction that if James II had not been deposed, and if the rule of primogeniture passed through the female line, then he would have been Tommaso, Duke of York, at the very least."

She smiled sadly. "I think he has felt a little cheated all his life," she said.

"Reverend Mother," said Brough after a discreet pause, "our purpose, as you rightly say, is murder. Specifically, the Rogano murders in 1454. You know of them of course?"

"Yes, the story of the Rogano Strangler has been kept very much alive within the walls of the abbey. Not only was one of our sisters a victim of the murderer. Even after the killer was executed, there was an event in the abbey still spoken of in hushed tones."

"The suicide of Mother d'Aprillia."

"Exactly. Never before or since has such an event occurred anywhere in our order. The taking of a life, even one's own life, is a terrible sin in the eyes of God. But poor Mother d'Aprillia had been so distressed by the abduction and murder of young Sister Ruffo that she found she could live no more. She cast herself from the window of her cell and died."

"I know that is the tradition hallowed by hundreds of years of repetition," said Brough, "but I don't believe it."

"Why not?" asked Mother Sebastiano.

"Because, simply, poor Mother d'Aprillia was beside herself with grief nearly three weeks *before* the abduction of Sister Ruffo. My nephew discovered a diary penned by a member of the deputation of elders which arrived at the abbey seeking the mother abbess's guidance after the murder of Ruggiero Festa. When the elders left her she was weeping."

"Perhaps she was moved by the dreadful events in Rogano."

"No. Something far more deeply rooted was troubling her. Mother d'Aprillia was not the anxious bystander tradition would have her. She was *involved*. She knew, even at that early stage, the truth about the murders."

"How do you know?" cut in Nicholas.

"The facts have been staring us in the face from the beginning," said Brough. "Now, I wonder if we might crave your indulgence, Mother Abbess, and ask to proceed to the final stage of our quest before acquainting you with all the complex facts of our investigation to date?"

"Of course, Mr. Brough. You must finish the job first. Tell me what it's all about later."

"Is the altar in the same position as it was in the fifteenth century?" asked the detective.

"Why yes, as far as I know. It is the original altar constructed by the sisters who started the work of transforming the old fortress into an abbey back in the 1200s."

"May we see it?"

"Yes. Come this way."

She led them out of the room and along a series of narrow corridors, most of them lit by candles swinging in dusty chandeliers. Eventually they reached a door at the foot of a flight of steps that led out into the open air. They were now close to the central point of the abbey, from which all the buildings radiated in a rough spiral trisected by the two parallel roads. At the center of the abbey was its spiritual as well as its physical heart—the medieval Church of San Bernardo, built in the shape of a cross. Mother Sebastiano preceded them into the church. Apart from a choir chanting a mournful psalm and a solitary nun lying prostrate be-

fore a statue of the risen Christ, the dark ranks of wooden pews
were empty. The mother abbess genuflected and walked with rev-
erent lack of haste along the nave. Before the altar she fell again
on one knee and murmured a prayer.

"Might I look behind the altar?" whispered Brough.

"Yes, of course."

He ascended the emerald-carpeted steps and walked behind a
block of solid oak surmounted by a carved crucifix and candles in
silver sticks. Nicholas and Galen followed close behind.

"Behind the altar the true son of Peter is concealed," mut-
tered Brough.

There was an area about three feet wide between the altar and
the rear wall of the chancel. The wall, built of huge blocks of
stone as high as a man, towered above them for thirty feet before
it was broken by an immense stained-glass window depicting the
crucifixion.

The mother abbess had followed them, and stood watching
Brough over Galen's shoulder. Outside, the sun was low in the sky
and the shadows in the church had begun to lengthen. Behind
the altar the gloom was almost impenetrable.

"May we borrow a candle, Reverend Mother?" asked Brough.

Without a word, Mother Sebastiano scuttled nimbly away. She
returned a minute or so later with a large candle. By its light they
were able to distinguish the gaps between the dark stones of the
wall.

"The son of Peter is still here?" said Galen.

"Unless I am very much mistaken," said Brough.

"How . . . ? Who . . . ?" asked Nicholas. He had begun to
feel decidedly uneasy.

Wordlessly, Brough continued to examine every block of stone
in the wall for signs of interference. He worked swiftly but cau-
tiously, deftly exploring every gap with his penknife, withdrawing
the blade and moving on. After more than half an hour he bor-
rowed a chair in order to examine the stones above his head, and
continued tirelessly to probe every inch of mortar between the
great stones. At last he stepped down from the chair with a sigh
of exasperation and sat down.

"Nothing," he said in disgust.

"What about the floor?" asked Galen. The stones there were

not so large, he thought, but they were still wide enough to allow a man, or the body of a man, to pass through if there was some cavity beneath.

"Let's look," said Brough.

They all fell on their hands and knees and began grubbing around the floor, looking for cracks or gaps that might betray the presence of a hiding place.

"Nothing!" said Brough again after they had traced and re-traced every crevice. Standing up and brushing the dust from his clothes with his one free hand, he turned his attention to the rear of the altar itself. He moved along its length, one ear against the wood, tapping it with his fist.

"Solid as a rock," he said at length. "I *am* very much mistaken. No one has been concealing Peter's son here, of that you can be sure."

"Where then?" said Nicholas.

"Is there any other altar in the abbey?" Brough said, turning to the reverend mother.

"There are several small altars of course," she replied, "and there is the chapel by the gatehouse."

"Was that there in the fifteenth century?"

"The building was there, but it was not a chapel. It was origi-nally a guard room, and until it was converted into a chapel about 1800 it was used to house wagons and agricultural implements."

"Did Mother d'Aprillia have her own private place of worship?"

"Yes she did. Her cell is largely as it was when she died. No mother superior since has wanted to occupy it because of its un-happy associations."

"Where is it?" asked Brough.

"Follow me," said Mother Sebastiano, and she was off, so thrilled by the hunt that she almost forgot to genuflect at the end of the nave before scampering out of the church.

Hugging herself against a biting wind which had risen with the gathering dusk, she walked along the cobbled road until she reached the perimeter wall on the opposite side of the abbey from the main gate. Turning sharp left, she led them along under the fifty-foot-high wall to the entrance of the square, domed West Tower.

Mother d'Aprillia's cell was in the outer corner of the tower about halfway up. It had a window in one wall which looked down on the silver ribbon of the Pergino and the rooftops of Rogano. There was a chair, a table and a wooden bed. Through an archway in one wall was a small anteroom just large enough to contain a miniature altar draped in gold-colored fabric. Its crucifix and candles had been removed long ago. Brough could barely contain himself. He strode across to the altar and pulled it clear of the wall.

"Bring me the candle," he said to Nicholas, who promptly obeyed. Producing his penknife once more, Brough crouched down and began the tedious business of exploring every crack in the stone blocks of the wall.

"But the stones aren't big enough," said Galen.

"Who said so?" replied Brough. Starting at floor level and examining every stone in the whole seven-foot width of the room, he gradually worked his way upward, repeatedly reminding Nicholas to keep his working area properly lit. Between two blocks about three feet up from the floor, the knife did not encounter the customary resistance as he inserted it in the gap. It penetrated the wall right up to the hilt without meeting any mortar. Brough grabbed the candle and brought it close to the wall.

"Wood!" he exclaimed, withdrawing the knife and driving it into the center of the block. Suddenly he turned.

"Reverend Mother, I know this must seem desperate impertinence, but I must ask you to leave us alone at this point. May we see you in your office in a short while?"

Not for the first time in her life, Mother Sebastiano found the two sides of her nature at war with each other. The ever-patient sister of mercy struggled with the eager amateur detective who was outraged at the thought of being deprived of an exciting denouement. The fight endured for the briefest moment, the stoical mother superior emerging victorious and the vanquished sleuth disappearing inside her.

"Of course." She smiled, and withdrew from the chamber.

As soon as the door closed after her, Brough grasped the handle of his knife and pulled it toward him. The wooden block began to move. Nicholas and Galen, all the tension and confusion of the past weeks welling up inside them, watched speechless as the detective drew the false brick from the wall.

"Beech," he said, sniffing the wood before placing it on the floor. He reached inside the hole and felt around. "It goes in a long way," he said, his shoulder by now pressed hard against the edges of the hole. "I can't reach the end."

Then his fingers touched something hard. He strove to reach farther in so that he could grasp the object, but it was useless. Then his mind returned forty years to his days in India.

He who struggles and cannot reach his toes must relax, not strain. A muscle in repose is pliable and may stretch. A tense muscle only shrinks.

The words of the yogi echoed and re-echoed in his memory, and as they did so he allowed his entire body to relax. Of its own accord his breathing became deep and regular. He closed his eyes to allow the relaxation to pass in a two-way exchange between body and mind. He began to feel the arm in the wall grow longer. As the muscles relaxed more and more, his fingers crept ever closer to the mysterious object hidden away inside. At last he was able to identify it. It was a wooden box with some sort of metal handle set in its side. He curled his middle finger around the handle and gave a gentle tug. It moved easily. In a moment the box was out of the cache and standing on the beechwood block which had concealed it from all but Nostradamus for four and a half centuries.

"What in God's name is it?" asked Nicholas.

"The root of much evil," said Brough, rising and leaving the box unopened.

"I'll leave this to you two," he said gravely. "Your talents are greater than mine."

"What do you mean?" cried Nicholas.

"Open it," said Brough.

Galen fell to his knees and ripped open the plain wooden box. "Papers!" he said, staring at the contents.

"Yes," said Brough, "papers. And none of them will be in English, so allow me to hand over the reins to the linguists of our little coterie."

He walked into the main part of the cell and stood by the window, looking down on Rogano as the last light of day slipped away beyond the peaks at the end of the valley.

Nicholas sat on the floor next to Galen and eagerly scrutinized the bundle of papers.

"There are six separate documents," Galen called to Brough. The detective did not answer. "The first two are in Italian, and the third is in Latin."

"Let's take them in order," said Nicholas. "What does the first one say?"

Galen read it through quickly in silence. It was written with a rough pen, probably a quill, on coarse-grained paper.

"It is some sort of statement signed by Mother Maria d'Aprillia," said the German.

"Read it!" urged Nicholas.

Galen read, translating as he went.

"My time on earth grows short. The past months have changed my entire perception of our little world of men and shown me that I can never again be a part of it. The time has come for me to die. He whom I have most cherished has been taken from me, and alone I am bereft. Oh merciful God, forgive an old woman her sins and allow her into thy Kingdom. Let me not be damned to suffer eternally for the evil I am about to commit. Forgive me, Lord, for I am lost. Forgive us all for straying from the path of righteousness, I beseech thee.

"I do not know how best to act. I am unworthy of that which has been entrusted to my care, and so I am concealing it in a place where it might never be discovered. I pray that if ever in the tortuous history of mankind it does come into the light once again, that he who holds it in his hands is strong and righteous. If not, great misery will follow. . . ."

Galen broke off and looked at Nicholas.

"Are they the very words?" asked Nicholas.

Galen nodded. *"Great misery will follow.* Nostradamus' words exactly."

"Go on."

"Alone I cannot do what between us was planned. With dear Sister Ruffo murdered and Signor Aquilina committed to the stake, I am the last. I am a frightened, lonely old woman and all I beg is a speedy death."

"Is that it?"

"That's all."

"What is she talking about?"

"Remember what she told the deputation of elders," Brough called from the other room.

Galen and Nicholas exchanged a puzzled frown and moved on to the next document.

When he realized what it was, Galen's grip upon it loosened as if it were a priceless and fragile treasure.

"A letter from Giuseppe!" he said. "A letter in the actual hand of my former self."

"Don't drop it," said Nicholas heatedly. "Come on Galen, what does it say?"

"It is dated December 1454 and addressed to Mother d'Aprillia. . . ."

"I can see that much."

"It says, *Most Reverend Mother Abbess, our hopes of ridding the world of the tyranny of the Untrue have failed. As the only one of us free from suspicion, you must take charge of the papers. Hide them. I am trying to contact friends in France to beg them to come to our aid. It might yet be possible for us to smuggle the documents into northern Europe, or even back into the empire of the Turk. The greatest mistake Lorenzo and I made was bringing it from Constantinople at all. There we would have been safe to follow our design. We should even have had the help of powerful men. It is true the help would have been given for the wrong reasons, yet it would have been help.*

"*So many things might have been. When I bought the scrolls from the legless beggar in the bazaar I had no notion of their contents. They seemed to me but an interesting relic, an unusual souvenir of our pilgrimage. Only when we returned and Lorenzo showed them to Brother Domenico and then to you did we know for certain what was in our hands.*

"*Intelligence has come to me that I might be taken as the man who murdered our comrades. If this happens, there is one final hope. It seems they are uncertain whether it is me or Antonio they want. Their confusion might give us the extra time we need to flee. I only pray that Antonio comes to no grief over this. But in the worst eventuality, how can I save him without revealing the whereabouts of the papers and disclosing your own complicity? The one consolation is that Antonio believes it is only a question*

*of time before the Inquisition drags him away to trial for his
'heretical' work on the structure of the universe. Heresy seems to
run in our family. May the One True God smile on you and
preserve you. Giuseppe Aquilina.*"

"God, what is this all about?" cried Nicholas. Brough had
moved to the archway during the reading of Giuseppe's letter.

"The next one is a scroll," he said, pointing to the remaining
documents in Galen's hand. "By my reckoning that will tell you
everything."

Galen unfurled it gently. "It's in Latin," he said, handing it to
Nicholas, who alone of the three understood the language of the
Romans.

"It is a memorandum," said Nicholas, carefully examining every
word on the scroll, "from Eusebius of Caesarea . . ."

"That's the historian," interrupted Galen.

". . . to the Emperor Constantine. It says, *For your perusal I*
. . . Wait a moment, I shall have to write this down."

Nicholas spent the next twenty minutes writing his translation
of the document onto a page of Brough's notebook and a further
ten minutes polishing the syntax. While he worked, Galen rose
and spoke to Brough.

"If the Eusebius that Nostradamus was talking about was Eu-
sebius of Caesarea, it changes everything we have so far decided,"
he said. "We were working on the hypothesis that he was speak-
ing of Eusebius of Nicomedia, one of the chief proponents of the
Arian heresy."

"*You* were working on that hypothesis," said Brough. "I never
favored Eusebius of Nicomedia."

"But I remember your saying that you concurred with my
theory."

"About the *pious lady* of quatrain forty-six being Mother
d'Aprillia, yes. But I was careful never to make any comment
about your interpretation of the Eusebius quatrain. And if you
had thought about it, you'd have realized your choice of the here-
tic Eusebius was based on the supposed existence of the Gormini.
When we realized the Gormini had never existed it invalidated
your theory."

"Here we are," said Nicholas, scrambling to his feet at last. His
voice was taut, his breathing fast and shallow. "The full text

of the memorandum to Constantine says, *I attach for your perusal the new official versions of the epistles of St. Peter. The four gospels and the Acts of the Apostles, approved by you last year, are now being copied by my scribes. I have adhered to your instructions concerning the original, which is returned to you herewith. Where the previous writings required only scattered amendments and interpolations, Peter's account had to be rewritten completely. It proves beyond all doubt that the man Jesus was no more than a pretender to the throne of Israel, a soldier and a zealot. I must earnestly petition you to destroy the document forthwith. If it fell into the hands of our enemies it could do untold damage, and the religion we have done so much to unify could be discredited overnight. As you yourself have observed, crucifying the non-Christians and feeding them to the lions is not enough to establish Christianity throughout the Empire. If the fanatical beliefs of the various Christian sects are to be smelted into one solid Faith—so solid that it will provide the Empire with a unity that military might has failed to bring—then we must devise a factual basis to convince the intellectuals. All our careful eradication of inconsistencies, the insertion into the other gospels of all the carefully contrived accounts of miracles, would count for nothing next to the damning contents of Peter's true epistles. I urge you again, destroy the true progeny of Peter's pen. Even your own inspired idea about Jesus rising from the dead, embodied in the verses we added to the end of John's gospel, would have aided us little if the truth about Jesus had been propagated. I thank God that Peter's epistles have never yet been disseminated like the other gospels, which at their worst were ambiguous and, if one happened upon different versions, contradictory. But Peter's detailed study of Jesus the warrior, the man who believed he could overthrow Herod and the Romans and seize the throne himself, would overturn Christianity for good. We are fortunate the Council members were in general too obtuse to understand that the only reason Jesus was executed was that he set himself up as an earthly king in opposition to the Emperor. All this talk of God's kingdom on earth did not begin until long after the men who had known Jesus had passed away. We have now traced every Christian writing and consigned it to the flames. After this final step it will be out of the question for any dissident to prove that the man*

Jesus was not God, and the Council's majority decision will stand for all time."

"Which council?" said Galen.

"The Council of Nicaea," said Brough, "which decided by a majority vote that Jesus was divine and that the nature of God was threefold—Father, Son and Holy Spirit. It was from that council in the year 325 that the real temporal power of the Church dates. Before that, each bishop was autonomous and was free to teach his flock virtually what he wanted. Before Nicaea it was by no means an uncommon teaching that Christ was not divine. For the past fifteen hundred years the Roman Catholic Church has been the most powerful institution on earth, and for all that time its survival has been threatened by the continued existence of these documents."

"So Peter's son was not a man at all!" said Galen.

"No," said Nicholas, "this is Peter's son." He had withdrawn from the bundle a brittle scroll of what looked like leather. It consisted of three rectangular squares stitched edge to edge and covered on both sides with minute black script.

"It looks like Aramaic," said Galen, "the language in use in Palestine at the time of Christ. This little bundle of papers could overturn the world."

"God Almighty," stammered Nicholas. "Christianity is a *myth?"*

"A deliberately engineered myth," said Galen.

"From the evidence we had I expected this," said Brough. "But I allowed myself to hope I was wrong."

"Can it be true?" said Nicholas. The younger men seemed stunned.

There was a long silence.

"It all begins to make sense," said Galen at last. "When Guiseppe wrote in his journal about *the duplicity of that devil Eusebius,* he was referring to the official church historian's deliberate falsification of the gospels."

"And in wanting to expose it he was taking on the entire might of the Catholic Church," murmured Nicholas.

"He and his eight confederates," whispered Brough as if he stood before some awesome Presence.

"They were going to print thousands, perhaps millions, of copies of Eusebius' memorandum and of Peter's true epistles," said Nicholas.

"That was the message that would have delivered Christendom from bondage," said Galen. "There's a printed copy with that heading here among the papers."

"I wonder if it would have delivered anyone from bondage," mused Brough, "or would it have precipitated bloody religious wars far worse than anything we have ever seen? Even faced with evidence like this, there would have been hundreds of thousands swayed by the welter of counterpropaganda inevitably produced by the Inquisition. They were dark, unreasoning days. Imagine how in that witchcraft-ridden world the Inquisition could have convinced entire populations that the printed evidence produced by the conspirators was the work of the devil. Until that time, remember, no one had ever seen a printed document. No, I think Nostradamus was right when he said that the documents should be destroyed or great misery would follow. He saw the sense of that even though, by his rejection of the Church late in life, he plainly believed they were authentic."

"This explains Lorenzo's refusal to have his son baptized and why his piety vanished after he returned from the pilgrimage," said Nicholas.

"It explains Mother d'Aprillia's suicide," said Galen. "After learning that her life had been devoted to the perpetuation of a myth she had nothing left to live for."

"It explains everything," said Brough. "Doubtless we shall discuss it all in endless detail until we are sick of it."

"I'm sick of it already," said Nicholas.

They stood in silent contemplation for a great while.

At length, Galen stirred. "I know it's hard to imagine wanting more after this," he said, indicating the papers, "but we still haven't got to the killer."

Brough sat down on the beechwood block and took his pipe from his jacket pocket.

"The Rogano Strangler," he said, pulling some tobacco from his pouch and stuffing it into the bowl of the pipe, "was the man who benefited most from the deaths of the people engaged in exposing the Eusebius papers."

"Thousands of people would have benefited," said Nicholas.

"Yes, but in Rogano one above all others. By name, Vincenzo Palestrina."

"The Grand Inquisitor," said Galen.

"Yes. That brilliant and ruthless man who knew that he had to eliminate nine people without one breath of their secret becoming public. Had they been ordinary townsfolk or peasants he could have dragged them off and burned them on any vague old heresy charge. But there were powerful people among his intended victims. You can't just dispose of men like Lorenzo, Gatta and Giuseppe Aquilina without a damned good reason. Even in Italy in the 1400s, public opinion counted for a lot, as you point out in your notes, Herr van Galen. Imagine the outcry there would have been if the Inquisition had taken a sister of mercy and the daughter of a rich merchant and committed them to the stake. No, the devious Palestrina had to devise an infallible scheme to get rid of his enemies and keep public opinion on his side. So he invented the Gormini. He killed eight of the nine and blamed the murders on the band of heretics in the hills above Rogano. The people were whipped into a frenzy. Then, at precisely the right moment psychologically, he had the finger of suspicion pointed at his ninth victim, Giuseppe. By now he had everyone on his side. This, he told them, was the man who had assassinated their beloved duke, their chief architect, even two helpless women. His high birth was no longer an obstacle. Let the flames consume his evil heart."

The detective looked up from his unlit pipe. "He even managed to get rid of Antonio at the same time without having to complicate the issue by dragging in his astronomical *sorcery*. It really was a brilliantly conceived and splendidly executed operation. Its only failing was that it did not reveal Mother d'Aprillia's complicity and so lead Palestrina to the documents for which the agents of the Church had doubtless been scouring the world for centuries."

"Who is the Deptford Strangler?" asked Nicholas.

"The man who is lurking in Rogano at this moment, waiting to kill us," said Brough. "The reincarnation of the Grand Inquisitor."

"*Who?*" said Nicholas.

"Do you know one of the main clues that set me thinking about the true nature of the son of Peter?" said Brough. "Apart from all the other indications, there was one comment which made me think that the son of Peter might not be a man at all."

He stretched his legs out in front of him and lit his pipe. "Do you remember, Nicholas?" he said, words coming from one side of his mouth and smoke from the other, "do you remember back in Jermyn Street when you first told me about Carew? He had said that Nostradamus used many metaphors and figures of speech. 'For instance,' you quoted Carew as saying, 'he would often personify inanimate objects, and where he seemed to be talking of people would in fact be referring to *things*.' That really got me thinking about the son of Peter, I can tell you. I reflected that the French pronoun *il*, used by Nostradamus in alluding to the son of Peter, meant not only *he* but also *it*. And then only four days ago, when you and I were walking back to the pensione from the palazzotto, I started talking about Shakespeare's sonnets, which I had been reading. It had struck me forcibly that Shakespeare regarded his writings as his children, his *sons*."

"Yes, but what about the killer, Uncle?"

Brough seemed not to hear. "It was also common in the 1500s to play with words, to give one word or phrase several meanings. Once again, Shakespeare was doing it all the time. Having decided that the son of Peter referred to the writings of St. Peter, I could see its secondary meanings. The printing press, being the brainchild of *Pietro* Gatta, was also Peter's son. And I'll wager there is a third meaning that names the man we now have to set about capturing."

"Peterson," said Nicholas.

Brough half closed his eyes and savored the gray-blue smoke curling upward from the bowl of his pipe. "Who else?" he said.

55

"What will we tell the mother abbess?" asked Nicholas.

"Unless we want her to go the same way as Mother d'Aprillia we shall have to lie to her," said Brough. "We'll say we found nothing in the hiding place except an empty box."

"You can't ignore the truth," said Galen.

"Truth at all costs can be a dangerous policy," said the detective. "There are millions of people in this world of ours for whom faith in Jesus Christ is life's one hope. By means of an ancient story about a man who rose from the dead, they themselves learn to conquer the fear of death. For countless multitudes eking out their lives on the face of this mysterious planet, Christ is a living reality, a reason for being and a constant friend in suffering and loneliness. Does the truth really count for very much?"

"What about the evil that has been done in Christ's name? What about—"

"There is no longer an Inquisition," said Brough. "The Church no longer tortures those who oppose it. It can no longer wage war. What is to be gained from disseminating this new 'truth' of what happened in Palestine? How could you justify the great misery that would follow?"

"By the fact that it is the truth," said Galen.

"Oh, Gregers," said Brough. "We must read some Ibsen together when we get back to London. Have you ever looked at *The Wild Duck*?"

"No."

"Do. It might show you something of the iniquity of a blind insistence upon what one takes to be the truth. Illusions, sometimes, are more valuable than reality."

"But—"

"If, indeed, even this is reality," said Brough. His voice was hushed and solemn.

"What do you mean?"

"Four years ago a middle-aged lawyer called Secondo Pia took the first-ever photograph of an object that has been in the hands of Italy's Savoy family for more than four hundred years. The object has been known by Italians for centuries as the Santa Sindone, the Holy Shroud of Turin. It is, they say, the burial cloth of Jesus Christ."

"Go on."

"Pia's photograph revealed that the shroud is itself a photograph. A photographic image of a man taken eighteen hundred years before the invention of photography."

For a moment no one spoke.

"It must be a hoax," said Nicholas quickly. Too quickly, Brough thought.

"Must it?" said the detective. "Many people would argue that the shroud is at least as strong evidence in favor of Christ's divinity as the Eusebius papers are evidence against it."

Nicholas found himself unable to hold his uncle's steady, somber gaze. He looked across at Galen instead.

"Many committed Christians would tell you the *documents* are a hoax," continued Brough. "Atheists and devotees of other religions would say the *shroud* is a fake."

"It is certain both cannot be genuine," said Galen.

"Is it? Do we really know enough to be dogmatic even on that point? We speak of enormous issues, far beyond our comprehension, and yet we use words like *certainty* and *truth* with such confidence. Most of us don't even know for certain that our heart will make its next beat. Do we, in fact, really know anything at all?"

"Perhaps documents and shroud are *both* hoaxes," said Nicholas.

"Perhaps they are," said Brough with a strange, sad smile. "It is a curious coincidence that the shroud and the documents entered Italy within a few months of each other. Perhaps one is a hoax designed to discredit the other, which might be authentic. But if so, which? Perhaps, in some inconceivable way, both might be genuine." He shook his head disconsolately. "And perhaps both are incredible fakes. Perhaps . . . perhaps . . . perhaps."

Doubt and silence engulfed him.

"I'm sure the documents are genuine," said Galen.

"Yes. I thought you would be," replied the detective. "They are indeed impressive evidence of something, and perhaps you are right. But hesitate, if you can, for just a moment. The documents were bought in Constantinople, then the last and first bastion of Islam. From its ancient walls the so-called Infidel gazed defiantly across land and sea to the hated Christians of Eastern Europe. Is it not conceivable—I do not ask is it a certainty, but is it not at least conceivable—that some brilliant Turk could have forged these papers in an attempt to undermine Christianity? Is it not conceivable that they are the work of someone as accomplished in imagination and deceit as Eusebius is supposed to have been?"

"No," said Galen quickly, "I don't think it is."

Brough turned back to the window.

"Are you going to destroy the documents?" asked Nicholas.

It was now so dark outside that only the misty yellow reflection of Brough and his companions was visible beyond the pitted glass.

"I don't know," he said.

56

Mother Sebastiano accepted what Brough told her with a shrug of resignation. "Ah well," she said, "it was not to be."

"I am sorry, Mother Abbess. It would have been splendid if we could have shared the final scene of this ancient murder mystery. But it was a long shot hoping there would still be evidence in existence at this late date."

He moved to the door. "There is one consolation," he said, turning back to her. "There is no talking point more barren than a mystery solved. At least now we can go on debating the Rogano case to our hearts' content."

She smiled. "You are kind," she said. After a moment she added, "I wonder what you really did find in that box."

"Something, madam, that you would not wish to know about," said Brough.

"I'll accept that," she said serenely. "Farewell, Mr. Brough."

He gave a little bow and left her.

"When did you begin to suspect the real motive for the Rogano stranglings?" asked Nicholas as the cabby drove them at walking pace around the first bend of the unlit road down to the town.

"It came slowly, piece by piece," said Brough. "The first major clue of course was Lorenzo's queer carry-on when he got back from the Holy Land. Something either during the pilgrimage or shortly after it had made him turn his back on the Church. Something prevented him from allowing his son to be baptized. What it was I could not at that stage begin to imagine. But he had been a most pious Christian. It had to be something pretty big."

The cab began to jog along more swiftly as the driver became more certain of the road.

"Then you told me the words Mother d'Aprillia spoke to the deputation of elders. She said, 'Ask no intercession. Pray with all your souls directly to the Father and to the Father alone.' She was weeping as she spoke. This was an astonishing statement. Part of the unchanging ritual of the Roman Church is that one can pray not only to the Father directly, but also through Mary or the saints. In urging the elders as she did, the reverend mother was also turning her back on Christianity, because Mary and all the saints are products of Christianity. Only God the Father came before the Christian faith. It was not hard to see then that something had happened to turn both Lorenzo and the mother abbess against Christianity."

He fell silent and looked into the dark fir trees at the side of the road.

"After that, odd clues came from all sorts of directions. The Deptford Strangler's second victim was Dr. Colin Manders, known as 'Godless Manders' according to Daubeney. He made himself very unpopular last year when he published a paper suggesting there was no historical basis for belief in Christ. Patrick Lovell was planning an expedition to Palestine and thought he was on the brink of a major discovery that would shed new light on biblical studies. And you two were both there when Mrs. Antrobus told us her son's subjects were European history *and religious studies*. He was, she said, a recognized authority on the early spread of the Church.

"Then there was the case of Nostradamus, who of course knew everything about Rogano. Carew told Nicholas that in the prophet's last years the Inquisition had him under close observation. Toward the end he was a hunted man because in the early 1560s *he had renounced his allegiance to the Church*.

"The last positive clue that the truth about Christianity, which meant the truth about Christ, had been cast into doubt was in Herr van Galen's regression. Remember how Giuseppe angrily ripped the crucifix from the study wall and threw it on the fire?"

"Of course!" said Galen. "As you said, all the clues have been there."

"Then there was the strange behavior of the Inquisition. That they were hiding something became clear when Nicholas discovered that the registers for the period October 1454 to February 1455 had been deliberately removed from the cathedral crypt.

"There was also that fire at the cathedral in 1781, by coincidence the same year as Nostradamus' prophecies were proscribed by the Vatican and thousands of copies burned. It was after the fire, according to Superintendent Matteotti, that the dungeons under the crypt were sealed up and all trace of them hidden."

He got out his notebook and read several pages before speaking again. "The Grand Inquisitor himself was a sinister figure. I mentioned early on how strange I thought it that in his account of Lorenzo's life he omitted to mention Lorenzo's prolonged blasphemy. The Grand Inquisitor's use of the Lorenzo pamphlet as—I quote Nicholas—'a fanatical reaffirmation of the supremacy and the infallibility of the Roman Church,' was also suspect. As no one had openly been challenging the Church, this was a virtual admission that its infallibility was not so certain as it made out.

"I have told you how I came to suspect the presence of a printing press in the cave. For the Grand Inquisitor to get so hot under the collar about a printing press, the evidence casting doubt upon Christ had to be some particularly dangerous document.

"All the 'facts' about the heretics, you will remember, were produced by the Grand Inquisitor and his promoter fiscal. All these facts turned out to be lies, which put the Grand Inquisitor in it up to his neck. By this stage I was confident that the motive for the crimes both then and now was the suppression of some document that undermined the divinity of Christ. This was strengthened when Nostradamus started talking about 'the great untruth of Eusebius' and we discovered that no extant copies of the gospels predated those produced by Eusebius of Caesarea.

"With all the information at our fingers' ends it was not difficult to identify the 'Peter' of the quatrains as St. Peter, the man venerated as the first Pope and the 'rock' on which Christ is traditionally supposed to have built his Church."

"I am amazed that so many facts could have been staring us in the face and we be blind to them," said Nicholas.

Brough did not reply. They were now clip-clopping along the road to the East Gate. Thoughts of how best to deal with Peterson were filling the detective's mind.

"You know," he said, "I am certain that Peterson must be unaware of his real part in all this. In his incarnation as the Grand Inquisitor it was his aim above all to suppress the Eusebius documents, and he killed in order to do so. But as far as Peterson is concerned, I am sure, he is just out to kill me for revenge. Fate is using his hatred of me for a purpose of which he is not even dimly aware. Perhaps it even caused him to commit his first crimes and me to track him down so that his hatred could evolve."

"I keep coming back to the question, why should this fellow Hutchinson want to kill us?" said Galen.

"I had an answer to that until Hutchinson himself was murdered," said Brough. "His death upset that little theory."

"Where now?" said Nicholas as the cab entered Rogano.

"To the police office," said Brough. "We are going to need all the brawn we can muster to bring Peterson back in chains."

The German called up to the cabby to take them to the police office, where they arrived nine minutes later.

"Captain Fabriano is not here," said a sour-looking *carabiniere* behind the counter.

"When will he be back?" said Galen.

"Tomorrow."

"Has he gone home?"

"Not yet."

"Where is he?"

"At the infirmary. He has gone to collect the post-mortem report on the murdered man, Signor Hutchinson."

"We can try to catch him there," said Brough when the German had translated the *carabiniere's* words. They hailed another cab and set off for the infirmary.

"Ah, signori," said Fabriano when he found the three men waiting for him in the entrance hall, "you have come to view our corpse?"

"Oh yes, the corpse. We might as well do that while we're

here," said Brough, "but chiefly we are here to help you catch a murderer."

"You know who killed Signor Hutchinson?"

"Yes. The murderer's name is Peterson. He escaped from prison in England about seven weeks ago."

"This is good news, signor. We must start our search immediately. Come, I shall quickly show you the body." They followed him along a corridor and into a white-tiled room on the left. The corpse lay on a table and was covered with a rubber sheet.

"It bears some interesting clues," said Fabriano, marching up to the table and grasping the corner of the sheet. "For instance, the marks on the neck tell us we are looking for a left-handed killer."

"That's as I expected," said Brough. "Peterson is left-handed."

Fabriano drew back the sheet and revealed the body, considerably whiter and more cadaverous than when Nicholas and Galen had first seen it. Brough's eyes widened in astonishment and he stopped dead in his tracks. He turned away from the corpse, the same stunned expression frozen into his face.

"What's wrong?" cried Galen urgently.

"Uncle, what is it?" Nicholas had never seen Brough so dismayed. The old detective looked at some point midway between his two friends. "It is the body of Peterson," he said.

57

"How *can* it be Peterson?" cried Nicholas in anger. "It is Hutchinson."

"Hutchinson *is* Peterson," said the detective. "He was hardly going to tell you his real name when you met him in the street, was he?"

"But . . . but . . ." His nephew was lost for words.

"When you first told me about Hutchinson I thought he must be Peterson," said Brough. "He hadn't been trying to kill *us*, he'd been trying to kill *me*, just as he tried in England. But when

Hutchinson was murdered I decided I was wrong. Who else but Peterson could have killed him? I was wrong there, too, evidently."

"So Peterson was the reincarnation of Mercurio Ferruccio," said Galen.

"Yes," said Brough, slowly shaking his head. "It must have been an accident that he was a killer in this existence. Fate somehow ordained that he must be murdered in this life as well as his former, and by some means we shall never know he was enabled to make his escape from Dartmoor to keep his appointment with his killer."

"Then who in the name of the devil is the Deptford Strangler?" said Nicholas.

"Tommaso!" said Brough.

"What are you saying?"

"Tommaso and Luigi," whispered Brough, hardly aware of the others, and without another word he walked quickly out of the room.

"Uncle," said Nicholas, "wait!" He ran into the corridor.

"Go back to the pensione," called the retreating detective. "Leave this one to me." He ran down the steps of the infirmary and climbed into the cab, which moved away with a jerk and disappeared into the darkness.

"He might get himself killed," said Nicholas, staring after Brough when Galen and Fabriano arrived at his side. "What shall we do?"

"I have learned to trust him enough to do as he says," said the German. "We must return to our room and await events."

58

Brough did not return to the pensione that night. The two men sat up waiting for him until after three in the morning. Nicholas wanted several times to call out Fabriano and his men, but Galen persuaded him to sit it out. At last they lay fully clothed upon their beds and drifted into fitful sleep.

They were awake again before it was light. There was still no sign of the detective. After an uncomfortable breakfast with Lombardi, they stepped outside for a breath of the crisp mountain air. Still no word came.

"If he doesn't turn up before ten I'm going to get Fabriano to turn this whole town upside down," said Nicholas. "He might be lying murdered in some gutter at this moment."

His ultimatum had only seventeen minutes to run when Fabriano arrived at the pensione in a police carriage. Nicholas, who saw the vehicle draw up, ran downstairs with Galen close behind.

"Where's my uncle?" demanded Nicholas, throwing open the front door as the policeman crossed the pavement.

"He is not with you?" asked Fabriano after Galen had translated the question. "I came here to ask him what he had found out."

"He did not return last night," said Galen.

"How strange. Perhaps you will ask him to contact me when he returns."

"He's not going to return," shouted Nicholas. "This bloody strangler must have got his hands on him."

"You think so, signor?" said Fabriano in alarm. "Then I must leave you with your visitor while I telephone for advice to my superior in Venice."

"Visitor?" said Nicholas, and as he spoke Fabriano moved to one side. Meg Brandon was standing on the pavement near the carriage.

"Meg!" he whispered. "How did you get *here?*"

"Train," she said simply. "I just arrived."

Fabriano and Galen discreetly moved inside the pensione. "Nicholas, what's going on?" they heard her say after a moment.

"Didn't you get my letter?" said Nicholas, taking her traveling bag and following her into the vestibule.

"What letter?"

"I wrote to you on Saturday. Of course, you must have left London before it arrived." He paused. "Meg," he whispered, ensuring Fabriano could not hear, "neither of us is the killer. Another strangling took place here on Sunday and both Galen and I were in the hills together when it happened."

"Who is the killer?"

"We don't know yet. Uncle is out somewhere now trying to track him down."

"I met your uncle at the railway station," said Meg.

"At the station?"

"Yes. He asked me to give you this." She took Brough's note-book from inside her muff. "He asked me to hand it to you with-out reading it myself."

Nicholas took the notebook and opened it. Many pages of notes had been removed.

My dear Nicholas and Herr van Galen . . .

"It was rather odd," said Meg, interrupting Nicholas' reading. "He said he knew I would be there."

"Who?"

"Uncle Brough. He said he was expecting me. I asked him how he could possibly have known I was coming, but he replied with another question. 'Am I right in thinking that you left home on Saturday night without telling anyone you were going?' he said. I replied, 'Yes, I crept out of bed after everyone was asleep. How did you know?' But again he didn't answer me. He just said, 'You are an extremely fortunate young woman. This time your twenty-ninth birthday will come and go without misadventure.' And with that he boarded the train I had just left and it chugged out of the station."

"He left Rogano?"

"Yes."

"Where was he going?"

"I don't know."

My dear Nicholas and Herr van Galen . . .

"What did he mean, Nicholas?"

"Mean? About what?"

"About my being fortunate. And about my birthday."

"I don't know." He paused. "Hold on a moment—it's your birthday today!"

"Yes."

"December thirtieth. This is the day of the year that the body of Sister Ruffo was found. It would have been her twenty-ninth birthday that day. She had disappeared three days earlier. . . ." He looked at her searchingly. "And you didn't tell anyone you were leaving. *You disappeared from your bed three days ago.*"

"What does it mean?"

"You are the reincarnation of Sister Ruffo."

"*What?*"

"Why did you leave home secretly?"

"I don't know. I had to see you, to find out what was happening. It was torture stuck there in London not knowing. But something almost outside of me seemed to be guiding my actions. I can't think why I should behave like that. Father and Mother will be beside themselves."

"Fate," said Nicholas.

"What?"

"Fate was guiding you. Don't feel bad about your conduct. You were not in control. There was no way the predestined pattern could have been broken. It is probably as old as creation."

My dear Nicholas and Herr van Galen . . .

"You mean *I* am caught up in this web too?"

"What? . . . Yes, it rather looks like it."

My dear Nicholas and Herr van Galen . . .

"But now I'm safe?"

"Yes. Your murder would have been three days ago if it had been going to happen."

My dear Nicholas and Herr van Galen . . .

"But what if—"

"Meg, will you let me read this letter!" Nicholas cried in exasperation. He went and sat in an armchair by the window and read.

My dear Nicholas and Herr van Galen,
By the time you read this you will know that I have left Rogano. Our debate about the future of the Eusebius papers has shown me that it is scarcely my part to play God and decide what will happen to them. As to their authenticity, I'll leave you

*to make up your own minds. You know their history as well as I.
Finally, though, it matters little whether they are genuine or
whether they are brilliant forgeries. A misuse of the documents
could bring such unspeakable suffering that I have no choice but
to seek infallible guidance as to what to do with them. There is
only one place I can hope to find that guidance—India. I can
think of one man alone who can help me. I haven't seen him for
forty years and he was over seventy then, but I have every reason
to believe he would still be alive. I pray he is, for there is some-
thing else I must discover, and I believe only he can tell me. The
question is one that I have posed to Herr van Galen before: Is
the soul of a murderer necessarily damned for all time? Is it a
case of "once a murderer, always a murderer"? There seems to be
some evidence that this is not necessarily so, for Peterson was
about as brutal a killer as you could imagine in this life but there
is nothing to indicate that as Mercurio Ferruccio he was anything
but a normal, law-abiding citizen.*

*How can I tell you what I have to say next? It is nigh impossi-
ble to begin. As I write I sit in the dungeons of the old cathedral.
Superintendent Matteotti was kind enough to lend me his key. It
is nearly dawn.*

*I came here after realizing the significance of a vital clue in
this appalling case, the clue of Tommaso and Luigi. Do you
remember, they scared the daylights out of me when they rushed
into the palazzotto for Emilia's tablets while you were both un-
conscious? I knew at the time there was something very odd
about the incident, but I could not pinpoint what it was until
last night. They were speaking in Italian. Of course they were,
you will say. Although Tommaso speaks perfect English he is
hardly likely to use it in conversation with his Italian brother-
in-law. But I understood every word they said. I speak no Italian
but a few basic traveler's phrases. Yet I understood perfectly.
How can I tell you, my friends? I am the reincarnation of the
Grand Inquisitor. It is I who am the Deptford Strangler. The
fearful images of the interrogation and torture of the Aquilina
brothers which have come to me during my solitary vigil in these
dungeons confirm that beyond all doubt. Yet the clues have been
there from the beginning.*

*What a devil's dance my subconscious has been leading us.
Each time I began to see the significance of a certain clue, the
mind of Vincenzo Palestrina somehow filled my own, pushing
me in the wrong direction, and the significance was lost.*

What I am still unclear about is whether the London murders were committed by my physical self or by my soul in physical form as I slept. Certainly Peterson was murdered while I was asleep at the infirmary after those injections, as you know.

We even spoke, I remember, about my out-of-the-body experience in my youth. But somehow we never even considered the part played by my soul in this sickening saga.

It was of course ludicrous to suppose that I was the only person embroiled in the case who was not a reincarnation of someone involved in events at Rogano, when everyone else—not only you two but all the victims, Peterson, Meg, even Bruno—had fifteenth-century counterparts.

I had been feeling restless and miserable since the first London murder, and I had been having troubled nights for the same period. But the real cause of my state of mind never occurred to me.

The Deptford Strangler was left-handed. So am I. Rope Walk was familiar to me when I went to examine the site where Antrobus' body was found—not, I now realize, only because I had been there thirty years before on the Toynbee case.

The Grand Inquisitor, among many other things, was a detective. That aspect of his ability reproduced itself in me just as Herr van Galen told us certain qualities are apt to do.

I can't remember if I told you, but little Bruno had been following me around for weeks after the first murder. And whenever he got the chance he said to me, "I didn't tell the big man, Mr. Brough. You're my friend. I didn't tell the big man where you were." After Peterson tried to kill me in London I thought the "big man" was Peterson and that the dwarf was bragging that he had not told him of my whereabouts. But the "big man" was Daubeney. Bruno found the body of Antrobus. For all I know he saw the murder take place. He obviously thought I was aware of strangling Antrobus, and was reassuring me that he had not told Daubeney that he had seen me in Rope Walk.

We narrowed the field of suspects down to someone who had heard Quentin Carew spouting drunkenly about his brother at the Beggar's. I even remembered hearing him talking about Nostradamus, Rogano and the rest myself, as I told you. But still it didn't dawn upon us.

Then we discovered the murderer was someone with an intimate knowledge of the photographs on my walls in Jermyn Street. When Nicholas was ruled out, who could that leave but me alone?

When we first saw the palazzotto on Christmas morning, a sort *of shiver of recognition ran through me. It looked exactly as I had imagined it. At the time I was astonished. Now I know why. I had been there before. Then—do you remember?—I led you both through the pitch darkness of the baptistery without faltering. You asked me if I had been there before. I hadn't, of course, in this life.*

It should really have been obvious that Peterson was not the reincarnation of the Grand Inquisitor, but in this whole case my mind seems to have been sabotaged from within. Peterson was only forty-two. In Herr van Galen's notes it is stated plainly that Palestrina was born in 1393, making him sixty-one at the time of the Rogano stranglings. Sixty-one. My age.

And finally there was the evidence of Nicholas' dreams. He dreamed of strangling on the very nights the London murders took place. We even spoke about the telepathic link that seems to exist between the two of us at certain times—how, for instance, Nicholas had once had a clear vision of me at Stonehenge, but we never took it that crucial step further and applied this link to his dreams.

I have pinned to this page the blank sheet of paper from the top of Patrick Lovell's note pad. It bears the indentation of his writing from the sheet above. The name of the person he went to meet on the night he disappeared. Hold a light over it and you'll just be able to read "Insp. R. Brough." I met Lovell once when I was investigating a burglary at his mother's place in Kensington. It puzzled me from the beginning how the strangler's victims were tricked into taking their notes and papers with them to meet their killer. I can't imagine what pretext the Grand Inquisitor used to lure them out, but he used my name to inspire confidence.

Forgive me for referring to the modern killer as the Grand Inquisitor. Even now I find it impossible to think of myself as a killer. My life has been spent tracking down and punishing murderers.

It is not I who kills, I beg you to believe, but whatever remnants there are in my brain of that fearfully shrewd and wicked man Palestrina.

In all humility I ask you both to understand, and, if you can, to forget the misery you have suffered at my hands. I think I shall never be able to wash away the blood of seven people from my hands. Perhaps, though, if I act righteously over the Eusebius papers, my guilt might be somehow mitigated in the eyes of God —assuming, of course, that God is more concerned about Right than the neutral absolute force envisaged by Antonio would be.

One day, perhaps, I shall return to London. But perhaps I shall not. I have thought often lately that I should never have left India after the army. I discovered something there that I can only describe as a portal to the miraculous. In my youth I didn't need it. Now death is not so far off I need it more and more. It might be that it is no longer there, that I have missed my chance, I don't know.

And that seems to sum it all up, my friends. I do not know.

Nicholas looked up from the last page of the notebook. Galen was standing nearby with Meg. Fabriano had retreated to the farther end of the vestibule with Lombardi and a bottle of wine.

Nicholas looked at the German. "Read this," he said.